POWER,
EFFECTIVENESS
AND SPIRIT

*A New Paradigm for
Human Potential
and the Practical Steps
for Achieving It*

Lynn Woodland

Beaver's Pond Press

Edina, Minnesota

Credits

Cover artist, Egil Jonsson, is an award-winning Minnesota artist listed in *Who's Who of America*. He has exhibited throughout the United States and Canada and has a studio in St. Paul, MN. To contact him call 651-224-7837, 649-4464, or write to P.O. Box 580902, Minneapolis, MN 55458.

Author's photo by Randy Libersky. To contact him call 1-888-433-4506.

ISBN: 1-890676-46-2

Library of Congress Catalog Card Number: 99-066668

First Edition

Printed in the United States of America.

02 01 00 99   5 4 3 2 1

With deepest love and gratitude,
I dedicate this book to my greatest teacher
of unconditional love and spiritual power,
Cheryl Rehovsky.

Contents

CHAPTER FOUR

Discovering True Power 131

CHAPTER FIVE

Uniting in True Relationship 175

CHAPTER SIX

Accessing the Limitless Source 223

CHAPTER SEVEN

Recognizing We Are More 271

Listing of Exercises

Acknowledgments

By the time I got around to writing the acknowledgments for this book I was so weary from months of editing and finishing touches that I just wanted to write, "I'm sick and tired of this book, thank you all very much!" and leave it at that.

But I know the power of gratitude. I often teach in my seminars that gratitude makes us magnetic to our highest good. So hearing my own teachings echoing in my mind (I think we wind up teaching what we need to learn so we will eventually learn to practice what we preach), I pushed past my inertia and applied myself to the project with a feeling that it would take me somewhere I needed to go.

Without a thought in my head, I started to write. The words flowed quickly and easily and when it was done, I was surprised by what came out. The process clarified who and what have been most instrumental, not just in the writing of this book, but in the formation of my Self. When I finished, my weariness had been completely replaced with excitement, gratitude and love, even for people I didn't always like so much along the way. I encourage everyone to write your own Acknowledgments. Don't wait until you write a book!

****

Thank you to everyone I have ever known who failed to live up to my expectations. Your participation in my life has helped me see my blocks, my shadow and ultimately my strengths as I transform the illusion that my happiness, success and quality of life are somehow determined by you. I thank you for playing this difficult role in my life. If you hadn't been there, I wouldn't know my own creative power in the way I do now. In particular,

I thank and honor my father as my spiritual teacher. He received little appreciation during his lifetime and I wish to amend this by acknowledging the spiritual gifts he gave me.

Thanks to the people who assisted my growth and training early in life when it was most difficult, especially Reed and Sheila Morrison and Thom Mumaw. You, for some reason, saw something worth nurturing and encouraging in a painfully shy, frightened twenty-year old. Without your support that spanned more than a decade, I don't know how I would ever have found the wonderfully fulfilling path my life has taken.

Thanks to the many, many people who participated in my groups and workshops over the years. You helped me learn my trade. I thank all of you who believed in me and gave me so much wonderful encouragement (and who participated so good-naturedly in some of the truly bizarre exercises I came up with as I learned what worked and what didn't!)

I am grateful to the many friends who have supported the actual writing process of this book. A big thank you to those of you who have been readers, unofficial editors, morale boosters and cheerleaders. In particular, thank you to Jenni Lessins for your early input and to Deni Dantis for your final editing. To Steve Tiffany, thanks for being so cheerfully willing to come to my rescue every time my computer got the best of me, and for all your help with the web site. Thank you to Egil Jonsson for the cover art.

Special thanks to Anton Christiansen for your help in making this book happen. Thank you for teaching me the power of "Yes!"

My deep appreciation goes to my beloved friend and spiritual sister, Deb Teramani, for things too numerous to mention. Thank you for being the kind of friend who, after having read much of the material in this book umpteen times, was still moved to tears of joy and excitement when reading the finished product.

Many thanks to the whole Teramani family: Mr. T., Nan, Jay and Cindy, Sarah and Emily, for welcoming me into your family. Thank you for teaching me things about family I didn't learn from my own.

Thank you to Rosanne Bane, who guided my first attempts at professional writing when she was editor of *The Phoenix*, and who showed up again later, very synchronistically, to become the editor of this book. Rosanne, you seem to be around for my writing "firsts," — my first articles and now my first book. Your encouragement and enthusiasm for my work has made a big difference in my willingness to persevere in my various writing projects. I even wonder if this book would have come into being if you had not been the first editor I approached with my work many years ago.

Last, but certainly not least, I thank you, the reader, for participating in making this book worthwhile by reading it. Thank you in advance for the service you will do for our world as you increasingly live from your spiritual power.

Introduction

Taking the Quantum Leap

We live in an amazing time when all aspects of life seem to be speeding up. No sooner have we bought the latest high tech piece of equipment than it has become obsolete, replaced by something better, quicker and cheaper. The pace of life gets faster and faster. Who hasn't felt, from time to time, overwhelmed by the challenge of keeping up with life? Just as we think we've got our lives on an even keel of quiet predictability, some great change erupts, turning everything upside down, for better or worse.

Even the heavens are reflecting this quickening. For the last fifty years or so we have been living under the fastest phase of Pluto's elliptical orbit, meaning that this normally slow moving planet is traveling faster than it has in generations, as measured from the earth's perspective. Interestingly, astrologers have always attributed to this tiny and distant planet the experience of deep, slow, powerful metamorphosis: change that is absolute and impersonal, destroying everything old and outmoded; a force of nature that lifts us up whether we choose to go or not, and drops us down in unfamiliar territory. A good metaphor for our times — metamorphosis speeding up.

At the heart of this quickening is a reshaping of the whole nature of reality as we have always known it. The findings of quantum physics are exploding our most deeply-ingrained beliefs about the nature of matter, time, space and consciousness. This expanded paradigm of reality is showing us that everything in the universe is part of an intricately connected web where consciousness itself has the power to effect change, and matter can leap from one point to another without passing through all the points in between. When we take some of these findings out of the physics lab and look at them in the everyday world of our lives, they become startling, amazing, miraculous even. Science is quietly proving that nothing is what it seems. While this has the disconcerting implication that nothing is solid or predictable, it also suggests undreamed possibilities. The one thing we can all count on is that nothing will remain the same for long.

Periods of great transition are always unsettling. Any new beginning is preceded by some amount of dying away. This is the natural order of things that makes room for new growth. We have all experienced this at a personal level. Recall the last major breakdown period of your life and see if it wasn't soon followed by a powerful growth spurt. As we stand at the threshold of a new era, we all sense change in motion whether or not we consciously embrace it. We have the choice to look back and see only the end of what has been, or we can look ahead to see something very new and different on the horizon.

The inclination to look back is a strong one. We are deeply attached to what we know. There is the illusion of safety and comfort in what is familiar. Yet, all we see when we look back are the signs and symptoms of an old way of being coming to an end. We see a picture of loss instead of growth.

For many of us this has precipitated a flurry of survivalist activity as we enter a time that has been the focus of so many predictions of doom, ranging from the Biblical prophesies of Revelations to technological crashes, environmental catastrophes, nuclear wars and world plagues. Some of us are stockpiling food, water, even weapons and preparing for the end of civilization. Others of us have gone more deeply into denial, feeling so out of control and powerless over the magnitude of breakdown we see around us that we choose to do nothing at all.

Personally, I am not stockpiling food. Neither am I dismissing the breakdown of our world. Yes, most certainly there is breakdown. However, I don't see in our future one single catastrophic event that will send the world reeling. In a way I think we almost wish for this because it makes the problem into one that we can comprehend. After all, we've seen countless TV movies about the end of the world as we know it. We can wrap our brains around that. It's familiar. What's more, there's something about a major catastrophe that brings out the best in us. It gives us something to rally around and brings us together.

Have you ever heard the story of what happens when you slowly boil frogs? I have no idea if this is true — I've never actually boiled a frog (and please don't try this at home) — but I've heard it said that if you put a frog into cool water and slowly bring it to a boil, the frog won't jump out. It will be lulled to it's death, not noticing the rising temperature enough to take action. This is the way I perceive our growing challenge of breakdown. Nothing so easy as one catastrophic event that hits all of us all at once. More like a complex brewing soup that challenges us to become conscious and to take action even when it doesn't feel like we absolutely have to.

As slowly boiling human froggies, we have tried everything. We've protested the fire under the pot, developed heat-resistant suits, even tried standing on our fellow frogs so they go down first and we buy ourselves a bit more time. We've tried everything — short of jumping out of the pot.

The leap out of the pot is not simply about averting danger in time. It's not just a matter of taking the right action to save the environment, feed the hungry or right injustice. Neither is it about going into denial that there is a problem, or hunkering down with our own survival provisions waiting for the world to end. The leap that is being asked of us is something altogether new. It is a change in being, not just a change in doing. To borrow a term from physics, our next step needs to be a quantum leap. Just as physicists have observed subatomic particles to miraculously leap from one point to another, spontaneously, without passing through all the points in between, so must we leap to a new paradigm of understanding ourselves, the universe around us and our place in it. This leap changes everything. It introduces solutions we couldn't see from inside the pot.

Paradoxically, this type of leap requires less effort, less pain and struggle than everything else we've tried. It is, however, something completely different. It means using familiar resources in unfamiliar ways, stretching our imaginations to places they've never been before, surrendering where we usually exercise control and most of all, going bravely into the unknown.

In this era that can so easily leave our minds boggled, nerves frayed and guts filled with free-floating anxiety, there is, at the same time, a sharply contrasting sense of wonder growing. Just as we intuitively sense that we will increasingly have our old comfortable guideposts of sameness torn away, so do we also know at the deepest level of our being that new wonders are becoming possible that will take us Home in a way that is joyous and marvelous in its unfamiliarity.

Although based on a visionary premise, you will find this book to be exceedingly practical. It is a guide for applying the new reality to the mundane affairs of life. For truly, it is in the everyday that life is lived. It is in the day-to-day, particularly those times when we act from habit, that we see the roots of the old reality paradigm most powerfully alive and at work within us, keeping us limited and in fear. Even the most dedicated spiritual seekers still tend to react from old ways of being when stress mounts or the routine of life invites unconsciousness. This is why so many spiritual and self-help practices may produce isolated results but ultimately fail to change the overall quality of life.

You will find here many exercises and small, practical, sometimes mundane steps that touch upon many different aspects of life experience. Rather than focusing on creating a specific result, the totality of this book is designed to create a shift in the fabric of life. The difference is akin to changing the soil of a garden so that a whole crop can grow easily, rather than learning to grow individual plants in spite of poor conditions. One way supports continued growth and harvest with ease. The other way takes ongoing effort, diligence and struggle, and peters out as soon as constant attention is broken.

What can you personally expect? Please expect no less than the fulfillment of your dreams. Specifically, _____ (fill in the blank with your personal goals). Understand, however, that stepping into your spiritual power will open the door to many things your heart longs for that your mind hasn't learned to name. Things you never thought to dream of. This is the nature of the new paradigm of reality. It offers the potential of power in ways we have never experienced. The power to create what we want is just the tip of the iceberg. It is the tease that motivates us to pursue. The bigger results are beyond what we currently know.

And now, I hope you are excited, a little afraid and ready to begin.

1

"...taking the quantum leap means taking a risk,
going off into uncharted territory with no guide to follow.
Such a venture is an uncertain affair at best.
It also means risking something that no one else
would dare risk."

—Fred Alan Wolf,
Taking the Quantum Leap

A Shift in the Nature of Power

The Path to Power

This book is about power — how to have it, how to use it and how to avoid the most common ways we throw it away. The true proof of power is not in how much money we make, our job or social status, our sexual power, our power to control people or circumstances or any of the other external forms we use as symbols of power. True power is much simpler than all of these things. It is the capacity to know and manifest our heart's desire. It is the ability to feel content, happy, at peace with our lives and to follow a path that will sustain our state of inner peace.

Our heart's desire is not a selfish thing — not to be confused with greed, narcissism or self-absorption. It is, rather, the highest aspirations of our heart that, when all distractions are cleared out of the way, naturally seeks a path that serves all as it serves one. There is a harmony, a divine order in following our heart's desire. It brings personal joy and inner peace, and it allows us to make a contribution to the whole at the same time. Our heart's desire is synonymous with our highest good.

Yet, our true heart's desire is often an elusive thing, covered over by years of disappointment, feelings of unworthiness, fear that there is not enough of anything good to go around and learned habits of resignation that tell us we can't get what we want so we may as well settle for what we can get. Many of us have turned to numbing habits of addiction to fill the void left by the absence of our heart's desire. We have indulged in over-eating, over-working and the abuse of alcohol or drugs. As we filled our lives with things that didn't fulfill us, we further separated ourselves from what we truly need and undermined our power to get it.

This is not a book on spiritual development. Our spiritual power does not need to be developed. It is already there. This book offers steps for stripping away all that dims and diminishes who we already are. Essentially, this is a process of letting go, opening, listening and surrendering.

The first thing we need to let go of is the layer of limiting beliefs we inherited from our family and culture — beliefs that tell us we can't, we shouldn't, it's not possible. We need to shed beliefs rooted in fear that tell us we are separate and alone, that we must adopt a defensive stance to survive. These beliefs shape our reality, whether we know it or not.

The next layer we need to peel away includes the many habits we use addictively to numb ourselves and help us cope with unfulfilling lives.

Spiritual power requires being fully conscious in each moment because consciousness itself is a creative force. The power inherent in our state of mind is one that few of us fully utilize. It is a force that can skyrocket us into new dimensions of healing, achievement and joy. Of course, it requires that we come un-numb, shedding addictions and other habits that help us go unconscious. Spiritual power requires us to feel. This is quite the opposite of what we so often strive for when we are seeking relief from painful and stressful lives.

Releasing addictions opens a Pandora's box of feelings that we have routinely suppressed, and brings us face to face with all that we have worked to avoid. Fortunately and paradoxically, as we relax our efforts to avoid, control and compartmentalize pain, pain loses its power to hurt us. No longer a frightening and devastating force, it ceases to be pain altogether and simply becomes intensity. As we stop fearing the power of our emotional intensity, we allow the full presence of passion and ecstasy.

The process of opening fully to our natural state of power must also include the release of fear, anger, dishonesty and everything else that keeps us locked into separateness: separate from other people, separate from our own inner wisdom, separate from God. Separateness and fear are antithetical to true power.

As we relax our tight, fearful grasp on life, we are more able to be still, to hear the quiet voice of inner guidance and to see the bigger pictures that lead us to our heart's desire. We open to the presence of a Universal Intelligence, a Limitless Source, an all-embracing force of Love. We allow a Higher Power to be the guiding force of our lives. Separateness gives way to synergy. We find that we are no longer stuck in the past or obsessed with the future. We begin to live in the moment with passion and enthusiasm. Miracles happen. Struggle diminishes.

This way of being is not without an element of risk. It requires stepping out of the familiar and stripping away protective layers that dull our sensitivity to both pain and pleasure. It means coming out of hiding to show who we truly are. Most of all, it is a journey of faith, and it is on this odyssey of inner discovery and miraculous unfoldment that I invite you.

My Story

I was eighteen when my father died of a heart attack. There was no grief, no tears, just a weary sense of relief — finally it's over. I was out of town visiting a friend when I heard the news. I didn't go home immediately. I spent the day by myself. As I thought about him I felt strangely detached. I prayed for him and spent much time tuning in to see if I could sense where his consciousness had gone after it left his body. I thought I could feel his fear and I sent him as much strength as I could, though with little love or feeling attached.

My father died an alcoholic. At the time of his death, his life was beginning to crumble around him. My mother had just left him, his debts were escalating, his business was failing, his health was deteriorating.

I did a lot of remembering the day my father died. I remembered the usual routine of my childhood: being eleven, twelve, thirteen, spending evenings in my room with the door closed. There was little socialization in our house at night. My mother, father and I all retreated to separate rooms a good deal of the time. My mother went to bed early to escape my father. I, too, went to my room to read and do homework, hoping to be left alone.

My father began drinking gin early in the day, and by evening he was a sloppy and angry drunk. There was usually a period in the evening before he passed out when some desperate combination of pain, fear and frustration drove him to engage with someone. With my mother asleep, that left me. He would burst into my room glaring at me with such hatred and rage. He screamed on and on about my worthlessness. The older I got, the more sexual his insults became. He told me how ugly and repulsive I was, how no man would ever want me, accused me of a multitude of perverted sexual acts. He would leave for a while and then come back, sometimes again and again in a single evening. I always thought of him as a monster.

Once my father started one of his rampages very little could stop him. I learned not to talk back because that would trigger violence. I learned not to lock my door because he would just break it open. When I tried pretending he was invisible or that I was invisible, it kept him from getting worse but it didn't make anything better. I felt powerless.

As I reflected on that day of my father's death, I realized his powerlessness, too. I think I had always known it, felt it even more acutely than his power. But recognizing his weakness was even more painful than his bullying and bluster. My father, my mother and I were all imprisoned together in our belief that we had no power to change our circumstances.

I became interested in metaphysics when I was sixteen. It gave a context of meaning to my life and helped me to put painful experiences in perspective. It gave me hope. I was very intense and diligent in my studies: I meditated, I read every spiritual text I could get my hands on, I practiced astral travel and psychic development techniques, took classes in astrology, numerology and Tarot. While still in my teens, I moved into a spiritual community and worked for spiritually-based, nonprofit organizations. To use the New Age terminology of that time, I wanted to be a "Light Worker." Whatever that meant.

After four or five years of this, I was struck by the question: Does all this spiritual knowledge and practice have any effect on the quality of my life? At the time it didn't seem to. At age twenty I asked myself, "If I'm doing all this 'Lightwork' why am I so miserable?" My spiritual studies seemed to be all up in my head and didn't feel like they had much to do with rest of my life. It felt to be more of an escape than a recovery from my childhood of growing up with my father.

No matter how much I meditated, I still came back to myself — a young woman terrified of practically everything who had painfully low self-esteem. I was horribly shy and could barely bring myself to speak to anyone I hadn't known for years. Though my father had been dead for two years, I still carried the messages he drilled into me in his frequent drunken rages, that I was worthless, ugly, unlovable, no good. I still felt powerless and unable to create love and happiness in my life.

My need to somehow understand and heal what had happened to me in my earlier years led me to volunteer my time to a group of friends who were starting a spiritually-based counseling program, an alternative to traditional addictions counseling and general psychotherapy. Within three months, this talented group of young people, hardly any of them over twenty-six, received a grant from the Maryland State Drug Abuse Administration and suddenly I was offered a paid staff position.

This was a major turning point in my life. In retrospect, I believe that some higher power was at work — perhaps my Higher Self giving me an opportunity to push past my fear. Although I felt compelled to accept the job, it didn't feel like a lucky break at the time. It was more akin to being booted into deep water completely unable to swim. I was sent to training classes, given supervision and pushed into rooms with clients I was expected to help. I was terrified. Yet I stayed. The alternative seemed worse; I knew that I was drowning in my life and had to do something. I believed that if I somehow learned to reach out to these people who were assigned me as their counselor, I would have to break out of my own shell that kept me so alone and afraid. I promised myself that I would stick with the job until I stopped fearing it.

This began one of the most challenging times of my life. As I learned the rudiments of psychotherapy, I learned about myself. As I forced past my fear to meet with a client or to facilitate a group meeting, I gradually broke through some of my walls of shyness. My own healing process was often slower, more cautious and painstaking than the participants in the groups I led! And, amazingly, people claimed that I helped them.

I have since come to believe that the teachers and healers we choose (or wind up with) are not accidental or random. We attract into our lives the people who are going to take us to whatever next step we have consciously or unconsciously chosen. I also believe that when we are in the role of healers or teachers, we attract people whose healing is going to reflect and assist our own. When I encountered Jerry Jampolsky's philosophy of attitudinal healing, that we are all equal students and teachers to one another, it felt very natural. I had no illusions that I was more healed than my clients! To this day, I feel deeply grateful to those first clients who were my early teachers in healing.

After about four or five years, I reached my goal. I was no longer terrified of my job. Once that happened I found myself in love with it. What's more, I developed social skills and psychological insight that gave depth and balance to my metaphysical studies and spiritual practices.

Over the years, this group of young therapists grew up and moved out of the experimental attitude of the early 70s into the more conservative professionalism of the 80s. We all worked on advanced degrees and became a mainstream group private practice. As I neared 30, I once again found myself asking if all this psychotherapy was improving the quality of my life. While I certainly had grown and changed for the better in many ways, happiness still wasn't a big part of my experience. I understood a great deal about what made me as I am, but I still felt powerless to change my experience.

In 1983 I helped to found and became the Director of the Baltimore Center for Attitudinal Healing, a support organization for children and adults dealing with life-challenging illnesses. The Center was modeled after a similar center in Tiburon, California, started by psychiatrist Gerald Jampolsky when he decided to bring children with life-threatening diseases together in groups with adult professionals (who were instructed to take off their credentials before entering the group room) for the purpose of extending love and learning from each other as equals. The philosophy of "attitudinal healing," as defined by Jampolsky, is based upon principles drawn from *A Course in Miracles*, a lengthy three-volume text of philosophy and lessons that guide students through a step-by-step process of shifting perception from fear to love. *A Course in Miracles* and the philosophy of attitudinal healing pulled together many strands of truth that I had encountered in other spiritual paths and texts.

Much of the focus of attitudinal healing is on letting go of the past and the future and opening to love in the present moment. While I thought I understood this conceptually, I had little awareness of what it meant to live in the moment. Most of my attention seemed to be focused on painful things that happened in the past or what I wanted to happen in the future — things I felt I just couldn't be happy without. All of life seemed to be such a struggle.

Around this time, I attended a workshop given by spiritual teacher Louise Hay, author of *You Can Heal Your Life*. Something she said set off a lightning bolt inside me. Hay's electrifying observation was, "Our point of creative power is always in the present moment." Power! What a concept! Psychology helped me to understand and cope with the pain of life, and spiritual practices helped me to rise above it, but nothing had offered me power to create something different. A sense of my own power, faith that I was the creator of my experience not just at the mercy of it, was what had always been lacking in my life.

All of a sudden I understood that my inner experience creates my outer reality, not the other way around. And, if I want my life to change, I have to start right here and now, not with more goals and plans, but by harnessing my own power to generate joy, love and inner peace.

This new revelation came just after a painful relationship breakup. Starting with my father, my relationships with men were often fraught with fear, pain and feelings of powerlessness. When a relationship ended badly, as they usually did, I felt that I had little power over what happened. I would plunge into a well of hopelessness that went all the way back to my childhood, immersing me in a pain much bigger than the situation triggering it. I had always seen these painful thoughts as an uncontrollable reaction to my circumstances that just had to run their course. With my new awareness, I suddenly saw my thoughts as a powerful creative force that was calling my future into being.

I had never before felt motivated to create the present moment differently because I didn't understand the connection between what I hold in my thoughts right now and the external results I attract into my life. I believed I needed certain external circumstances to be happy. It seemed pointless to use my energy and will to conjure up a moment of happiness when I believed it would surely be short-lived without the external rewards I thought I needed to sustain joy. So I told myself that I would be happy when I had a perfect relationship (or home, or work situation, or whatever else I was focused on at the time), and until then I would cope with being unhappy, putting energy into finding new ways to get what I wanted.

This time however, instead of just suffering, or finding ways to distract myself from my suffering, I started consciously creating my state of mind. I watched my thoughts and, for the first time, really noticed where I gave my attention and what negative messages I told myself over and over again. I was horrified by the possibility that I was creating my life from the painful jumble of thoughts that ran through my mind in a day.

I replaced hopeless, disempowering beliefs with new messages. Instead of focusing on how no one loved me or on being a victim of someone's unfair or cruel actions, I affirmed to myself again and again that love is my only reality, that anything is possible, that my highest good is now unfolding. I recorded these messages and played them over and over. I wrote them, I said them to myself. I surrounded myself with reminders to reach up for spiritual assistance. I realized that my spiritual practices of the past had not transformed the painful, stuck places of my life because I did not believe they could. I had used meditation and spiritual pursuits as a way to tune out worldly concerns. Now my spiritual practices were more meaningful because I believed that as I connected with my Higher Self, I called forth my highest good. I played music that lifted my spirit, I read inspiring books, I took myself to beautiful places. I gave attention to how much love was in my life and what I had to be grateful for instead of what was missing.

As I spent my time focusing only on the moment, none of the circumstances of my life changed immediately, but I changed. I found myself looking forward to getting up in the morning, enjoying my days, even though I still didn't have many of the things I had always thought I needed to be happy. I just was happy, not because of anything. I still had goals but I was no longer so focused on them. I wasn't postponing my life until I got "there."

After a while, without having to struggle for it, my life underwent a huge change. I settled into a long term relationship, started my own business and moved into a beautiful home in the country. The outcomes that I had been grasping for fell into place, but they were no longer the point. The point was that I was happy. Not because of what was happening around me, but because I had created it within myself. For the first time in my life I felt my own power.

A Shift in the Nature of Reality

We live in an era when the definition of reality is undergoing a fundamental shift. The findings of quantum physics throughout the twentieth century have introduced many mind-boggling paradoxes that are completely changing our previous understanding of matter, time, space and consciousness, proving beyond a shadow of a doubt that the physical world cannot be neatly observed, measured and predicted. Physics is proving what Eastern religions and metaphysical paths have taught for years, that there is a reality beyond what we can see and know through the limited perceptions of our physical senses.

To explain briefly, for more than a couple of centuries now, the Newtonian model of reality has prevailed. This view holds that the universe, whether it be at the macrocosmic level of planets, or the microcosmic level of atoms, is mechanical. In the Newtonian view, the universe is made up of separate components that move and interact in predictable ways that can be observed, precisely measured and expected to behave the same way at every observation.

But in this century, scientists have shown that the seemingly solid, predictable nature of matter is far more complex and miraculous than we had ever imagined. We now know that, at the subatomic level, matter does not behave consistently. Instead, it shows statistical *tendencies* to behave in certain patterns and has the potential to change spontaneously in ways that have no clearly apparent physical cause. What's more, at this quantum level, matter can exhibit the qualities of solid, separate particles and the qualities of unified light waves. The way matter shows up has to do with the way it is observed. That is, when the scientist observer is looking for particles, particles are found and have characteristics exclusive to particles. But when the observer is looking for waves, waves are found and have characteristics exclusive to waves. As physicist Fred Alan Wolf writes about this phenomenon in his book, *Taking the Quantum Leap*, "How matter appears depends on our minds' choices; reality is a 'matter' of choice."

The phenomenon of two seemingly incompatible realities coexisting, as with matter appearing as particles *and* waves, is known as the Principle of Complementarity, first formulated by physicist Niels Bohr, an early pioneer of atomic physics. Wolf says, "[Complementarity] taught us that our everyday senses were not to be trusted to give a total view of reality. There was always a hidden, complementary side to everything we experienced." Furthermore, "The more we determine one side of reality, the less the other side is shown to us." In other words, the more we focus on one perspective of reality and hold it to be the only truth, the less we are able to see other perspectives. In fact, perspective itself seems to have an influence in determining the reality that shows up.

This crucial factor of perspective, the power of consciousness in and of itself, is one that has never been taken into consideration in the methods of classical science. Once assumed to have no power to influence when separated from action, consciousness is now proving to be a powerful force. Physicist Helmut Schmidt of the Mind Science Foundation in San Antonio, Texas did extensive research on the power of consciousness to affect matter, using random event generators that produced random patterns such as those produced by radioactive decay. His studies, which have been successfully replicated by other researchers, showed undeniable evidence that mental intention could influence these random patterns, proving that thought alone can influence matter.

Another of the many mind-bending findings of quantum physics shows that at the quantum level, motion does not happen in the linear, flowing, point A to point B way we had assumed. Instead, subatomic particles have been observed to "leap" from one place to another, all at once, without passing through the space in between — something that is impossible to explain using the old Newtonian model of reality.

We can no longer even assume that time and space are the known quantities that we perceive with our physical senses. In the words of well-known physicist, Stephen Hawking, "[Einstein's] theory of relativity combined time with space and said that both could be warped, or distorted by the matter and energy in the universe.... No longer could we think of space and time as running on forever, unaffected by what happened in the universe. Instead, they were now dynamic quantities that influenced and were influenced by events that took place in them."

Along these lines, Helmut Schmidt in his experiments with random event generators showed that subjects could not only mentally influence random patterns occurring in the present, but could also affect random results that had been collected *in the past*, so long as these results had not yet been observed. We actually have the power to change the past with our consciousness as long as that past has not been "fixed" in time and space through conscious observation.

It is becoming increasingly clear that the universe is not an assembly of separate particles, planets and entities in set, predictable relationships to one another. Instead we are finding that all the pieces making up our physical world are dynamic, interrelated and able to affect and be affected by one another. It is impossible to separate ourselves from the whole sufficiently to observe it without our very observations having an impact.

These new truths, by their very nature, must radically reshape how we perceive ourselves, our relationships to one another and how we live day to day and relate to the world around us. Taken out of the realm of science and applied to daily life, these new laws of physics suggest a reality where we have far more power to influence our environment than we've previously known. Our very thoughts have the power to affect the physical world. What's more, movement at the physical level can happen instantaneously, through a "leap" in time and space rather than a linear, mechanical process.

Exercising our power begins with perspective. Just as matter shows up as particles or waves depending upon what the scientist observer is looking for, if we see ourselves as separate and vulnerable beings defined by the boundaries of our skin and the limits of our physical bodies, we will find a reality that validates this perspective. When instead we believe ourselves to be unlimited and having power beyond that of our physical interventions, this is the reality we will find. We will leap to new levels, or plod through life, according to our expectations.

As we begin to know our own nature as being part of a unified wave of existence instead of separate entities, our desire for power undergoes a shift as well. As separate particles we are more inclined to seek influence over the world around us through dominance and control. When we live from a perspective of separateness, we see the world as a place to survive in and ultimately master. When we come to know the power of wave energy, we also become aware of our oneness with all that is, since a wave cannot be separated into competing pieces. In "wave" reality, dominance loses all meaning because it requires a separation between the dominator and the dominated that "wave" reality denies.

The Newtonian model of reality is more than a scientific concept. It reflects a long-held collective belief system that humanity has shared and lived by. This belief system defines reality as limited to that which can be observed with our physical senses. It has led us to find our identity in our physicality and define ourselves by the strengths and frailties of the physical body. We believed ourselves to be separate because our physical bodies are separate. We believed ourselves to be vulnerable because our bodies are vulnerable. We believe that our power is limited to our physical interventions. For the most part, our whole way of being in the world, from the way we think to the ways we act and pursue goals, has been geared toward getting from one place to another in a mechanical, linear, step-by-step fashion.

Collectively, we still have relatively little comprehension of the process of "leaping" where change happens instantaneously instead of mechanically. "Leaping" is when we arrive without moving, we create without working, we know without learning. For most of us this seems impossible, too paradoxical to fathom. Yet, these are the paradoxes that we are now finding to be the core nature of reality. This way of viewing All That Is is so radically different that, as it slowly makes its way out of the relative obscurity of physics and metaphysics and filters into mainstream consciousness, it cannot help but change us, deeply and fundamentally.

Imagine how different life would be if the intrinsic nature of everything you know to be true, things so solid and certain that you never even think to question them, suddenly shifted? Imagine what it would be like if you knew with certainty that what you think of as "You" is not defined by your body. There is mounting scientific proof that consciousness is nonlocal, that is, not limited by distance or even time. In other words, it is becoming increasingly evident that our consciousness is *not* our physical body. And, if the power of our consciousness is not limited by physical constraints, why would it follow that it could be destroyed by the death of our physical body? A trip to any bookstore reveals among the top sellers countless stories and research on near death experiences, offering compelling evidence that life and consciousness exist beyond the life we know only through our physical senses. Imagine what life would be like if you truly knew your "Self" to be essentially beyond harm; that the life of your body did not define and limit the life of your "Self."

While many of us who ascribe to spiritual teachings may think we live according to these beliefs, few of us, including the most dedicated spiritual seekers, actually do. The old model of reality is so ingrained that we continue to act from it even as we fill our minds with metaphysical and spiritual concepts. For most of us, pursuing our spiritual path requires constant diligence and faith; it does not come naturally. It requires such an effort of faith because we are so conditioned to believe the reality that our physical senses show us. We must constantly put aside what we "know" at the most visceral, cellular level of our being in favor of what we want to believe, what we hope to be true.

When we do truly believe our spiritual teachings, they stop being hard work. When we truly *know* a different reality, then we don't need to keep fighting our conditioned instincts. We allow our spiritual beliefs to work, and we receive the peace of mind that all spiritual paths promise.

It is significant that science is now verifying concepts that have been a part of various spiritual and metaphysical teachings throughout the ages. Religion has lost much of the power it had in past centuries to inspire wonder and guide our lives. It is no longer the unequivocal voice of truth. Today that voice comes from science. Science in this century has given us many miracles, from walking on the moon to incredible life-saving technology. It has become a new religion of sorts and the voice that we believe in without question. When science speaks, we are ready to believe. As science introduces these new views of reality and they slowly trickle into our collective awareness, it signals a wide-scale readiness to assimilate a new perspective. It means that these ideas are no longer just for an esoteric minority. Rather, they are gradually forming a new collective belief system.

As we move into a new millennium we are all on the brink of leaping into this new paradigm of reality (what I refer to as "spiritual reality"). Some of us will make the leap sooner and some later. As we make this shift in consciousness and know ourselves to be one wave instead of individual particles, it will matter little who goes first or last as competition dissolves along with separateness, no longer having a place or meaning in the new order of things. I have few predictions as to how this process of transition will look since I firmly believe the future is not fixed in any predictable way.

I especially do not ascribe to any of the many predictions of doom that have become so popular as we close a millennium. "Doom" is by nature part of the old paradigm of reality (what I refer to as "physical reality") where vulnerability is assumed and fear is a powerful motivator. As we stop defining ourselves by the frailties of our bodies and the vulnerability of our separateness, fear loses its power over us. Consequently, "doom" also loses its meaning and disappears as we make the leap.

Essentially this book is a tool for making the leap in consciousness to this new order of reality. It offers practical steps and exercises for going beyond the "head-level" of understanding to actualize it at the "heart" and "gut" levels. As we begin to know and act from this new paradigm, our power increases exponentially. What's more, the whole nature of power becomes something entirely new: the power of consciousness instead of effort, the power of synergy rather than competition, the power of love over fear.

Spiritual Power Principles

It is widely accepted that the ability to feel power in our lives is crucial to our well-being on every level. Forms of therapy, healing and spirituality that don't enhance our experience of power do us little good. Well known medical intuitive, Caroline Myss, author of *Anatomy of the Spirit*, found in her years of work with physical illnesses that feelings of empowerment generate emotional well-being and physical health while the lack of it triggers illness. She goes so far as to say, "Power is at the root of the human experience" and, "Our relationship to power is at the core of our health."

Yet for many the very idea of power conjures up harsh images of force, hierarchies, greed, power over others, victims and abusers. This old paradigm of power is based in fear and has no place in the new order of reality. It disappears as we leap into our true power, which I term "spiritual power" to refer to the power we have beyond that of our physical nature. Fear is antithetical to spiritual power. It keeps us limited, focused on defense and protection rather than creation. Fear can easily permeate every aspect of our lives and shape our experience of reality. There are a number of "fear" beliefs that are so predominant in the world today that most of us have them incorporated into our way of thinking and living by a very early age. Our state of fear becomes so habitual that we may even cease to recognize it. Yet, the more we collectively hold fear-based beliefs to be truth, the more we perpetuate a fearful world. The "reality" that fear would have us believe looks like this:

Fear Beliefs Predominant in the World Today

Separateness. The fear perspective holds that we are all separate, unrelated to other living beings and disconnected from the world around us. Therefore, what happens to one person doesn't necessarily impact upon others and, ultimately, we are alone in life.

Vulnerability. From a place of fear we believe that the world is a dangerous place and we need to always be on the defensive to keep ourselves safe. We believe that our fear protects us.

Scarcity. Through the filter of fear, it appears that there is not enough of anything — be it money, material resources, love, joy or time — for everyone to have all they need. Therefore we feel compelled to compete to get our share. We are fearful about letting go of what we have because we might not get any more. We are guilty about receiving abundantly because having "more than our share" must be at the expense of someone else.

Powerlessness. Fear tells us that we are victims of circumstances beyond our control and that one person cannot make a difference. We feel at the mercy of senseless, random forces of the universe.

Spiritual power results when we shift perspective. When we make this shift, we assume that instead of being separate we are joined. We begin to see that we are safe because the essence of our being, something greater than our physical body, is beyond harm. We recognize that there is enough of everything for everyone, so we can give freely without fear and receive without guilt. We transform painful experiences through forgiveness and love.

A paradigm shift is needed to make this leap out of fear and into love. This can be impossibly difficult or astonishingly easy. A paradigm shift is hard for someone else to explain to you, but when you've had one, you know it and wonder why you never saw things that way before. It's the experience of suddenly recognizing many simple and obvious options in a situation that previously felt impossibly limited. It's the "Aha!" experience of suddenly seeing the bigger picture as though someone removed blinders from your eyes that you didn't even know you had been wearing.

Price Pritcett, begins his book on personal effectiveness entitled *you2*, telling a story that perfectly illustrates the idea of a paradigm shift. He described watching a housefly bashing itself to death trying to get outside through a screen window. All of its limited housefly senses told it that straight ahead was the most direct route to freedom. It could see it, smell it, practically taste it, yet the more it tried, the more beaten and battered it became. If only the fly could have seen the bigger picture it would have been able to turn around in the opposite direction and fly easily through an open door. This is how we often operate in life. We become fixated on the linear route that is most obvious to our physical senses and assume that it is not only the best but the only route to our goal. Then we limit our possibilities and wind up pursuing a path that will not take us where we want to go, and may even destroy us in the process.

Paradigm shifts come when we expand our consciousness. While there are many techniques and spiritual practices designed to facilitate this process, ultimately expanding consciousness is not about "doing," it's about "being," so no amount of exercises and activities are guaranteed to bring it about. This concept in and of itself requires a paradigm shift to comprehend because our culture worships doing as the path to achieve all outcomes, even spiritual ones (as in, "If I meditate long enough eventually I will become enlightened"). But a shift in consciousness can't be measured in exercises performed or time elapsed. Go back to the housefly metaphor: increasing effort wasn't effective. A new approach was required. Flexibility, openness and vision lead to paradigm shifts, not necessarily hard work. Expanding consciousness has more to do with how we experience the moment and how we choose to perceive the world around us.

The following spiritual power principles become operative when we let go of fear. They represent a shift from "housefly" thinking to a perspective that allows a greater range of possibilities.

Spiritual Power Principles

We create our reality through our state of mind. Therefore, we have limitless possibilities in all situations, and are never victims of circumstances beyond our control because we can always choose to change our state of mind.

Our point of power is in the present. Because we create our reality through our state of mind, and our state of mind exists only in the present, manifesting any desired future outcome begins with a change in consciousness in the moment.

Love is the only true power there is. Therefore, our experience of safety, health, creativity and success increases as we give attention to love rather than fear.

Our true relationship to one another is unity rather than separateness. Our power increases synergistically as we shift from "me" consciousness to "we" consciousness and replace competition with a paradigm of win/win.

There is a limitless spiritual source of power, wisdom and love we always have access to. Therefore, we don't need to live in fear of scarcity, and we are never alone.

We are more than our physical body — we are spiritual beings. Therefore, we don't need to be afraid of death, separation and illness.

In essence, these power principles all hinge upon recognizing the connection between our inner state and the outer reality of our lives. Our thoughts create the blueprint of our lives. Our emotions provide energy. Our intuition shows us the highest path, speaking to us constantly through subtle sensations, visions and passing thoughts that most of us have numbed out or learned to ignore. To use all of the power available to us, we must begin to pay attention to what we have perhaps spent a lifetime learning to dismiss.

In working with this book you may find yourself thinking about power in a whole new way. You will get to know the quiet power of inner peace that allows you to turn over your struggling fear-based control to a higher, wiser part of yourself. You will find your power to act with faith and certainty upon intuition. This power replaces the loud voice of discipline and "reason" with the gentler voice of Inner Guidance. Those who have learned to listen to this soft and sometimes elusive voice have the appearance of being "lucky," always in the right place at the right time, at peace with life. This is an ability that can be learned, and it is what differentiates ordinary people from truly extraordinary ones.

Working with this Book

There are many exercises in this book, enough to keep you very busy for a long time if you choose to do them all. There is no one right way to work with this book. I suggest you let yourself be drawn to whatever calls you the loudest and do whatever exercises feel right in whatever order works best for you. You may choose to start at the beginning and work your way to the end, or begin with an exercise in the middle. Or you may choose to read the whole book first before you begin a single exercise.

The exercises lend themselves well to group exploration and I encourage you to form a study group to work with this book, or to simply gather a few friends together from time to time to do an exercise. Most of all, I hope you will use what's helpful, pursue what feels exciting, take in what rings true and leave the rest, for you are the only one who knows where your path of growth lies. Trust this!

2

"Consciousness is that by which this world first
becomes manifest, by which indeed, we can quite calmly
say, it first becomes present; that the world consists of
the elements of consciousness..."

—Erwin Schrodinger, physicist

Creating Reality Through Our State of Mind

We create our reality through our state of mind. Therefore, we have limitless possibilities in all situations, and are never victims of circumstances beyond our control because we can always choose to change our state of mind.

Choosing Heaven or Hell

A Course in Miracles states, "What you see reflects your thinking....
Accept a little part of hell as real,... and what you will behold is hell indeed.
Yet the release of Heaven still remains within your range of choice."

One day, the start of which truly felt like a day from hell, I learned what it means to create my own reality. It was many years ago and the idea that my outer life experience could be directly reflecting my inner state was a brand new concept to me. I understood it in theory but it hadn't fully sunk in yet. On this particular day I had a million things to do. Paper work (all with imminent deadlines) piled up at my office. I had a class to give that evening and I hadn't even started to prepare for it. But instead of being at work plowing through all this, I was at a busy shopping mall about to pay an overdue phone bill that my housemates had neglected to pay before they left for a month in Europe. The phone was going to be turned off tomorrow. I was in a money panic because I had to come up with my housemates' share of several months worth of long-distance phone bills. I was stressed, angry, feeling sure that I was the last responsible adult left on the planet, and to top it off, I had a splitting headache.

As I walked impatiently through the mall searching for the phone company office, I accidentally kicked myself in the ankle so hard that it stopped me in my tracks and sent blood trickling into my shoe. When I could move again, I limped the remaining distance to my destination only to discover the longest line I had ever seen. I almost broke down in tears when I realized the long wait I had ahead of me.

The wait, however, turned out to be a gift from God. With nothing to do but stand there, I was left alone with my thoughts. I thought of how I had kicked myself and wondered if it was perhaps a metaphor for what I had been doing to myself all day in many different ways. This strange new concept that my thoughts create my reality popped into mind, and I shuddered to think of what this day's batch of thoughts must be creating. Since I had nothing else to do, it occurred to me that perhaps I could change my thoughts right then and there as I stood in the phone company bill-paying line.

I was so distressed, I knew concentrating on "happy thoughts" and New Age affirmations was not going to do the job, so instead I started by simply forgiving myself. I thought of how I had been "kicking myself," and forgave myself for being angry, for feeling unsupported, for not being a superwoman. As I thought about these things, an image came to mind of myself as a young child, and I realized that, in my overwhelmed state, I felt very young. I continued to explore this image because it felt soothing some- how. As I did, the phone company office seemed to disappeared and I lost all awareness of the crowd of people around me. I imagined myself becom- ing the child, first feeling her rage and then her abandonment. Next, I was looking at her; little, vulnerable and crying. Instead of feeling angry, now I felt compassion. The knot in my stomach relaxed, my mind stopped racing and my heart opened. I imagined taking this little girl in my arms and com- forting her, letting her rage until her anger turned to fear and sadness.

As the image faded away, I found myself suddenly at the beginning of the line. I paid my bill and left, not at all the same person I was twenty minutes earlier. I felt healed. In spite of my head still hurting, I was more relaxed, peaceful even. Somehow I didn't seem to be worried about my class or money or anything any more.

When I returned to my office there was a message that had come in while I was at the mall from a woman in the class I was to teach that evening. She said she had a special presentation she would like to make to the group that evening if I would be willing to put off whatever I had planned. As I had nothing planned, this couldn't have been a more wel- comed request. Minutes later, I opened my mail and found a substantial check made out to me with a note that the giver had been so inspired by my work that she wanted to make a tithe to me. It covered the phone bill with some left over.

The rest of the afternoon flowed by easily and I breezed through the work I needed to complete. I arrived at my class several hours later. Almost as soon as I walked in the door, a woman in the group who was a skilled healing practitioner took one look at me and decided that I needed to receive some healing attention. She proceeded to do some Reiki healing and massage on me that relieved my headache and relaxed my tense muscles, while I settled back and enjoyed the evening's presentation that I did not need to be responsible for.

On this day I truly "got it." I understood the connection between my thoughts and my life. And what was most striking to me is how little effort it took to put "the day from hell" back on course so that it ended up being one of the nicest days I had experienced in a long time.

We begin the creative process through thought. Quite literally, what we think is what we create, and what we hold in our thoughts is what we keep alive in our lives. As the quote from *A Course in Miracles* at the beginning of this chapter states, shifting from "hell" to "Heaven" is always among our range of choices. Making this shift doesn't need to be hard work. It is simply a choice to focus our attention differently. Perhaps the hardest part is catching ourselves in the midst of a downward spiral and recognizing that we do, in fact, have a choice. The exercise that follows is one I think of as "emergency care" to stop a bad day midstream and turn it around.

Exercise: Emergency Self-care

Step One
Stop. Stop running, stop thinking, stop talking, stop worrying, stop controlling.

Step Two
Close your eyes (or, if you happen to be in the middle of a shopping mall, simply turn your attention inward) and take a few deep breaths. Relax. Let your shoulders drop. Let the muscles in your stomach relax. Feel your brow become smooth and free of worry lines.

Step Three
Take a moment to just be with whatever you are feeling without

judging it or trying to change it. If it is rage, let the rage be there. If you are feeling afraid or guilty or sorry for yourself, just notice as much as you can about how that feels.

Step Four

Ask yourself, how old do I feel right now? Don't think too hard about this. Simply let an age pop into your mind or an image of a younger you appear in your mind's eye.

Step Five

Ask yourself, as myself at this age what do I need now? Don't concern yourself with what you needed then. Rather than going into old family history, imagine what the child feelings in you now are calling out for. For example, as I stood in the phone line, if I asked my adult self that question she would have answered, "I need my housemates to be more responsible! I need more money! I need to get back to my office and get some work done!" However, the four-year-old feeling that I was in touch with had an entirely different answer. First she wanted to kick and scream and rage. And then her tantrum quickly gave way to wanting to be taken care of, wanting to be held, wanting to have somebody notice her pain. She wanted things that my adult self wouldn't have admitted to.

Step Six

Use your imagination to create an inner experience where your child self gets whatever it needs. You might imagine an inner healer or nurturer holding you while you cry, or keeping you safe while you have a tantrum, or taking you on a magic carpet ride where you can feel free and rise above stress. You might imagine yourself as an adult caring for your child self. Play with different images and scenarios until you find one that gives a sense of release, relief and comfort. Let your imagery become as real and vivid as you can so that you actually fill up your own emptiness.

Step Seven

Let this imagery experience go when it reaches a natural completion and you find a feeling of relief. As you go back to the activities of your day, consciously choose to interrupt any returning "hell" thoughts that want to plunge you back into the day you were having. In other words, if you find your thoughts automatically returning to the resentments, worries and burdens that were in your head before you did this exercise, choose to replace them with thoughts of whatever fills you with peace, love, gratitude and joy. This could be someone or something in your life that you love, it could be something in the future that you are looking forward to, it could be an affirmation such as, "I am at peace," or "My highest good is now unfolding."

As you do this exercise, hold as your only goal that of creating the inner experience of peace in the present. Don't do it with expectations of dazzling results because this train of thought in itself will distract you from simply being present. The value of this exercise is in finding acceptance and joy in the face of what is.

Our outer world reflects the state we have created within. When we are so full that our happiness no longer relies upon the occurrence of external outcomes, then our world reflects this back to us in wonderful abundance. After completing this exercise, spend the rest of the day giving thanks for the blessings that are already present in your life. Keep reminding yourself that you always have the choice between "Heaven" and "hell." *As A Course in Miracles* says,

"No one remains in hell,...
You will find Heaven.
Everything you seek but this will fall away.
Yet not because it has been taken from you.
It will go because you do not want it."

What Are You Creating with Your Thoughts?

Where does your attention go when you are not actively engaged in some specific mental focus, when you are alone driving in your car, taking a break from work or cooking dinner? Do you tend to dwell more upon all the things that are wrong in your life — resentments, past hurts, future worries? Or, do you fill your thoughts with what you love in life — things that have gone well, love that you have shared, contentment in the present and pleasant anticipation of the future? If you looked at each thought that goes through your mind as a seed that will grow all the events of your future, how do you feel about the quality of the seeds that you are planting? Are your thoughts in the moment growing success, joy and love, or bitterness, pain and disappointment?

Most of us have certain patterns of thought that are so habitual we are not even fully conscious of them. The type of thoughts that go through our minds when we are not trying to think about anything reflect habits we learned, probably when we were very young. We may have learned habits of worry or of optimism, faith or bitterness. We may tell ourselves many times a day that life is unfair, or that we are unsafe, or that we don't deserve to be happy. We may be so unaware of this inner conversation that we don't even call these messages thoughts; we call them reality, and what we believe to be true is the reality we create. The areas of our lives that flow easily for us reflect learned beliefs that are positive and helpful. The areas of life where we struggle and feel stuck show us where we hold limiting beliefs.

When we have experiences of disappointment and not getting what we want, especially early in life, we tend to form expectations of a harsh reality that will always let us down. These expectations become a blueprint we continually think about and use to create more events that match our beliefs. We may become afraid to imagine anything better for fear of more disappointment, or we may simply have forgotten how to imagine anything better for ourselves. We let our imaginations become rusty from lack of use.

To create something better in life, therefore, we must first be willing to shift our attention away from all that's wrong, to what is good, successful and fulfilling in our lives. We must do this not just once, but consistently, moment by moment. This doesn't need to be a painful or difficult process. In fact, it feels good to shift out of fear thoughts to a more peaceful frame of mind. It does, however, require the energy and commitment necessary to change a habit.

Affirmations are a powerful tool for doing this. An affirmation is a statement of what we want to create in our lives and what we are willing to have be true for us. It does not need to reflect what we believe to be true now. Affirmations work on the principle that our subconscious mind acts upon whatever messages we tell ourselves over and over again. Unfortunately these are often limiting and fearful messages we learned in childhood. By writing and/or repeating an affirmation over and over, we literally begin to reprogram our unconscious beliefs about reality in much the same way that we might reprogram a computer by giving it different information.

In creating an affirmation, it is important to always state it in the present tense. Our unconscious mind is very literal. If we affirm "I will be happy," we are perpetuating a state in which happiness is always in the future. Or, if we affirm, "I want to be happy," we perpetuate the state of "wanting" happiness rather than being happy. Affirm instead, "I am happy," or "Every day I become happier and happier."

It is generally more effective to state an affirmation in positives rather than negatives. In other words, state what you want to experience rather than what you want to eliminate. Instead of affirming, "I am no longer depressed," affirm, "I am now joyful." I have a friend whose negative affirmations worked all too well. After affirming continually that she wanted to leave her job and her living situation, she managed to "disappear" them both and found herself jobless and homeless for a time. This unpleasant struggle was not at all what she wanted and yet it is just the kind of results that we so often create when we focus on what we want to eliminate instead of what we want to create.

Keep affirmations focused on yourself. That is, instead of affirming, "My husband loves me unconditionally," affirm, "I love and am loved unconditionally." You are the only person you can change and yet, paradoxically, as you change yourself, the way others treat you will usually change, too, reflecting back to you the inner changes you have created.

If you feel uncomfortable with your affirmation because it seems too far removed from how you feel in the present, experiment with affirmations that state willingness or deserving rather than being. For example, if it feels uncomfortable to affirm, "I love myself unconditionally," then affirm "I am willing to love myself unconditionally" or "I deserve unconditional love."

Make sure that the wording of your affirmation truly states what you want. For example, when I ask people in my workshops what they most want in life, I often hear answers like, "I want to understand all of my problems." Upon questioning it becomes clear that understanding problems is only a perceived means to an end. What the person really wants is more along the lines of inner peace, freedom, joy and love in various forms. Rather than affirming the means to a desired end (as in, "If I understand my problems, I will be able to free myself of them") it is more powerful and effective to affirm the end result that you want as in, "I now feel deeply at peace and enjoy every moment of my life." Affirming the end result will call the appropriate next step into being, and it may be a much different and more efficient route than you had envisioned.

Many of our limited beliefs are so ingrained that they permeate even our positive affirmations, in ways we may not immediately recognize. For example, on the day that I wrote an earlier section of this book about leaping to a new paradigm of reality, synchronistically, I saw a bumper sticker that read, "Subvert the Dominant Paradigm." Although, at first glance, this message seems to bear similarities to "leaping to a new paradigm," it's actually quite different. In the first, our attention is directed toward the "Dominant Paradigm" rather than a new one, and how we can "subvert" it, which leads us to imagine all the things wrong that are in need of subverting. This message keeps all of our energy wrapped up in what's wrong. The second message, however, draws our attention toward something new and we begin to imagine what this could be. As our energy moves toward "leaping," we automatically give less energy and, consequently, less power to what we are leaving behind.

Quite often we undermine our efforts to actualize the most well-intentioned change and growth by pursuing new-reality goals through old-reality methods. We "fight against war" rather than "create peace" (or even more simply, "be at peace"); we fight hunger, homelessness and abuse instead of creating well-being; we strive to overcome depression rather than to be joyful. As we define our process as "fighting" or "overcoming" rather than "being" or creating," we immediately establish through our expectations, the reality that the end result we want can only be attained through struggle and battle. We set our goal within the paradigm of fighting and, while we may succeed at feeding someone who is starving or sheltering someone who is homeless, our efforts don't affect the root causes of these things. Though we may win a battle, we never end the war.

So, as you create affirmations, continue to refine them, being attentive to any ways your wording expresses limits rather than open-ended potential. Also, notice the affirmations you have chosen to surround yourself with in the form of bumper stickers, tee shirt slogans, humorous sayings on refrigerator magnets, coffee mugs or desk plaques. Do they reflect the reality you want, or do they affirm that "shit happens"? Remember, the messages we feed into our subconscious mind become the reality we create.

To work with your affirmations, spend time each day writing one or two of them over and over again. Say them to yourself out loud or silently throughout your day, especially when you notice your thoughts sinking back into negativity. For example, there are times when I become stuck in painful thoughts. Often the start of it will be an event that in and of itself is a small matter, but I will interpret it according to past painful experiences and project into the future the worst possible outcome. Then I'll think this thought over and over again, like picking at a scab until it becomes worse. I've found at those times that outer circumstances, too, become worse and worse, adding fuel to my most negative thoughts. To turn this cycle around, I will sometimes take a simple affirmation or two (such as "I surrender to love," or "I am at peace,") and say them to myself over and over, all day long, whenever my mind is not actively engaged with work, or relating, or another specific focus. It takes very little time this way to turn my state of mind around and to see a shift in events as well.

Guidelines for Affirmations

1. Always state an affirmation in the present tense.

2. State an affirmation in positive rather than negative terms. That is, state what you want rather than what you want to eliminate.

3. Keep an affirmation focused on changing your own experience rather than on controlling the behavior of others.

4. If an affirmation feels so far from current reality that it is difficult to say, then begin with an affirmation of willingness and/or deserving.

5. Affirm the end result you want, not what you believe to be the means to that end.

The following exercise uses affirmations to transform old beliefs and to shift attention from what is lacking to what is already working well in your life. To learn more about working with affirmations I recommend the books *Creative Visualization* by Shakti Gawain and *You Can Heal Your Life* as well as the many other books, tapes and videos by Louise Hay.

Exercise: Transforming Old Beliefs

Step One: Identify Fears

Write each of your fears, doubts, worries or resentments on a separate 3"X5" card. Include things from the past that you are afraid will happen again, loss or lack that you are focused on in the present, fears and worries you have about the future, and resentments that occupy a lot of your attention. Do these quickly and spontaneously, writing until you can't think of any more.

Step Two: Identify Successes

Start another stack of 3"x5" cards, this time writing on each one something that is a success or source of joy in your life. Include past and presents achievements, people and things you love and are grateful for, things that you are excited about and looking forward to in the future. Keep writing until you can't think of any more.

Step Three: Turn Fears into Affirmations

When you are finished, place your two piles side by side and notice which pile is bigger. This will give you an idea about where you direct most of your energy. Remember that what we give energy and attention to is what we keep alive in our lives. Using your two piles as an indicator, notice how much of your creative energy is being directed toward what you love, and how much of your energy is going toward what you fear. Now, take out each "fear" card and turn each fearful message into a positive affirmation of what you now want to be true for you. For example, if one of your fear statements is "I never have enough money," you could turn this into, "I have plenty of money for everything I need and want." Write the new affirmation on the back of each "fear" card.

Step Four: Work with the Cards

Over the next week, at least once a day, read over your stack of "love" cards and review all the things in your life that inspire love and appreciation. Read the affirmations on the backs of the "fear" cards at least once or twice a day, too. You can also work with your cards by posting them on mirrors and other places where you are likely to see them frequently. Write your affirmations over and over, filling up a page a day, working with one or two affirmations at a time. Choose the ones that have the strongest emotional appeal for you.

Another way to work with these fear/affirmation cards is to randomly choose one each day, without looking, with the intention that the one you pick is the one you most need to work with today. Or, you can think about a problem you need guidance for and randomly pull a card. Again, hold the intention that the card you pick will have special significance to your current situation, the fear showing what is blocking your path and the affirmation showing the path of healing. You can add new cards as more fears and affirmations come to you, creating your own personal card deck for healing and guidance. The use of randomness in this way is a powerful means for inviting spiritual wisdom and guidance to break through the limits of our physical perceptions and linear thinking. You may find yourself amazed at how perfectly the messages on the cards you pick fit your situation.

Turning Imagination into a
Powerful Creative Tool

Because there is such a strong connection between our thoughts and our circumstances, our imagination is one of our most powerful creative tools. It is difficult to create what we can't or won't imagine, therefore an important step in creating something better in life is being willing to imagine it and practice imagining it again and again.

Creative imagination is something quite different from day dreaming where we long for things that seem out of reach. Day dreams such as these leave us with an empty feeling and tend to reinforce a belief that we can't be satisfied with life as it is. Creative imagination is empowered dreaming, where we create the inner experience of what we want so vividly that we feel full in the present and have a feeling of having already attained what we are imagining.

There once was a woman in one of my groups named Martha who was reading a book by Richard Bach called *Illusions.* The main character of the book, Richard, received instruction from his teacher on how to make something materialize instantly, in this case, a blue feather. Martha, who was very pragmatic and not inclined to believe such things, was nevertheless intrigued by what she read and decided to try the experiment herself to see if she could make a blue feather appear. So, she did the exercise described in the book of vividly imagining the feather as if it had already appeared, and then went about her day, waiting for the blue feather to show up. She was in the midst of doing an errand, paying for something at a convenience store and thinking about her blue feather experiment. She was feeling a bit foolish for even entertaining the notion that she could cause a material object to appear with her mind and a little relieved that her beliefs about the nature of reality had not been shaken by success. She was all set to go back to group and dispel the airy-fairy, New-Aged optimism of some of her fellow group members, when she saw at the register right in front of her a canister filled with feather dusters all made with blue feathers.

Martha was changed for life. She bought a duster and brought it to our next group meeting to share the experiment with all of us. She invited everyone to pick a feather from the duster and silently make a wish on it. As we held our feathers, we all did the visualization exercise, imagining our wish as though it was already here. The magic started working almost immediately. I had been searching for someone to do some work for me and in our meditation period it occurred to me that a young woman in the group would be perfect for this job. I approached her after group and she was overcome with emotion — the wish she had made was for a job. By the next group meeting others also reported receiving the things they had visualized.

I often hear stories like these about people who experience immediate and seemingly miraculous results after doing some form of inner visioning or healing. A woman attending one of my workshops once came to the difficult decision to call her estranged mother to offer and seek forgiveness. Neither had spoken to the other in years and she resolved to call as soon as the workshop was over. However, she didn't get the chance because her mother called first, also with the same intention. Another person opened to receive abundance and several days later received in the mail a completely unexpected check for $5000 from a grandparent, with the note "Be happy!" written on the bottom. Soon afterward she was offered a new job at more than double her previous salary.

While these stories offer exciting glimpses into the true nature of our creative power and the vast possibilities that most of us haven't even begun to tap, creative visualization techniques alone are not a panacea. I have also heard stories of those who have practiced various affirmation and positive thinking techniques diligently and have been sadly disappointed with the results. Sometimes the results comically backfire, as with Arlene who visualized a vehicle coming to her. She envisioned the make, model, even the color, and she did in fact, succeed in attracting a gift of just such a vehicle. However, the gift vehicle came with no engine so she received it just as she envisioned it — standing still! Another woman, Gina, affirmed adamantly that her next boyfriend was going to be rich. She did soon enter into a new relationship with a man who was not terrible wealthy but was named Rich!

Many use "New Age" techniques in the context of old world paradigms based upon fear and separateness. Sometimes the techniques don't work because we planted the right seeds in the wrong climate and soil. We may even succeed in creating the desired results but not get the desired feeling of satisfaction and peace from them. Or, we may create dramatic results and then find they disappear as quickly as they arrived because our deeper beliefs about reality won't let us have success that easily.

Our Beliefs Determine Our Experience

I know a woman who is single and looking for a partner. She goes to singles' dances, has placed personals ads and has a busy active life. Yet she had no luck at meeting a compatible partner and seemed at a loss about how to find the right person. I know another woman who says she doesn't understand singles' events and personals ads because whenever she is single she has no trouble at all finding a new partner. Both of these women are attractive, intelligent, interesting people. They live in the same city and work in the same office. Why such a difference in their experience?

A number of years ago, when I was in my mid-twenties, my closest friend and I agonized over a similar question. Carol and I had everything in common, from values to clothing size. The one big difference was that I was chronically unhappy because I wasn't dating anyone while she was chronically unhappy because too many men were pursuing her at once. I was always looking for someone while she was forever trying to disengage from complicated relationships.

We were confused as to why we should have such radically different experiences in this area when we seemed to have so much in common otherwise. One day we were discussing our favorite topic (men) and she said something that suddenly shed light on this perplexing issue. In describing the feeling she had in relation to men, she compared her energy to a fire that kept unintentionally leaking sparks. She said she didn't feel much control over people coming and taking this energy from her.

As she spoke I realized that I, too, had an image of myself in relation to other people that had lurked at the back of my mind, not fully conscious until that moment. It was of myself in a glass bubble, able to see out, but separate from contact. It felt very difficult to break through this invisible barrier to connect with others.

As I shared this with Carol, it became acutely clear to both of us that what we created in our social lives perfectly reflected these deep core beliefs we each held. Since we both wanted a little more of what the other had, we came up with an experiment. We decided to intentionally practice visualizing each other's image.

The results were immediate. Over the next two months, virtually every man who had ever been romantically important to me — my first high school crush, first lover and every other significant relationship since — showed up in my life in very coincidental ways. I also attracted a couple of blind dates unexpectedly. None of these were men I cared to pursue a relationship with and I realized that Carol's image of leaking sparks didn't work any better for me than it did for her.

What I gained from this experiment, however, was the certainty that my experiences are determined by my core beliefs, and not because there aren't enough good men out there, or I'm not attractive enough, or I don't meet enough single people or any of the other external justifications I could come up with. More importantly, I learned that I can change my core beliefs and create a different experience. I eventually came up with a more positive image. I pictured an aura of light around me that magnetically attracts people who are for my highest good and repels those who are not. It was not long before I created a long-term relationship, as did my friend, Carol.

What we believe and give attention to is what we create in our lives. It is that simple and that complex. Many of the attitudes we hold that limit our capacity to create joyful lives are so deeply ingrained that we do not question them any more than we question whether grass is green or sky is blue. These unconscious beliefs reflect what we have learned to expect from life, probably at a very early age. The easiest way to unearth these beliefs is to simply look at the circumstances we find ourselves in. Observing what shows up in our lives can be an excellent source of feedback about the unconscious expectations and beliefs we hold.

For example, I had to let go of many negative beliefs about money before I could attract a steady flow of it into my life. One of my beliefs was that if I had money and someone else needed it, I should give it to them. Having too much money left me feeling vaguely guilty and uncomfortable. Throughout my early adulthood, my mother was chronically in a state of financial disaster and I often felt manipulated by her demands for money. My inner program said that I had to give my money away if someone else needed it, but I resented having to do so. I resolved this dilemma by making sure that I never had any more money than I needed to get by. I didn't consciously make this decision but I always managed to change jobs for something lower paying whenever my income started increasing. I could then say I didn't have the money rather than I didn't want to give it.

Some years after my mother's death, I worked on releasing this pattern so that I could allow more money to flow in. Just as I thought I had it licked, I attracted one more test. Money had been flowing in more abundantly and steadily than ever before, then suddenly a windfall of money came to me unexpectedly, all at once. The very next morning, I was awakened by a pounding on my door. I sleepily answered it to find a man I knew only from one of my workshops that he had recently attended. He was in a state of panic and desperation, begging me to give him money to pay his rent. Knowing that he had addictions to both gambling and drugs, the higher part of me knew better than to hand over the cash. My inner program, however, kicked in with guilt pangs. Though I sent him away with suggestions for getting help that did not include giving him my money, I had an opportunity to see that this negative belief pattern, while no longer incapacitating, was still in action!

We can begin to identify limiting core beliefs by assuming that whatever experiences we have reflect something about our belief systems. For example, if you tend to have loving supportive relationships with women and disappointing relationships with men, it's not because of the way men are. It's because, on some deep level, you believe that men are going to treat you differently than women, and subsequently you attract people into your life who will play along with these beliefs. Or, if you are chronically unable to find a satisfying job, it's not because of the job market, it is because some part of you believes that you can't have, don't deserve or is afraid to have the kind of job you want. When we project all the blame on other people and external circumstances, we usually go on to create similar experiences over and over with new players. We can break this cycle by using a painful experience to give us valuable information about our core beliefs (which tend to remain stubbornly invisible until we begin to change our perspective as well as our outer circumstances). Once we uncover what we believe, we can change it. The following exercise will help you to identify and transform these deep-seated beliefs.

Exercise: Changing Limiting Core Beliefs

Step One

Focus on a repeating pattern of experience that you don't want any more. Write a simple sentence that describes this pattern. If you are not aware of a repeating pattern, you can simply use a situation in your life now that is not what you want. Some examples are: "I am being blamed for things I didn't do," "I always have to struggle financially," "My romantic relationships never seem to last," or "People always leave me."

Step Two

Turn these beliefs into positive affirmations. Remember, an affirmation is a statement of what we now want to become true. Create an affirmation that counters each negative belief statement using similar language and style. For example, "It's too hard to meet anyone I could love" might turn into, "It's easy to meet interesting, desirable single men(women). I now attract the perfect partner for me." "There aren't any good jobs out there" might become "There are many wonderful jobs for me. I now have the perfect job."

Step Three

Repeat these affirmations to yourself often. Say them over and over silently or out loud, and write them, filling a page or more a day with an affirmation. The more attention you give to them, the more quickly they will take root in your subconscious creative mind and become your new reality.

Step Four

Next, imagine a metaphorical image that represents the feeling of your negative belief. In other words, let a picture come to mind that describes how you feel in the stuck pattern. This metaphor will show you how manageable or insurmountable you perceive the challenge of your situation to be.

For example, Tim, a friend of mine, once described his career situation in terms of having painted himself into a corner with no way out but to leap out the window. This image felt dangerous and extreme with visions of Tim plummeting many stories to his death. Someone suggested he imagine himself on the first floor so he could easily step out of the window onto solid ground. In this image, the only negative consequence is that he might get his pants dirty! Then someone else suggested that he could step out of the window and fly instead of fall. By playing with his image in this way, Tim diffused the power of it. Now every time the old fear comes up he can quickly diffuse it by calling up the modified metaphor where he has power.

Write your own metaphor and notice how much power it has. Does your image describe a small inconvenience or a life-threatening obstacle? Play with your own metaphor the way Tim did until it is an easily manageable challenge. Bring this manageable metaphor to mind whenever you feel fear, pain or stuck around this pattern.

Step Five

Now create a new, positive image that describes the experience you want. The positive image is not about disappearing what you don't want any more the way you did in Step Four. This is an image of what you want to replace your current situation. So, for example, Tim could imagine what it would feel like to have the perfect job. He might picture himself opening the door to a beautiful garden where many people greet him and welcome him. He might see himself busy doing work he loves, being productive, attracting positive recognition and financial reward. He wouldn't even need to know what kind of work this is. He could still make the experience vivid and real by imagining how he wants to feel at his job and by feeling the emotional intensity of his joy, empowerment and satisfaction.

You may need to work with your image for a while to get it right. Giving energy to a new metaphor will often produce dramatic results. You may find that what you thought you wanted doesn't feel quite right either (as when I envisioned my friend's leaking sparks image). Keep modifying your image over time until it feels just right.

Step Six

Make your new image a part of your belief system by giving it energy. At least once a day, take time out to relax, close your eyes, take some deep breaths and imagine your new scenario as vividly as you can. Place yourself in it rather than seeing it from an observer's perspective. Make it clear and real by experiencing it with all of your senses as though it is actually happening. Make the colors bright, feel it as a physical sensation in your body, add sound, etc. Say your affirmation as you create this inner image. Let the experience reach a peak of intensity, then take a deep breath and let it go.

Step Seven

Between these intensive imaging sessions, remind yourself frequently, many times a day, of the whole inner experience of this new image. Say your affirmations many times to yourself. Picture the scenes of your imagery and allow a wave of loving well-being to wash over you.

Many of these suggestions begin with a paradigm shift. The old paradigm of reality holds that only physical action produces physical results. To tap into a higher paradigm of power we must first recognize the power we are exercising in every moment through the thoughts we are choosing to think. Remember "Sticks and stones will break my bones but words will never hurt me!"? Not true! The words we choose direct our creative energy. Try saying to yourself three times, "Something terrible is going to happen!", and then say three times, "Everything is turning out just fine!" and notice how different your body feels. The energy you feel in your body is the energy that is directing physical matter around you, calling into being circumstances that will match the quality of this energy. Fear calls fearful things into being, joy calls joyful things. And the choice is yours.

Blame, Shame and Self-responsibility

Self-responsibility, that is, the concept that we create our experience through our thoughts, beliefs and expectations, is one that makes many people bristle because it seems abusive, self-punishing, even egotistical to assume credit for all the things that happen to us in life. If you have a difficult time with the idea of self-responsibility, if it feels unfair, burdensome, preposterous or if it makes you angry, then very likely you have been taught early in life to carry a lot of shame. Blame and shame go hand in hand, one giving rise to the other. For those of us who have been taught shame, it is unbearable to let go of blame because all the energy that had been going into blaming external forces for everything that is wrong has nowhere to go except toward feeling shame. In other words, if we are in a habit of blaming others, when we stop we are likely to start blaming ourselves instead.

The concept of self-responsibility becomes abusive and harmful when it is applied in a blame and shame context. For example, many have applied the idea of self-responsibility to physical illness in a way that assumes an ill person has done something terribly wrong to create their disease. Others hold a perspective that they are somehow less spiritually evolved if the outer circumstances of their lives do not reflect joy and abundance. Some become overly zealous with the idea of responsibility and equate it with personal control, thinking that if they control every act, thought and habit well enough, their lives will go just as they plan. They blame and shame themselves when challenging and painful experiences happen.

"Personal control" breaks down because we can only have control over those aspects of self that are within the range of our conscious awareness. When painful and unexpected challenges arise, they can be a way to become conscious of limiting beliefs and patterns that have been operating at an unconscious level. Most of us have an assortment of conscious and unconscious, sometimes conflicting agendas, all operating to create our experience in life.

An example of an unconscious agenda conflicting with a conscious one would be a person consciously wanting to heal from an illness while receiving so much benefit from the caring attention and rest that the illness has necessitated that there is an unconscious investment in maintaining whatever circumstances are needed (i.e. the illness) to keep these rewards coming. Another example would be someone who consciously wants to succeed in life and grow beyond the limited success of his parents, yet at the same time holds an unconscious agenda of family loyalty that prohibits outshining his mother or father. Or, a person may long to be in a relationship yet have an unconscious belief that an intimate partnership would mean the loss of personal freedom and sense of self. When these unconscious agendas are present, we often have the experience of spinning our wheels. Even though we direct a lot of energy toward our conscious desire, we don't seem to make any progress. And we won't until the unconscious agenda is somehow addressed or released. It is often through the challenging experiences in life that we have an opportunity to see and change these hidden agendas so that we can stop wasting energy being at cross purposes with ourselves.

There is never a context in which blame or shame serves us or motivates us to be a better person. They are disempowering, often immobilizing emotions. To shift from blame and shame to self-responsibility, look at what you don't like about your life, not as something you did wrong (shame), or as something done to you by circumstances beyond your control (blame), but with the question, "How does this situation show what I've learned to expect from life?" For example, in the event of being a target of violent crime or abuse of any sort, the distortion of self-responsibility would be to assume, "I must have done something to deserve or ask for it." The more positive application is to examine how you have been taught to expect danger or abuse as part of life. How have you been taught that you are not safe? The opportunity here is to learn compassion for yourself, forgiveness for another and to begin to develop a deeper understanding of your own safety that will ultimately keep you safer physically. As a counselor many years ago, I noticed that my women clients who had been raped had almost all been subjected to sexual or physical abuse as children. They had learned to expect to be harmed. No one had ever taught them they had a right to be safe.

Ask yourself about the value of a painful situation and how it serves you. If you look closely enough there is invariably a gain. Sometimes we fill up our lives with energy-draining obstacles because on some level we are not ready for what we think we would rather be doing. If we never have time or opportunity to pursue our dreams, we never have an opportunity to fail. If we are constantly a victim of circumstances beyond our control we can ask for people's support and empathy and have less expected of us than if we had not fallen upon "hard luck." There are hidden gains in even the most unpleasant life experiences.

Once, for example, I was driving to an appointment feeling very irritated and rushed. I had made a promise to myself a week earlier to break a pattern of angry thinking where I focused on an irritating situation and played it over and over in my mind until I made myself feel terrible. On this particular day I had succumbed to my old habit and my mind was going wild playing over angry scenarios. All of a sudden a car in front of me slammed on the brakes and I was just able to screech to a stop without hitting it. The car behind me, however, kept right on going into my bumper. The collision wasn't my fault and in my state of irritation I could have felt victimized and chosen to experience it as one more crummy event to add to a really bad day. Instead, the accident had a totally different effect. It literally shook me out of anger and into a place of surrender. It occurred to me that the minor accident was a perfect reflection of the state my mind was in when it happened. It even seemed to be an answer to my prayer for help in releasing angry thoughts. There was no serious damage done, I was only slightly bumped and bruised, and it had completely knocked all the angry thoughts out of my head. As I drove the rest of the distance to my appointment I felt very much at peace for the first time that day.

The power in self-responsibility is that once we start seeing our own contribution to our circumstances, we can change them. If the world is treating you badly, look to see how this could be a reflection of how you treat yourself. Are there ways you are treating yourself badly? Are you self-critical? Do you put everyone else's needs before your own? Do you get so caught up in doing what is expected of you and what you think you should do that you have no time left to explore what you want to do? These are just a few ways that we may manifest our lack of self-love and acceptance.

When I talk about self-responsibility in my workshops, there is usually someone who says, "But I believe God creates my reality, not me!" I agree whole-heartedly. Harnessing the power to create our reality is all about putting fears, doubts and egotism to rest so that we can come into greater alignment with the plan God has for us. It is about listening within for higher guidance and courageously acting upon it rather than letting fear and habit move us.

Acceptance

When we move beyond blame and shame, we can experience challenging life situations from a place of acceptance rather than judgment. Far from being an attitude of weakness, it is through acceptance that we unlock surprising powers and resources to transform our situation. I know a woman who has lived with melanoma for many years. This extremely dangerous form of skin cancer required her to have painful surgeries every six weeks to remove precancerous growths. She struggled through periods of anger, fear and depression over her illness and related to the cancer as an enemy to be combated. Finally, after reading a book on spiritual healing, she decided to make friends with her body and her disease. Every day she wrote pages of the affirmation, "Thank you, God, for cancer." At first the words felt untrue and hard to write but she kept at it week after week. Gradually she stopped feeling like a victim of her illness and soon her six week check ups were detecting no precancerous tissue. More than a year later she was still clear of cancerous growth.

We always have a choice about how to perceive the life circumstances we have experienced in the past or present. The most harsh or tragic events may be the greatest turning points of our lives. That doesn't mean we need to call pain into our lives in order to grow. I believe that growth happens as we release our need to respond to life with pain or call forth the circumstances that will affirm our belief in pain. As we let go of our perception of ourselves as victims, we take a big step toward releasing pain from our lives.

Many of us feel victimized by our past and "damaged" as a result. Yet perhaps on some level we have called these wounds into our lives to help us tap into our greatness and to transcend the belief in our vulnerability. I lived for many years with a cruel, abusive parent who went out of his way to shame and torment me. On one hand, I can blame much pain, poor self-esteem and many failed relationships on this man. But, on the other hand, I don't believe I would be doing the work I am doing today, or have the values, joys and love I have in my life now if it weren't for the experiences I had with my father. Because love was not given to me easily I had to learn about it and become an "expert" in it. I have had to learn that I don't need to be a victim and consequently have this belief more firmly implanted than I would have otherwise. As we stop calling our circumstances "bad" and our experiences "painful" they lose their charge to hurt and control us. As we stop defining ourselves as victims we stop being victims.

Exercise: Transforming Painful Life Experiences

Step One
Write down a challenging experience that you would like to transform.

Step Two
Imagine that you have a Higher Self — a part of you that can never be harmed or do harm — and that this Higher Self has created a

playground for enacting all kinds of situations that will enable you to stretch, develop strengths and ultimately open to your highest good. The greatest challenge of this playground is to break through the illusion that you are not safe, supported and loved. All the pain you experience in life is a result of fearfully resisting this truth and as you remember that you are always safe, whole and have all that you need, pain and fear disappear. In this playground your consciousness is powerfully creative. Remember that what you think, feel, believe, desire and fear all have an impact on the physical world, turning your inner experience into your outer reality.

Step Three

Ask yourself: How is this challenge serving me? What is it helping me/allowing me/forcing me to do, be or have that I wouldn't otherwise experience? Is it forcing me to let others help me? Is it causing me to spend my time differently? Is it allowing me to put off doing things that are frightening or burdensome? Am I receiving attention that I wouldn't otherwise get? Am I developing strengths and resources I didn't know I had? Is it preserving a familiar identity? Am I comfortable being a victim? What is the opportunity in this challenge?

Step Four

If no answers come to the above questions (or even if they do) fill a page with an affirmation of gratitude for this situation. An example might be: "Thank you, (God, Higher Self, Spirit, Universe), for this experience in my life." Keep working with this affirmation every day until you feel the truth of what you are writing and a sense of peace around the situation.

Step Five

Pray for a way to receive the lessons or gains of this situation differently without pain and struggle. If you have never prayed before, imagine handing over your pain and struggle to a Higher Power. Speak silently or aloud whatever heart-felt words express your desire for and openness to receive help with this situation. Imagine that your prayer is heard by a Higher Intelligence. You can envision this as your own Higher Self or any form of God, Spirit or Universal Intelligence that is meaningful to you. Fill yourself with faith and certainty that healing is already underway.

Step Six

Look at how the world is treating you through this experience as a reflection of how you treat yourself. Let go of any inclination to look for what you did wrong and instead see how you could direct more compassion, forgiveness and love toward yourself. Imagine the part of you that created this painful situation as a small child who is afraid, in pain, innocent. Allow the adult in you to embrace and reassure the child. Let the child in you feel loved and accepted.

Self-responsibility and Keeping Our Word

How much thought do you give before verbally committing yourself to things? When you give your word are you speaking what you hope to accomplish or what you are certain you will do? How important is it to you to do what you say you will? Is there a big difference between your intentions and your actions?

And, is there any reason to make a big deal about whether we keep every promise we make? Of course, there are some obvious consequences to chronically breaking promises. We let people down and must then deal with their disappointment and distrust. But for many of us, these consequences never reach epic proportions. Our friends and family learn to live with our frequent lateness or occasional cancellations and we give the whole matter very little thought.

Yet, there is another less visible factor in operation every time we use our words to define our intentions. When we speak, we are giving expression to our thoughts, and our thoughts are creative. Remember, what we think is what we create.

Our subconscious creative mind is like a computer, very literally creating the reality we program into it through our constant thoughts and words. All the current circumstances of our lives reflect some component of what we think, believe or where we give our attention. If we want to know what we are telling ourselves over and over, all we need do is look around at the life we have created. If we believe life is hard and speak of it often, we will certainly live a hard life. If we believe we are at the mercy of circumstances beyond our control, and offer frequent excuses for why we can't keep the promises we made, we will perpetually call into our lives circumstances that overpower us and necessitate more excuses.

Just as repeating a positive affirmation directs our subconscious mind toward creating that affirmation as reality, all the rest of our conscious and not so conscious self-talk becomes our reality. Every thought we think and every word we casually speak is a creative force. Every time we speak an intention and then fail to carry it out we give the message, not just to others, but to our subconscious creative mind that we do not have the power to carry through. While this may not seem significant when it comes to keeping a social engagement, this same message can have a devastating effect when applied to the more important areas of our lives. When we can't carry through with our intentions to make a relationship work, or pursue our life purpose, or create what we want most in life, we enact this message that we can't trust ourselves.

Developing the ability to keep our word is not just about being a "good" person. It relates directly to our power and ability to turn any intention into reality. Have you ever made a wrong turn to a particular destination and then the next time found yourself making the same wrong turn again automatically? Soon the wrong turn is firmly anchored as an unconscious habit that has to be unlearned. In the same way, when we have a significant number of experiences that start with a promise being made and end with that promise being broken, our subconscious mind begins to automatically put these two things together. Remember, this unconscious part of us is very literal. It doesn't know the difference between a promise to someone else and a promise to self, or which promises are important to us and which are not. It simply generalizes our own personal reality that promises aren't always kept. Then when a crucially important promise arises, our subconscious creative mind applies the same belief system to the process of keeping it. Whatever resistance we bring to keeping the smaller promises of life — lack of motivation, unforeseen circumstances getting in the way, lack of time, struggle — will find their way into our bigger promises as well.

When we establish a habit of keeping every promise we make, we set in motion a similar automatic conditioned response. Only this time our subconscious creative mind sets about keeping our promises from the personal reality that all promises are fulfilled. All of our creativity is directed toward this end and we don't find ourselves battling against insurmountable obstacles or running out of steam. As in learning a new route to a destination, the more we travel it, the more it becomes automatic and does not require any thought or effort.

When I present the concept in my workshops that we create our own reality, it invariably meets with massive resistance. "But, surely there are circumstances that really are out of our control!" people say and then mention the multitudes of circumstances that could prevent them from keeping their word. And as they speak, they are directing creative mind power into envisioning, speaking and unknowingly calling all of these possibilities into being. Instead they could choose to imagine, and thereby create, a different reality.

I have seen circumstances shift in a "coincidental" way to accommodate someone's clear intention so often that I have long ceased to consider it coincidence. For example, a woman who had attended several of my 5-day workshops had been late every Friday evening due to a regular work commitment. The fourth time she attended, she announced on Thursday that she was going to experiment: she decided very firmly that she was going to be on time the next day. She didn't know how that would happen, she just pictured it happening and nothing else. The next day she was not only on time, she was early. Her last several clients of the day unexpectedly canceled, leaving her with hours of free time.

Then there was a time when I was preparing to board a flight home after a long work trip. I was exhausted and not looking forward to getting off the plane and driving right to a group I was scheduled to lead that evening. What's more, the flight was packed with a group of very boisterous twelve years olds who were already driving me crazy in the waiting area. I dreaded the thought of stuffing my exhausted self into a small space with all of their energy.

Just as these thoughts were rumbling through my mind, a flight attendant approached me and apologetically said that I would have to wait for a later flight as the plane was overbooked with passengers unable to accommodate a delay. I jumped at the opportunity to avoid the plane full of preteens and to have a good excuse for not leading my group that evening ("It's not my fault — I was bumped from my flight!"). What's more, there was the bonus prize of the free air ticket they offered for my inconvenience. Life was bliss!

But then, I got to thinking about the "importance of keeping a commitment" talk I always give in my workshops. A little part of me actually started wanting to get to back to my group instead of indulging in the nice lunch, quiet flight and restful evening (not to mention the free air ticket) that I was envisioning. As I wished for some way I could return home in time, the flight attendant approached again, this time to say there was one seat left for me after all, only it was in first class. So, not only did I get home in time, I wound up having a very nice peaceful flight with first class service, removed from the noise and bustle of the kids. I also wound up having a wonderful experience in my group that evening. I went home feeling refreshed and happy.

A frequent reason I hear people use for needing to break their word has to do with self-care, as in "Sometimes it's just more important to take care of myself than to keep a commitment. After all, if I don't take care of myself, how can I take care of anyone else?". Feeling pitted between getting our own needs met and meeting the needs of others is a common experience for many of us, yet it, too, is a result of our thoughts and beliefs. It signals a basic belief that it's either you or them, and sooner or later someone will have to sacrifice. As you shift this belief you will stop attracting situations that force you to choose between your own well-being and that of others. You will find that where you previously saw only two choices, there are now other options that allow everyone's highest good to be served.

Whenever you feel torn between two choices, where either you lose or someone else loses, you need to expand your vision to take in a larger paradigm. The next time you firmly believe there are only two imperfect options, imagine that there is, in fact, a third choice, and a fourth, and a fifth.... You simply haven't seen them yet. It may be time to let your imagination stretch a bit to consider options of an entirely different nature.

Giving and Keeping Our Word in an Empowered Way

Before deciding upon how to keep your word, it is first important to carefully examine how you give your word. Many of us say yes quickly, because it's easier than saying no, without really giving thought to our willingness or capacity to carry through. We want to avoid the direct confrontation of saying no, or we sincerely wish we could mean yes, even though we are overextending ourselves and know we can't keep every promise we make.

Some people struggle with the whole idea of commitment. Once a commitment has been made they feel restricted, anxious, even rebellious. Of course, this, too, reflects learned beliefs about life. This particular pattern usually has to do with feeling that there is not enough freedom, not enough choice in life. Many people waste a great deal of creative energy on rebelling against commitment and keeping all options open, so they never fully receive the benefits of any option.

The flip side of this coin includes those who fulfill every commitment perfectly, yet do so because they are afraid not to. Here there is a belief that "I must be perfect to be accepted." Those who fear commitment and those who fear breaking commitments both are caught in a pattern of reacting to external forces. When we're caught in this reactive pattern it becomes difficult to hear the inner guidance that tells us when to commit and when to say no.

Consider making a habit of stopping and thinking before making a commitment, even a small one. Envision yourself keeping this commitment. If it's hard to imagine, it's likely that you won't keep it. Check in with your body and ask for a "yes" or "no" feeling. If you feel excited, peaceful, or happy, it is a sign that you have energy and willingness to carry through. If you feel heavy or uncomfortable in your body, then this commitment may not be in your best interest and will be harder to keep. By saying no more often, your subconscious creative mind will be less likely to call forth circumstances "beyond your control" to prevent you from keeping your promises. As you become more careful about making only the promises you intend to keep, it becomes easier to keep all the promises you make.

Should you find yourself in a position of having given your word with every intention of keeping it, yet somewhere along the way things have changed so that the commitment feels burdensome or even impossible, you still can find an alternative to breaking your word. This is an opportunity to transform your situation to find a solution more creative and expansive than you have yet imagined.

I once made a commitment to lead a six-month long training program, but three months into it, I unexpectedly left my job with the sponsoring organization. On one hand, I did not want to be burdened with three more months of work for a job I no longer held. On the other hand, I had emphasized to participants the importance of making a commitment to attend the full six months and felt that my integrity was on the line. I felt I had no choice but to keep my commitment, but was doing so grudgingly. After a week or two of this, it suddenly occurred to me that there could be another choice besides deserting my class or being burdened with work I didn't want. I decided to make the next three months the best group experience I had ever had. I had no particular plan for how to make it happen, I just held this vision in my mind. Very quickly the group reflected my intention back to me by becoming more bonded, open and willing to take risks. It did, in fact, evolve into the most powerful and fulfilling group experience I had ever had. I am very grateful not to have missed this experience by choosing to "take care of myself" by breaking my commitment.

Another alternative that many people never consider is to simply have a conversation with the person you gave your word to and see if he or she is willing to release you from your commitment. Sometimes it is important to the other person that you keep your promise and you have an opportunity to practice transforming a burdensome commitment. Sometimes it's truly not a big deal. It may be a gift that the other person is happy to give to you.

Keeping your word doesn't mean turning life into a terrible burden and pushing yourself beyond reasonable limits. Rather, as we decide to make our word into something solid and meaningful and direct creative power toward this end, it begins to happen easily, naturally, even joyfully.

If you do find yourself in the position of breaking your word, experiment with doing so in a more empowered way by letting go of the habit of explaining why it wasn't your fault. Every time you say that you wanted to do something but couldn't, you affirm your powerlessness and give more power to the part of you that is well-meaning but ineffectual. Instead, give up your excuses and ask yourself what part of your thoughts, fears or wishes are reflected in the current outcome. Imagine that you could have created a different outcome if you had directed your thought and creativity along different channels, and you can create a different outcome next time.

It's important, as you do this, to let go of all blame and shame. These attitudes pull your creative energy into a dark hole and keep it there. When you break a promise, instead of judging what you've done as wrong or resenting the person you made the commitment to, completely step out of the dynamic of victim or victimizer that goes along with blame and shame. Look at the experience as feedback, showing you how, where and why you block your own creative power. Use the experience to help you see how to become a more powerful channel.

For example, there was another time I was scheduled to fly home to Baltimore from a work-related trip in Minneapolis and go right to a weekly group that I led. On this particular trip I had had some very intense emotional experiences that felt incomplete. I wasn't quite ready to go home. My flight left on time but two hours into what was normally a two and a half hour flight, the pilot announced that he was turning the plane around and we were flying back to Minneapolis due to thunder storms around the Baltimore area. My unwillingness to go home manifested quite dramatically and I wound up back in the Twin Cities. I didn't get home until very late that night and missed my group meeting. At the next group meeting, instead of explaining about storms and the plane turning around, I talked instead about the emotional experience I had had and my divided attention. I apologized for this rather than for circumstances beyond my control. I used the evening to strengthen my commitment to the group.

Blame and shame constitute our greatest resistance to the possibility that we are the creators of our lives. If we are powerful enough to create ease and fulfillment, then we must also take responsibility for all the struggle as well. We are so conditioned to see through the filter of judgment and guilt that this becomes a terrible burden. Better to continue in a safe groove of mediocrity than to accept that we have called circumstances of our lives into being through our thoughts, fears and expectations.

Yet, keep in mind that much of what we have created stems from patterns of thought and expectations that we learned at a very young age. These thoughts have become semi-conscious habits. There is no guilt or shame in believing in and acting from what we were taught. Furthermore, there are some things we call into being, such as illness and hardship, that seem to have some deep soul purpose, helping us to learn lessons we would not learn any other way. Figuring out why and who's to blame is not so important as the truth that we always have the potential to transform our experience in the present.

Steps for Empowering Your Word

Step One

Before giving your word to anything, no matter how small, stop and check in with yourself to see if you are truly willing and able to carry through. Make only those promises that you are willing to keep. Give yourself permission to say "no" when something doesn't feel right.

Step Two

Once you have given your word, imagine yourself following through in a way that is joyful. Dispel any thoughts that pop up about what might prevent you from keeping your word, or visions of it being unpleasant and burdensome. As these thoughts arise, replace them with an affirmation such as, "It is pleasant and effortless to keep all my promises," or picture yourself going about your commitments in a way that is fun and easy.

As you carefully choose the commitments you make and only make those that you intend to keep and get an inner "yes" about carrying through on, you will be able to keep the promises you make. The great power in this is that you will then be more able to create your heart's desire simply by promising yourself that it will be so. The following exercise is a powerful one for strengthening your subconscious belief in your ability to keep your promises and directing this subconscious belief toward manifesting your heart's desire.

Exercise: Using the Power of Commitment to Call Forth Your Highest Good

Step One

Identify a goal that feels very important and that you deeply want to have, do or be.

Step Two

Think of a commitment to an action that you are willing to make as a symbolic act toward creating this heart's desire. A symbolic act is an action that you give special meaning to so that as you do this act, you affirm and call into being the deeper significance you have given it. For example, the act might be to clean out your house and the symbolic meaning you give it is that you are making a clear, empty space that is now attracting your highest good into it. The particular action you choose to take will not be as important as the act of committing and following through on your commitment.

To give it added power, come up with an action you will perform over a period of time rather than just once. Make it something you are capable of doing yet still challenges you with having to choose to do it. For example, promising yourself that you will successfully run a marathon or make a million dollars in the next year when you have never done these things before is too big. The idea is to come up with something where the challenge is about keeping your commitment rather than the act itself being a challenge. Also set a time limit rather than making it open-ended so you will succeed at keeping your commitment rather than having it fade away as you gradually forget about it.

Some examples of symbolic acts include writing a page of affirmations every day for a month, committing to being on time for work and other engagements for a period of time, committing to a program of self-healing or exercise, paying your bills on time every month for the next year, picking one or more unfinished business situations in your life and committing to cleaning them up within a certain time frame, or counting your blessings every day. A symbolic act is therapeutic and productive in and of itself. As you give it a deeper symbolic significance, it will become even more powerfully creative.

Step Three
Check in with your inner guidance to see if this is a promise you are truly willing to keep. Close your eyes and envision yourself keeping this commitment. Is it easy or difficult to imagine yourself following through? If it's difficult to imagine then you probably won't. As you imagine yourself keeping this promise, how do you feel? Remember, if you feel excited, peaceful, or other pleasant feelings, you are starting with the energy and willingness to carry through. If you feel heaviness, dread, anxiety or other discomfort, then this commitment may not work for your highest good and will be harder to keep.

Sometimes there is a risk factor involved in a commitment that will touch off some fear, yet there is excitement and an inner "yes" feeling at the same time. This is telling you that the commitment is a powerful one to make even though keeping it may make you stretch and grow. If you don't get an inner "yes," then scale down or change the commitment until you do get a "yes" from your inner guidance.

Step Four
Perform this act and keep this promise as though your heart's desire depends upon it. As you go about doing the activity, affirm to yourself often that the power of your commitment is now calling forth your highest good. If you find your resolve wavering, ask yourself if having your heart's desire depended upon keeping this commitment, would you? You will almost always find the answer to this question is "yes!" The power of a symbolic act is that performing it with your goal in mind actually does call your desired outcome into being.

3

"The absolute tranquillity is the present moment.
Though it is at this moment, there is no limit to this moment,
and herein is eternal delight."

—Hui-neng, Sixth Zen Patriarch

Focusing Our Power in the Present

Our point of power is in the present. Because we create our reality through our state of mind, and our state of mind exists only in the present, manifesting any desired future outcome begins with a change in consciousness in the moment.

The Power of Consciousness

Imagine a mother who is worried about her child's safety while he is away from home. According to the old rules of reality that say we only have the limited power of our physical efforts, she would have little power to help in the moment. She might come up with some ideas for keeping the child safer the next time he leaves home. Or, she could physically intervene in some way by going to where her child is or by sending someone else to her child's aid. Other than these physical interventions she is likely to feel powerless to protect the child in the present moment. In her helplessness she would not see the present as an opportunity to exercise power. She would be more likely to wait and worry, envisioning dangers that could befall her child and putting off the experience of inner peace until he came home safely.

If this woman knew that her creative power was unlimited and began with her thoughts in the moment, she would have more options. Instead of wasting her power on worry, she could hold in mind visions of her son being safe and protected. She could imagine wrapping him in the deepest possible experience of peace and well-being. She could release her fear because she knows that she had taken powerful action to help. Perhaps her son would come home and describe an accident that just missed happening to him.

Working within the limited paradigm of physical reality, when we want to accomplish something, we form a goal, then a plan; we take action, we move things around on the physical plane; we wait for the process to unfold step by step. Creating change on this level involves much waiting — waiting for the opportunity to use our power of physical intervention, waiting for that intervention to bear fruit, waiting for external events to come along and make us happy. Consequently, our attention is often focused more on the future than the present. However, if we create our reality through our state of mind, then our power must lie in the present moment because our consciousness exists only in the now. We are often unaware of our power in the moment when we believe in the limited reality of our physical senses. From this perspective, movement is locked into a predictable linear process limited by our perception of space, time and physical energy. As we stop believing that we are defined by the limits of our physical body, we create results that defy the limits of physical reality.

Simply living in the moment as fully and richly as possible is powerfully creative. As we access our power of thought in the present, life starts to unfold differently. We experience miraculous coincidences and "lucky" breaks that are difficult to explain in the context of physical reality. For example, a friend of mine, after being unemployed for several years due to illness, decided it was time to work again. The prospect of finding an appropriate job that would interest her, use her creative skills and accommodate the physical limitations she still had seemed daunting. But rather than scouring the want ads, updating her resume and going on endless job interviews, Deb devoted her attention instead to prayer. She focused on releasing her fear that she would not find what she needed and imagined something wonderful showing up. One day as she and I were out together, she felt compelled to stop and explore a small shop that neither of us had ever been in before. The store sold beautiful jewelry similar to what Deb made herself. Talking to the shop employee, Deb discovered that much of the store's jewelry was made in a factory upstairs and they were desperately in need of a new jeweler. She quickly applied for and was given a job that satisfied her desire for challenging creative work, supportive co-workers and flexible hours. She created all this without doing anything other than changing her state of mind and listening to her intuition when it guided her to the shop.

Changing consciousness in the moment can help us to "leap" to a goal with a minimum of effort in situations where working harder gets us nowhere. I know a woman who put out tremendous effort for several months to either find a compatible roommate or a more affordable living situation. After three months, she had exhausted herself emotionally and financially with placing ads, distributing flyers, interviewing roommates who didn't work out and shopping for new apartments, all with no results. Finally, at a loss as to what more she could do, she wrote down everything she wanted in a new living experience, lit a candle to her new home, said some prayers and asked God to guide her. When she finished she had shifted out of fear and into a place of peace around her situation. Even though it was now 3 o'clock in the morning, she felt a strong urge to get in her car and drive for a while, something she often did when she needed some quiet time. On the drive, she found herself in a neighborhood and on a street where she felt she could enjoy living. She stopped her car in front of a house and had a strange feeling that she was meant to live there. There was no "for rent" sign or any indication that the house was a rental property at all. She just had a feeling. Frustrated at having so little to go on, she asked God to give her a sign if she was truly meant to live in this house. Immediately, the front porch light went on. In spite of this clear sign, she went home confused about how to act on it. The next day she checked the apartment listings in the paper as she did every day and found one in her price range. It turned out to be an apartment in the building she had been guided to the previous night. She was the first person to call about it and immediately rented it. After she moved in, she quickly became friends with a number of her neighbors and these connections led her into a new and exciting phase of life. Interestingly, she found the front porch light that had given her the sign didn't work.

Viewing life from the limited parameters of physical reality, we assume that if our physical efforts are not working, we must apply more effort. When we act from our spiritual power, quite often the opposite is more effective. When we use the power of our consciousness and no longer rely solely upon the interventions of our physical efforts, we can eliminate a good deal of work. We can even break through apparent log jams where no amount of physical force is going to help.

Exercise: Shifting into Spiritual Power

At least several times a day for the next week, affirm that in order to create your highest possible future, all you need to do is release thoughts of the past and the future and create this instant to be as full, rich and loving as you would like the rest of your life to become.

With this thought, fill yourself for an instant with the inner experience of joy, love and appreciation. Create this feeling so vividly that you experience it as a physical sensation of well-being in your body. Bring to mind any images that fill you with joy and peace, and say to yourself any words that help to trigger feelings of peace.

Know, as you do this, that each instant you devote to fully experiencing peace and well-being is a potent seed that is taking root and growing the joyful future that you desire.

Living for the Future

Our culture is extremely goal oriented, and consequently, future oriented. Most of us have this tendency ingrained to some extent. We believe that our happiness depends upon achieving certain external outcomes such as a successful career, lots of money, the perfect relationship, a nice house, and so on. Then we postpone happiness, doing whatever we have to do to achieve our goal, telling ourselves that we will get our reward later. And, while we may succeed in getting the external things we aim for, the experience of happiness often remains elusive. By the time we reach our goal, we may not even stop to take joy in it because we have already formulated a next goal, and a next.

Because what we tell ourselves quite literally becomes our reality, if we affirm that we will be happy when we reach our goals, we perpetuate a state of waiting to be happy. We perpetuate a reality that is about striving to be happy rather than being happy. When we live for a future goal, we are more inclined to settle for an unsatisfying present and believe that the end justifies the means. We don't listen to feelings of pain and unhappiness that are signals from our inner guidance telling us that what we are doing is not in harmony with our highest good. We grit our teeth and bear it because we believe in some future time when we will be rewarded. But this future panacea always remains in the future. As we wait for our reward, we wind up with a lot of unpleasant time to kill. We have much pain, discomfort and emptiness to escape from. We learn to suppress our emotions and turn to addictions of all sorts to make life bearable.

The more we brace ourselves against the pain of our lives and numb ourselves with addictive substances and behaviors, the less we are able to hear the small, quiet voice of intuition. And it is this voice that will lead us to the marvelous coincidences through which we leap into our highest good, as opposed to struggling toward it. Living in the moment and harnessing our full creative power requires opening to the full force of our feelings. Our physical senses and our emotions are the channels our intuition and creative power flows through. When we shut them off we are disempowered.

Without a full range of emotion flowing through us, we lose touch with what's most important. We forget what we want from life. Our "heart's" desire, (our highest joy in life) and our "gut" feelings (the intuition that directs us to our heart's desire) are messages from our higher self that we receive quite literally through the physical sensations of our body.

This may be difficult to comprehend without first understanding the extent to which we as a culture have learned to disconnect from our bodies. In a multitude of ways we are taught not to listen to our feelings. When something hurts, we take an aspirin. If we are emotionally stressed and physically tense after work, we drink a beer to "unwind." If a loved one dies, our doctor prescribes a tranquilizer lest we feel the full impact of our grief.

The result of these learned habits of numbing ourselves to pain and disconnecting from the feelings in our physical bodies is that we lose our sensitivity to all feelings. This means our capacity for joy and pleasure is diminished, our intuition is harder to discern and we literally forget what truly makes us happy. We lose our passion for life. We fall into a rut and feel depressed.

This is when we grasp for substitutes that will lessen the pain. Our culture has developed a multitude of strategies for "coping" with stress. These solutions, which include all kinds of addictive habits and ways to avoid painful emotions, mask but do not heal the pain and separateness that cause stress. As we settle for "coping" as an alternative to healing, we numb our body and spirit and diminish our capacity to perceive inner guidance and experience ecstasy. To fully utilize the power of our own consciousness, we must first stop numbing our consciousness though addictions.

When Coping Becomes Addiction

In the last few decades, it has become easier to identify serious addictions. A generation ago, addictions to alcohol, food and other substances were often disguised as normal social behavior or were strictly closeted and kept hidden within families. Now a barrage of literature, support groups and TV talk shows are educating us on the symptoms of addiction and making it easier to seek treatment.

But what about those of us who don't have severe symptoms of addiction that create havoc in our lives and place us clearly outside the "normal" range of behavior? Those of us who can't get through a day without coffee or cigarettes? Who can't unwind at night without several or more hours of TV or a beer or two? Those of us who order a pizza or turn to a chocolate cake when we're not really hungry, but just want something? Or who can't seem to stop working, or shopping, or exercising?

According to my dictionary, "addiction" is the "state of being given up to some habit, practice or pursuit," which probably includes all of us to some degree or another. Addiction has become a modern day coping mechanism for most of us, though not necessarily in an extreme or life-threatening form. So perhaps the question of "Am I an addict?" needs to be refined to "How am I addicted? What habits have I 'given up' to?"

Ask yourself the following questions:

1. Do I have habits that are an integral part of relaxing, socializing, having fun or performing adequately?

2. Do I routinely turn to a behavior or substance to help cope with times of stress?

3. Have I gone from a heavy pattern of regular drug/alcohol use to what feels like a moderate (i.e. acceptable) pattern of regular use (for example: from a past pattern of heavy daily marijuana use to a current pattern of one or two beers a day)?

4. Do I have difficulty knowing what I'm feeling or what I want?

5. Do I have difficulty feeling intimacy and sustaining it?

The Cost of Coping

If you said yes to any of these questions, you may have a low-level coping habit. What's wrong with these habits that help us "get by?" After all, they make it easier to live in our fast-paced world that stresses "doing" over "being" and future accomplishment over present happiness. When we believe that achieving a future goal will make all our present pain worthwhile, "being" in the moment seems a dangerous distraction that will lull us into complacency (as in "no pain, no gain").

Addictions help us to keep going in spite of the pain. There's no time to relax until a headache eases, so medication is taken. A beer at night numbs out the stresses of the day so there is no need to evaluate the causes and impact of such daily stress. A 90's TV ad summed up this outlook in its remedy for stress-related indigestion. It said we could try a change in diet, or a change in life-style but, better yet, we could just take an antacid!

Yet, our highest power lies in the present, so the more we turn off our "being" with numbing habits, the more we disconnect from our spiritual power source.

What's more, when we reach for an instant fix to turn off pain, the pain doesn't really go away. We simply manage to keep it at arm's length. Elizabeth Kubler Ross, a pioneer in the death and dying field, knew this decades ago when she protested the practice of tranquilizing people in grief. She found that when people were denied the opportunity to fully experience their pain as it came up, their grieving period dragged on longer. The same holds true for all feelings that we identify as painful. Turning them off creates a perpetual stalemate that requires increasing amounts of energy to maintain.

At their root, addictive habits are attempts to heal and nurture ourselves by alleviating discomfort and filling up where we feel empty. And these attempts are not ineffective. Addictions work, but generally only for a limited time, within a limited range and with some negative side effects. Because the addictive substance or activity is not what we truly need, we never get full or healed and we crave more and more. At worst, addiction escalates, requiring so much energy to sustain it, and causing so many negative side effects, that it loses it's initial capacity to give relief, and sometimes becomes life threatening.

An addiction can seem benign when it doesn't escalate out of control or interfere with our daily functioning, yet it still draws us further and further away from our true needs for healing and fulfillment. The consequences of these contained, low-level addictions might not be as easy to see. They may show up as a lack of ecstasy, or a slow deterioration of physical health, or difficulty finding fulfillment in intimate relationships. And these symptoms are easy to dismiss. After all, lots of people get divorced these days, we expect more aches and pains with age, and who ever expects ecstasy anyway? Ecstasy plays little part in a "doing" lifestyle. It's too immeasurable, intangible and internal, a part of the lesser-known realm of "being."

What's perhaps most insidious about even low-level addictions is that as we increasingly lose touch with what truly fulfills us, we think the effects make us feel good because we have forgotten the possibility of greater feelings. We think we can bear to spend a large part of each day doing work we don't enjoy because we don't believe we have more desirable options. We endure emptiness and separateness even in our most intimate relationships because we simply don't know how to do otherwise. We don't know that we have built a prison around ourselves.

Stop Paying the Price

To undo the self-made prison these seemingly innocuous habits can create, begin by considering what substances, activities or behaviors you turn to when you feel in pain or empty. These are habits that don't really address the source of what you are feeling, but instead provide a temporary "fix." We can create an addiction out of almost anything — drugs, alcohol, work, food, sex, falling in love, watching TV, playing computer games or surfing the Net, reading, smoking, shopping, gambling, keeping busy. All kinds of activities, behaviors and thoughts can become compulsive. What differentiates an addiction from a harmless, enjoyable pastime is that addictions provide comfort and gratification in the moment but, instead of leaving us feeling fulfilled, we feel empty afterward and often worse for having done it.

In dealing with any kind of addiction, it's important to take the shame and secretiveness out of it. We tend to feel out of control in the face of our addictions. We shamefully think that if only we were stronger, better or more disciplined, we wouldn't have this habit. So we may tend to keep the full extent of our habit secret. Yet, self-discipline is not the true key to breaking addictions. Since what we do compulsively is really an attempt at self-healing and self-nurturing, applying discipline to eliminate the habit leaves more emptiness and pain that needs to be dealt with in some way.

This is why many people break one addictive habit only to replace it with another. Alcoholics Anonymous groups, for example, have been notoriously infested with cigarette smoke and coffee drinking. People who go on diets often become addicted to exercise, while people who quit smoking may take up compulsive eating. Focusing only on breaking a habit without addressing the emotions and situations that caused us to turn to the habit in the first place usually results in another habit.

The following suggestions can help you stop paying the price of the seemingly benign habits you use as addictions. This approach stresses filling up rather than simply breaking the habit through discipline. The following won't work when you are actively using alcohol or other drugs because the process emphasizes becoming more conscious, which is not possible when your consciousness is chemically altered. If you know you have a problem with drugs or alcohol, or even think you might, seek out assistance immediately to support your recovery. Find a 12-step program, support group, or therapist to guide you through the process. Don't try to stop alone. Even if you feel you can handle the immediate detoxification process, the long term effects of releasing chemicals from your system can include many physical shifts and emotional changes over months or years as your body detoxifies and you begin to experience a wide range of emotions that have been suppressed for years. It's invaluable to have a guide who can frame all these experiences as predictable and manageable aspects of recovery. What's more, being unwilling to reach out for help probably has a lot to do with why you reach for alcohol or drugs. Learning how to receive help will likely be an important part of the personal and life-style changes needed to support your continued sobriety.

Steps for Healing Addictions

I. Make the habit "legal."

Stop telling yourself the activity is bad or forbidden. Don't deny yourself the addiction and don't shame yourself. See it for what it is — an attempt to care for yourself.

II. Make the habit conscious.

Addictions are about becoming less conscious — they numb out our pain, unpleasant emotions and bothersome thoughts. Whether it takes the form of a food binge or working obsessively, we tend to lose track of what we are doing. We stop tasting what we are eating, we stop noticing how much of life we have let go to get our work done.

When you feel a craving for your addictive behavior or catch yourself in the middle of doing it, acknowledge that some part of you is calling for healing. Take a moment to close your eyes, breathe deeply and give your full attention to what you are feeling in your body. Notice everything you can about how your body feels. Notice what physical sensations and emotions are there and give them your full attention, letting them get even bigger. Giving attention to a painful or uncomfortable feeling and trying to make it bigger actually has a paradoxical effect of diminishing the pain of the sensation. By making it bigger, you begin to move through it rather than avoid it. (The next section in this chapter on emotional clearing gives more specific information on dealing with feelings.)

Addictions, even ones that are very physical, such as masturbation or eating, are about escaping from something uncomfortable. Allow yourself to feel the discomfort and ask yourself what it is that you truly want.

Recognizing what we really want is a significant part of becoming conscious. Let yourself daydream about what is most important to you. What do you love most? Write down anything that comes to mind. Ask yourself, "What are my dreams? What is my highest life purpose?" and let more answers come gradually over time as you're ready for them.

As you recognize what you really want, notice what you give yourself instead. Notice how much time and attention you give to what you think you should do or have to do. Notice how much time and attention you give to avoiding things you don't want. Is there any time and energy left for pursuing your dreams? Remember that what we give our attention to is what we perpetuate in our lives.

III. Find some alternate forms of self-nurturing and comfort.

Make a list of as many things as you can think of that are relaxing and nurturing, such as deep breathing, a warm bath, writing in a journal, listening to music, calling a friend, meditating or walking. As you do this you may become aware of how little attention you have given to self-care. Be careful not to simply replace one addiction with another. Remember, a self-nurturing activity leaves us feeling better afterward. An addiction contributes to our feeling of emptiness. Break the routine of your addiction by doing one of these new activities instead. These new rituals can help carry you through the recovery process and gradually develop into a new habit of self-love.

If you have practiced a new comfort activity and still crave your addiction, don't deny yourself. Instead, proceed with Step Four.

IV. Turn the addictive behavior into a self-healing ritual.

We generally have negative messages attached to our addictions. For example, a workaholic's message might be "If I don't keep working everything will fall apart." A food addict's message might be "It's bad to eat sweets. They make me fat." A shopaholic might think "I shouldn't be spending so much money. I can't afford this." Whenever we engage in our addiction we wind up consciously or unconsciously affirming these negative beliefs, keeping ourselves stuck in a downward spiral.

To break the cycle and heal the addiction, make the practice of your addiction into sacred healing time. Attach a new message to the behavior and practice it consciously so the familiar addiction behavior helps you to become more conscious instead of less so.

For example, if sweets are your addiction and you are having a craving for ice cream, instead of going right for the Ben and Jerry's, first practice Steps I, II and III. Check in with yourself to discover what deeper needs and feelings the craving is signaling. Perhaps you have been taking care of other people all day and you feel unappreciated and in need of nurturing. Explore other ways to meet these needs. You might call a supportive friend and talk. Afterward you could take a warm bath. After treating yourself to some alternate forms of "sweetness" you might not want ice cream anymore.

And if you still do, don't deny yourself what you crave. Instead turn it into a healing experience. First put aside all distractions such as TV or the newspaper, so you can give your full attention to what you are eating. You might create a healing atmosphere with soft music or candlelight. Then, eat slowly, savoring the taste and affirming that you are loved and appreciated. Imagine that you are feeding yourself love and pleasure and that each bite is turning to health and beauty. Instead of feeling guilty or numb, or picturing fat already starting to form around your waist, use the experience to become more conscious of what you're feeling and to send yourself the message of self-love.

The result of giving yourself what you crave while changing your consciousness about it, is that you will find yourself needing much less to feel satisfied. Instead of reinforcing habits of guilt, shame and numbing out, you will be creating a new pattern of addressing your deeper needs for self-love and caring attention.

This same approach can be applied to other addictive behaviors with a little imagination. For example, if you are a TV addict, instead of sitting passively in front of the tube, watch programs that really engage your mind and imagination or use your TV time to write in an affirmation journal. Or turn off the TV at the end of a program and do something else for a bit before choosing to watch another show.

If you are a shopaholic feeling an urge to go on a binge shopping spree or impulsively buy something you don't need, acknowledge the empty feeling underlying the urge to shop. Allow yourself to shop but set a goal of buying one single item (within a set price limit) that will address rather than mask your inner emptiness. Come home with a $10 self-help book, a perfect flower or some other object that will enhance the quality of your life instead of an expensive new wardrobe and a burdensome debt.

If you are a workaholic consumed by business, set a timer to remind you every hour or two to take a moment to stop, relax and take some deep breaths. Envision yourself completing your work easily and effortlessly, leaving you time to spare. Imagine yourself at peace and supported. Picture other people showing up in surprising ways to offer unexpected assistance. In other words, build into your work process the exercise of being conscious and reversing the negative messages you usually tell yourself.

V. Reach out for help.

Begin by simply noticing how many opportunities for receiving help you turn down. How many times can you remember saying no to someone in your life offering help, either in specific or general ways? What went on in your mind at these times? Did you think that the offer was not really genuine? Did you think it would be easier to do it yourself? Did you feel that there would be too many strings attached to accepting help? Did you fear being drawn into a deeper level of intimacy by accepting someone's help? Did you feel embarrassed to let someone help you? Saying no to help may be such an ingrained habit that you are not even aware of how much you do it. As you pay closer attention, experiment with breaking this habit by saying yes sometimes when help is offered.

In small ways at first, find ways to reach out to people you trust and ask for help. The best way to get support is to make your requests specific enough that people know what you are asking of them, yet not so controlling as to leave people feeling manipulated by your requests. For example, "I'm going through a hard time right now and could really use some support" is very vague. Someone might want to help but not really know what you want. On the other hand, asking someone to take care of your cat and plants while you are away and leaving ten pages of instructions as to how and when to do every little detail may leave people never wanting to help you again. A good way to begin is to share with someone you trust your intention to learn how to ask for help. Ask them for suggestions. Ask your friends for feedback about how easy or difficult it is to support you. They might be able to help you see ingrained habits that you are not aware of.

It is important to give people permission to say no. If you have never developed a habit of asking for help, it can be devastating to work up your nerve to ask and then not receive what you want in the way you want it. You may have a conversation running in your head that says, "I'm always there for everyone and never ask for a thing myself and now the one time I ask for something I don't get it. See! This is why I never ask for help!" If people sense that you will feel terribly let down if they don't say yes to you, they will feel manipulated and less willing to support you. Just as it is important for you to learn how to say no to people sometimes, so is it equally important to let people say no to you without taking it personally and reading too much into it.

VI. What are you feeling and needing?

Examine your cravings. When you feel a craving, ask yourself if you are trying to control your situation too tightly and may need to let go, delegate or ask for help. Notice if you are feeling needy, and if you are, how you can receive nurturing from yourself and others. Consider if there is something you are not saying about how you feel, what your needs are or where your boundaries are. Ask yourself what you are trying to avoid.

VII. If you choose to release your addiction altogether, make it a symbolic act.

Connect the release of your addiction in your mind with the achievement of an important goal. Then, every time you resist the urge to indulge in your addictive pattern, hold the thought that this choice is bringing you a step closer to your goal. Every time you are tempted to give in, ask yourself if having your desired outcome required abstaining from your addiction, would you? By making the process a symbolic act, you are filling the empty space left by the absence of a familiar comfort with excitement about an important life goal.

To give this even more power, I recommend a three-month time period in which you make a commitment to abstain absolutely from your addiction and never cheat (not even once). Three months is enough time to break a long-term habit and yet it is not so long as to feel unmanageable. If you do cheat and wish to continue the 3-month symbolic act, you start over at day one. The aspect of never cheating is a powerful exercise in developing will. When you succeed in keeping such a commitment, you will find this power generalizing to other areas of your life in surprising ways. You will find yourself suddenly unstoppable and capable of more that you ever imagined.

Ask a trusted friend to witness your 3-month commitment. This person's function is to lovingly hold you accountable if you cheat and to celebrate your success if you don't. After your three months of abstinence you may find that you can indulge in this behavior from time to time without it feeling addictive. (See the last exercise in Chapter Two, "Using the Power of Commitment," for more on symbolic acts.)

Of all the many habits we could choose to compulsively and addictively engage in, most of us have found one or two that "work" best when it comes to numbing ourselves to what's really going on in our lives. Each of these habits has a deeper meaning, and there is a reason you've chosen the habit or habits you use to cope. As you read the following sections on the deep meaning of several popular addictions, consider which habit(s) you use and why.

Cease the Rush to Seize the Day

Newsweek magazine once ran a cover story that profiled many highly successful people and suggested that success and exhaustion are part of the same package. While we scorn those who binge eat, we look up to those who binge "do." We consider exercise and attention to diet admirable, but getting plenty of sleep, which has been proven to be vitally important to health, conjures up more images of self-indulgence and laziness than success. Clearly, our culture values action and not stillness. Yet in the stillness comes inspiration, creativity and innovation. Stillness gives rise to wise and efficient action and is as necessary to "doing" as inhaling is to exhaling.

Rushing often ensures that we have no opportunity to find our highest path. We become less efficient and wind up giving more energy to every task than is needed. When we arrange our lives so that we are constantly rushing, it takes all of our energy just to keep up with what we have set in motion. We don't have time to stop and reevaluate where we're going. We relinquish our power to choose and let our lives carry us away. For some, the illusion of having no choice is easier than bearing the responsibility of wanting something and choosing it. Wanting something opens the door to disappointment and failure. For some people, choosing one path over others feels unbearably restrictive. Rushing around with no time to think avoids all this.

If you want a clear picture of your priorities, simply look at where you give your time. How do you spend the majority of your time? If a significant amount of your time goes toward things that don't feel important to you, trust that there is certainly a hidden gain. Ask yourself what you get from spending your time the way you do. If your lack of time doesn't allow for intimate friendships, for instance, perhaps you are afraid of closeness.

When life is consistently too chaotic and we're spending time on things we don't want to do rather than on what we say is most important, it's likely that we are working hard to avoid something fearful rather than working to create something joyful. When our energy is consumed in making sure something bad doesn't happen, we may avoid a particular consequence but fail to create happiness. We take the route of avoidance rather than creativity and settle for a life that is, at best, "not bad."

The first step in shifting from fear-motivated avoidance to joy-motivated creativity is to stop. "Stopping" might mean giving yourself an afternoon walk in the middle of a busy day. Or it might mean taking a break when you feel the most frantic to breathe deeply, let your body relax and your mind clear. It means making sure there is enough time allotted in your life for sufficient sleep. It means making time for just doing nothing.

For many who have a long standing pattern of rushing, the thought of stopping may be heavenly, but the reality is terrifying. Stopping may mean dealing with the fear of saying, "no" and setting limits. It might bring up fears of disapproval, of failure, or of being alone and still. As you take a break for a moment from what you "should" do and ask yourself what you want to do, you might discover that the organization of your life doesn't allow for what you want. Stopping for a moment may ultimately lead you to reevaluate and change the entire structure of your life. And change is always a little, if not a lot, frightening. Yet the prize at the end of all this change is that you will reclaim your power to pursue what is important to you. You will have choices about the circumstances of your life and not simply be at the mercy of them. You will find a way to "have it all" that doesn't entail "doing it all."

Hints for Healing the Activity Addiction

1. Replace obsessive worry thoughts with a simple affirmation such as, "I am at peace" or "I have plenty of time." Many people have found that affirming they had plenty of time instead of panicking resulted in arriving at their destination exactly on time, even when they thought they'd be late. Experiment with this the next time you are stressed about getting somewhere on time.

2. Set aside a day, or at least several hours, when you have nothing scheduled. Ask yourself what you most want to do and do nothing until you feel a strong inclination toward a particular activity (or non-activity). Continue this activity as long as it feels satisfy-

ing and until you feel drawn to doing something else. Spend the
day identifying and following your impulses and inclinations
without judging any activity as better or worse than any other.
Trusting and following inner urges is a way to let intuition guide
you to be in the right place at the right time and to open doors
that would never have been found in "rush" mode.

3. When you find yourself racing, stop. Give yourself a full sixty
    seconds to breathe deeply, let your body relax and form a mental
    picture of what you want to create through your present effort.
    Hold a strong intention that you are now completing your task
    in the highest, most efficient way, with plenty of time to spare.

4. Examine your life for other possible addictions. When there is
    serious activity addiction, there is often one or more substance
    addictions that need to be addressed as well: caffeine to get going
    and keep going, smoking or binge eating to manage stress or
    slow down, alcohol or drugs to relax and numb pain.

Coming Out from behind the Smoke Screen

Most smokers, it seems, are trying to quit, have tried to quit, want to
quit or wish they wanted to quit. Of course, smokers are physiologically
addicted to nicotine, but there is much more to the ritual of smoking than
the drug fix. It literally creates a smoke screen that separates the smoker
from feelings, other people, passion and purpose. When it comes to kicking
the habit, understanding and addressing the deeper roots of smoking can
make the difference between quitting for good or quitting again and again
and again.

Perhaps first and foremost, smoking is a means of stress-management
and self-comfort. Smoking is a part of relaxing and dealing with problems.
It begins with our hands. It gives us something to do, to handle, it keeps
our hands busy. Smokers tend to be people who are very concerned with

handling things. They want to "handle" things themselves. To a smoker, reaching out for help feels unthinkable, impossible, inappropriate, embarrassing, shameful, even terrifying. Consequently, recovery from the smoking habit and the patterns that keep the habit fixed in place must include learning how to appropriately let go of self-sufficiency and control. This means allowing help, and cultivating a greater degree of faith in the ability of others to handle things as well as you can.

Along with our hands, cigarettes engage our mouths. Our mouth is what we use to take in nourishment, or kiss or speak. It is how we receive oral gratification and a primal feeling of nurturing. Smokers, who want to handle things themselves, not surprisingly, provide much of their own nurturing and comfort. Smokers are more likely to reach for a smoke than to reach out for love and nurturing from another person. A recovering smoker needs to find alternate means of self-nurturing and develop new habits of reaching out to others instead of to cigarettes.

Smoking makes everything it touches "smoky," both literally and metaphorically. As smoke fills our mouth and throat, it makes our words smoky. As one smoker said, "I have often found myself in a conversation where I'm starting to feel angry and I want to say, 'No!' But instead I take a puff, cool down a little, and what finally comes out is, 'I don't know...'" Smokers are often reluctant to communicate directly and set boundaries. Consequently, another important aspect of recovery involves learning to communicate clearly, say "no," set limits and risk speaking the truth.

As we draw smoke deeply into our lungs, we are limiting the very air we breathe. In Chinese medicine the lungs, the function of breathing, and the element of air are related to taking in life and spirit. As we make this function smoky, we disconnect from our spiritual power and anesthetize ourselves. As physical and emotional pain come up, we don't puff it away, but we do breathe it back down to a place below the surface of our awareness. When smokers quit, suddenly this well of feelings — both from the past and the present — comes to the forefront. One ex-smoker said that after she quit, she found herself sobbing in the bathtub every morning. Another person noticed that he felt angry all the time for a while after he stopped smoking. Another was much more aware of physical pain. Learning how to release painful emotions and to be with intense feelings without becoming overwhelmed is an important part of the smoker's recovery process.

Smoking diminishes all emotions, not just painful feelings. Smokers are often afraid of emotional intensity, especially their own. Remember, smokers don't like to feel out of control and deep emotions are too much like ocean waves, unpredictable, overwhelming, difficult to handle. As one smoker put it, "All the rituals of smoking, from finding my cigarettes, to lighting up and puffing away, keep my attention never fully on the person with whom I'm speaking."

In a variety of ways, smoking creates a buffer between the smoker and other people. Not only does it diminish the smoker's own emotional intensity, it creates a reason to run out of gatherings periodically for a smoke break. This break diffuses whatever emotional intensity or intimacy may have been building.

Ultimately, smokers need to cultivate trust. Trust is needed to stop "handling" things so rigidly and allow others to lend a hand. Smokers need to trust that it is safe to feel, that their emotions won't lead them anywhere they cannot handle. There is a need to trust in love, to feel that intimacy is safe and that it is possible to love and be loved.

Hints for Quitting the Smoking Habit

1. Let others know how to help you. Smokers often have family members and friends who would do anything to help them quit. Nagging and pleading are rarely effective and people intimately involved with a smoker often are left feeling powerless to help. Family members can, however, play an important part in a smoker's recovery process by helping them to learn to receive and

trust support, nurturing and caring attention from other people.

2. Make a commitment to practice a deeper level of honesty in all of your interactions with people. Be honest about saying no when you need to. Be honest in expressing love and appreciation when you feel that as well. (Chapter Five presents more detailed information on how to cultivate an honesty habit.)

3. Practice Intimacy. If you are not already in the habit of this, practice making eye contact when you speak. In all of your interactions, practice truly seeing people. See if you can find one thing about each person you meet that you find beautiful, powerful, helpful or positive. Share these observations, especially with the important people in your life. Also pay attention to how people show their pain and fear. See if you can observe the totality of people without critical judgment. As you perceive pain or fear in another, see them through eyes of compassion. Only offer support if you genuinely feel willing. You don't need to do anything when you notice someone in pain. People will just naturally feel better in your presence when you practice non-judgment. This in itself is a gift.

    Intimacy is about showing more of who you are and trusting that it is safe to do so. As you practice seeing and accepting others as they are, experiment with letting others see more of you. Imagine and affirm that it is safe to trust, that you are acceptable to others just as you are and that you do not need to disguise who you are with a smoke screen in order to be loved and accepted.

4. Use your imagination to picture every person you encounter as emanating a healing vibration of love. Let go of whether or not you believe this to be true. Imagine yourself receiving and being healed by this powerful emanation. Use your imagination to replace any learned beliefs you may hold that intimate contact

with others is dangerous or takes energy away from you with a new assumption that contact feeds and nurtures you.

Food, Weight and Addiction

In our culture where food is abundant and few of us need to worry about where our next meal is coming from, food has become a substance many people abuse. Food and weight are, for women in particular, a national obsession. Even as our consciousness about food, nutrition, fat, cholesterol and sugar is on the rise, so are fast food chains. People are getting heavier while models, the standard of beauty we compare ourselves to, are getting thinner. The double messages about food and impossible standards of beauty make it increasingly difficult to develop a balanced, healthy relationship to food. I often overhear preadolescent and even grade school girls in conversation about dieting, skipping meals, starving.

Unfortunately, restrictive low calorie dieting actually tends to promote weight gain. Physiologically, starvation slows the body's metabolism down so that when the dieter begins to eat again, she gains weight more rapidly than before. Emotionally, the deprivation of dieting leads to cycles of bingeing followed by more starving. I suspect the reason for the growing problem with obesity in this country is our obsession with thinness and dieting. We literally create chronic weight problems by trying to force ourselves into a body type that is not natural for us.

I know much about this from personal experience. I went on my first diet at age eleven, following my mother's example. I wasn't genetically predisposed to being heavy, but from my preteens to late twenties, I struggled horribly with weight.

With the help of low calorie diets, I started a nightmare relationship with my body and with food. My life revolved around what I ate. When I wasn't dieting, I couldn't get enough food. I was too ashamed to eat all I wanted in public, so I binged secretly. I couldn't stop, even when I was full, and often ate until it hurt. Because it was so hard to stop, I was afraid to start eating and would put off taking my first bite until late in the day.

Nobody knew about my struggle. Because I am tall, loose clothing disguised much of my weight ups and downs. I seldom told anyone I was on a diet. This phase of my life didn't end until I was 27 and so sick and tired of dieting that I decided never to do it again even if it meant being fat and getting fatter (my fear was that if I didn't diet I would just keep getting heavier and heavier). Even though I was at my heaviest weight at the time, I let myself eat whatever I wanted whenever I wanted and stopped counting the calories.

The first thing I noticed was that after a few months of this, my appetite stabilized. I knew when to stop eating and no longer felt compelled to eat until it hurt. This made it safe to start eating. I could feed myself during the day when I was hungry without worrying that I would eat non-stop until I fell asleep at night.

As I grew accustomed to life without food restrictions, I let go of a lot of my food "shoulds." I experimented with giving myself whatever I most wanted to eat no matter how much it clashed with my food do's and don'ts. There were nights when dinner consisted of a milkshake. And then, late at night when I used to crave sweets, I wanted a giant plate of spinach. I was still eating ice cream but now it was a couple of scoops instead of a whole pint, and a plate of greens replaced a heavy "balanced" meal. Sometimes my food cravings were strange, but over time they led me to a balanced variety of foods.

As I released my rigid restrictions on what and how I could eat, my body's own natural wisdom came back. Eventually, my weight stabilized at a healthy level for me. There were some ups and downs, and even now many years later, I am not free of occasional food abuse. What's different is that instead of focusing on my eating and minor weight gain as the problem, I know that my eating is a sign that I am feeling empty and need to take care of myself. I have found that if I pay attention to my emotional needs instead of worrying about what I am eating, my body soon balances out of its own accord as I feel better.

We all have healthy instincts about what and when to eat. Dieting obliterates these. Dieting throws our body into such an extreme state of lack that our instincts (i.e., our appetites and cravings) tell us to eat everything in sight, especially those things that have been most restricted, to compensate.

Those of us who have struggled with food addiction know that food is much more than just physical sustenance. It's comfort, emotional nurturing, distraction, entertainment, a pain killer. Food abuse and weight gain are usually symptoms of feeling empty. This is one of the reasons diets don't work. If we are abusing food because we feel empty, taking the food away just creates more emptiness.

The following suggestions emphasize self-love rather than self-denial. This approach conflicts with many approaches to weight loss, including Overeaters Anonymous. It's may not be effective for everyone, especially for people who feel extreme discomfort with lack of structure or for people who have any medical condition that prohibits some of the following suggestions. But if you have tried numerous approaches and nothing has worked, then this one might be right for you.

Hints for a Healthy Relationship with Food
I. Stop dieting!

Eat what you want. If you have done a lot of dietary restricting and subsequent bingeing, take time to let your eating patterns stabilize. Eat what you want and forget about losing weight. Focus on paying attention to your body's cravings. Experiment with eating exactly what you want exactly when you want. Stop eating the minute you feel full and eat again the minute you feel hunger. Letting go of dietary shoulds and shouldn'ts will give your appetite a chance to swing back (perhaps with some pendulum-like extremes for a while) to a healthy balance. Soon you'll find that the foods you crave are the foods your body needs, not the substitute for emotional fulfillment your inner child yearns for.

II. Eat consciously.

Before you eat, eliminate distractions like the TV or reading. Become quiet and relaxed. Take several deep breaths and say to yourself, "Everything I eat turns to health and beauty." Picture the food you are about to eat being easily assimilated by your body and turning into health and beauty. Eat slowly, paying attention as you chew and swallow. Stop the minute you feel the first sensation of fullness. Afterward sit quietly for a moment, relax and take some deep breaths. Imagine a feeling of comfortable fullness and lightness in your body. Imagine that your stomach is filled not just with food, but with peace and well-being that radiates soothing sensations throughout your body. Do not eat again until you feel the first sensation of hunger. Then eat immediately, but only until you feel the first sensation of fullness. (This is an exercise in learning to discern and trust your body's appropriate messages of hunger and fullness. It will only be effective if you honor your body's wisdom by eating at the first sign of hunger and stopping at the first sign of fullness, regardless of what you think you should be eating.)

If you are tempted to binge, create a healing ritual around eating one of your favorite foods. Eat consciously, savoring each bite. Imagine that this food has marvelous healing powers that are making you healthier and more beautiful. Continue eating this way until you feel the first sensation of fullness. (You will probably find yourself eating much less and enjoying what you eat much more.) End by giving thanks for your healing food.

Forgive yourself whenever you eat unconsciously. Notice what the binge is telling you about your emotional needs. Forgive the binge and address the cause. How are you feeling empty, angry, sad, or scared, and what can you do about it?

III. Focus on filling up rather than on getting thin.

Replace your old regimen of self-denial and restriction with an equally intensive program of self-nurturing. Find ways you can nurture yourself other than food. A long bath, meditation, a good book and your favorite music, a walk, self-massage or calling a friend, are just a few examples.

If you believe that you will be happy when you are thin, or that you can't be happy until you are thin, know that you have been brainwashed by false messages of advertising, the media and our culture, in general. You may be using the problem of weight and eating to cloud deeper issues. The real block to your happiness may have more to do with your relationships, your self-worth, your sexuality or your power. Being thin will not make you happy. Being happy, however, may result in effortless weight loss, and if it doesn't you won't mind because you will be happy.

IV. Gently unlearn bad eating habits by adding new foods to your diet.

When your eating patterns and weight have stabilized, look at learned eating habits that you believe are unhealthy. Eating habits are how we have learned to eat, foods we eat simply because they are familiar. For example, you may eat a lot of high fat foods because you were raised on them or because you hate to cook and eat a lot of fast food. This is something different from food cravings, which are the foods we long for and turn to for comfort. Routinely denying food cravings is what leads to bingeing and losing touch with healthy instincts. Food habits, however can be changed without these negative effects.

Don't deny yourself foods you crave, but keep adding new foods to your diet. As you eat more of these new foods, you will naturally eat less of the other foods. As you break the connection between healthy foods and restrictive dieting, you will find yourself looking forward to eating healthy foods. Your tastes will change and gradually, without any painful restriction, your food habits will change. Comfort food is comfortable because you have developed a relationship with it over time. As you "make friends" with new foods, eventually they become comfortable too.

V. Exercise for pleasure rather than punishment.

Make exercise a part of filling yourself up rather than a punishing discipline. Find a form of exercise that will be a pleasure.

VI. As life becomes full, then start letting go.

What we do with food and with weight is usually reflective of what we do in other areas of our lives as well. Therefore, people who have difficulty letting go of weight often having difficulty letting go, period. This stems from a deep fear that there is not enough of whatever we feel we need. When we believe there isn't enough for us, we hold on to what we have, even if it's not what we want.

Letting go is an essential part of making room for what we want in life. If we want more love, there won't be room for it if our thoughts are continually filled with memories of past hurts, worries, judgments and bitterness. If we want a fulfilling relationship, we won't have room for it if our emotional energy is tied up in relationships that are not serving our highest good. If we want fulfilling work, we won't have room for it if we are spending most of our time doing unfulfilling things. If we want beautiful possessions, we need to make room for them by letting go of things that are not what we want. As we begin to feel safe with letting go on all these different levels, our body begins to feel safe letting go as well.

Start by letting go of material things you don't need. Get rid of clutter. As it feels safe to do so, let go of people, places and jobs that aren't supporting the fulfilled person you are becoming. Let go of anger, pain and self-defeating patterns of thought. Let go of isolation, loneliness, care-taking and other destructive patterns. Let go of the past. And, last of all (or possibly while you were too busy to notice it dropping off) let go of unwanted weight, allowing your body to reflect the lighter person you have become inside. Give special attention to the exercises in Chapter Six on letting go and opening to the flow of abundance.

VII. Learn to receive.

Along with difficulty in letting go, people who hold weight also tend to have difficulty receiving. There is a fierce self-reliance, a belief that "I must do all the work of supporting myself because I can't depend on anyone else." People with food and weight issues are often very good at taking care of other people and give the impression of being pillars of strength, not needing anything from others.

Letting go is inseparably tied to the process of letting in and filling up. Just as inhaling and exhaling must follow each other, so must receiving follow letting go. As you give attention to letting go of what you no longer need, it is essential that you also give attention to filling up.

Reflect on the part of yourself that wants — food, love, attention — a part of you that seems to want too much and never seems to get enough. Imagine this part of you as a child who is crying out. How old is this child? What is it that she or he really needs? As you fall asleep tonight, imagine a Guardian Angel or nurturing figure comforting this child part of you, giving you everything you need to feel full and complete. Say to yourself over and over, all day long, as many times as you possibly can, "I deserve love."

Coming Out of Numbness — Emotional Clearing

As we let go of addictions we find ourselves face to face with a wide range of emotions and feelings we had previously dulled our awareness of. We may become acutely aware of why we preferred to routinely numb ourselves. Coming out of numbness requires a more accepting stance toward feeling and emotion than is generally embraced by our culture. We tend to define pain, anger and grief as negative. Because of this we go to nearly any length not to feel these emotions. As a consequence, we actually give pain more power to hurt us. An animal in pain will adjust far more quickly and easily to the experience. It will minimize activity as necessary and get on with life as normally as possible. Long before we reach a place of such acceptance, we are likely to torture ourselves with fear of being in pain (Will it ever end? Will it get worse?), anger at being in pain (Why me, God?) and grief about being in pain (I'm losing so many possibilities because of my pain). All of this fear, anger and grief only perpetuates our physical pain. What's more, many of us have learned to fear these so-called negative emotions. We think it's not safe to get angry because we might hurt someone. We think sadness is an indication of weakness or that if we give in to our sadness, we may never come out of it again.

If instead we relax in the face of pain and offer no resistance, it loses much of its power to hurt us. In fact, many experiences that we call "pain" transform into something else — an intensity of experience rather than a hurt — when we stop resisting them. In an excellent meditation on pain from his book **Who Dies?**, Stephen Levine compares pain to a fist clenched around a burning ember — the harder we tense up physically and emotionally in response to the experience of pain, the more surely it will hurt us. Yet as we loose our grip and just let pain be there, it stops burning us and can even warm us.

Before we can open to our feelings in a way that is truly healing, it is important to understand the difference between feelings and thoughts. While painful thoughts tend to increase our pain when we dwell upon them, painful feelings need to be felt and released to lose their charge. Emotions are experienced as physical body sensations while thoughts are our inner self-talk. So, for example, the feeling of anger would be the knot in our stomach, the tension in our shoulders, the desire to clench our fists, the urge to scream or beat something. The thought of anger would be our inner dialogue about who is to blame, how often this has happened before, how life is unfair and so on. These downward spiraling thoughts intensify painful emotions. To release pain it is necessary to both change the negative thought *and* open to the feeling. Doing one without the other does not facilitate a complete healing. Emotional catharsis without a new thought attached tends to lead us more deeply into despair, rage and depression. On the other hand, a new thought without the emotional clearing often does not "take," like planting a seed in hard, arid soil.

Each emotion produces a physical action. Anger produces a great physical energy that wants to scream, beat and push out of us. Grief produces tears and a desire to fold into ourselves. Fear generally makes us want to freeze or run. Love causes us to feel soft, open and to reach out to others. Joy can make us want to jump and dance like a fountain overflowing. Every time we have an emotion and stifle this physical response, we become a little more numb and a little more armored, not just against pain but against joy as well.

When we allow an emotion its full response, it not only releases its pain, it turns into something we need. Anger released becomes power, tears released break our hearts open to love again, fear becomes exhilaration, love and joy become ecstasy. There is a great deal of energy in emotion. Directed energy becomes power. As we suppress emotion, we suppress our energy and limit our power, our joy and our health.

It's healthy to allow emotions to flow easily and spontaneously. Long before we manifest a physical illness, it is likely that we have developed some long-standing habit of numbing ourselves to discomfort. This numbing is often so habitual that we may be completely unaware of it until discomfort erupts in an extreme form that can no longer be ignored.

On occasion I have seen people in my workshops become very upset when other people begin to release strong emotions through crying, shouting or beating on a pillow. Often their response is "I did all that several years ago and I don't need to do it again!" The truth is that people who don't need to release anything are not emotionally affected by other people releasing. They feel energized by the process and can be supportive. When someone else's emotional reaction triggers our own, it doesn't mean that we took on another person's feelings. It means that those emotions were in us and the other person acted as a catalyst to bring them to our awareness.

I have often heard people use the metaphor of being like a "sponge," overly sensitive and susceptible to soaking up unpleasant vibrations from their surroundings. This metaphor is damaging because it assumes and perpetuates a position of powerlessness — a sponge can't help but soak up whatever liquid it encounters. It also distorts the truth about our own emotional state. It makes it easy to deny responsibility for our own emotions.

Releasing emotions is much like releasing accumulated wastes from our physical body. It's an ongoing natural process, not a pathological one. Imagine saying, "I had a bowel movement last year so I don't need to do it again."! Of course, if we only have one bowel movement a year it certainly becomes an extremely painful and pathological problem, requiring professional assistance.

We could choose to see what comes out of our bodies as a smelly, disgusting mess and hold it in as long as possible, but most of us don't focus so much on the product of what we eliminate as we do the process of it. Regular elimination is a sign of health, and is a comfortable, not a painful process. Emotions are the same. The more we let them build up, the more painful they are to release. The more spontaneously we let them go, the less focused we become on the "product" — the tears, the shouts — and the more it becomes a natural process that leaves us feeling better. This doesn't, however, mean losing yourself in a roller coaster of emotional catharsis. Separating the physical experience of emotions from the thoughts we usually attach to them is an important step in having feelings without becoming our feelings.

When most of us have an emotion come up, we immediately start thinking about it. If we are sad or angry or afraid, we dredge up old messages that affirm we are alone, nobody loves us, we will never have what we want, life isn't fair, we're not safe, and on and on. We may dwell on the experiences that wounded us, playing them over and over. We may even become identified with our wounds, as in "I am an incest survivor." The rise of support groups and therapy in recent decades has offered a reward for being wounded — we get to be part of a special club, part of a shared intimacy. Letting emotions flow freely is not about wallowing in our pain and victimhood.

Emotional clearing requires changing your thoughts as you open to your feelings. When you feel grief, for example, let tears come but change the inner dialogue that may usually accompany the feeling of sadness for you. Instead of telling yourself that life is hopeless, you are alone and will never be happy, tell yourself that your tears are cleansing you, emptying sadness from your body, preparing you for new growth. Tears are far more healing when they are shared. If you tend to cry alone, find ways to share your tears with people you trust. Grief experienced alone can sink us into despair while grief shared with others is more likely to turn into love.

Give yourself permission to cry whenever you feel the urge. You might find yourself crying more often even as you feel less sad. As you open the flow of your tears, suddenly they will flow when your heart is open, when you feel compassion or love. You will discover your tears of joy when you empty out your tears of grief. Rather than being an unacceptable sign of weakness and vulnerability, tears can demonstrate the strength of our love. Oprah Winfrey, who is often moved to tears on her show, has built a remarkably successful career based on showing her heart rather than hiding it behind a veneer of professionalism.

As you replace these painful thoughts with a different focus, as described in the previous chapter, it is also important to "allow" your feelings. Start inviting your feelings to come to the surface by simply paying attention to your body. Sit quietly from time to time and notice what sensations you are aware of in your body. Is there tightness anywhere, or pain, or a hollow empty feeling? Give attention to whatever is there and just let it be. Ask yourself what emotion the physical sensations seem most like. See how your body wants to move or position itself. Do you want to clench up, or push, or run, or collapse, or curl up, or stretch? Experiment with allowing your body permission to act your feelings.

If your emotions seem so deep and dark that they are inhibiting your ability to perform the normal activities of your day, or if you have had suicidal thoughts, then it is important to find outside help to assist you with this work. Seek out a therapist or support group. Don't be afraid to ask for help. Sometimes reaching out is just the act needed to break through a downward spiral of negativity.

The following exercise is for reconnecting with feelings and inner guidance.

Exercise: Rediscovering Emotions

Step One

To do the following meditation you can read it over several times until you are familiar with it, record it for yourself to listen to or have someone else read it to you. Have paper and pen available before you begin.

Find a comfortable position, relax and take some deep breaths. Inhale deeply and exhale just as deeply.... Let your breath find a comfortable natural rhythm and give all your attention to this rhythm. Let yourself breathe in feelings of relaxation and breathe out all tension, tiredness and any thoughts that you don't need right now. Breathe out everything but an awareness of your body and the sensation of your breath breathing in and out. Feel your muscles relaxing, everything letting go, your mind becoming still and quiet....

In a relaxed, peaceful state, bring to mind the experience of being angry. You may wish to bring to mind a specific situation when you have felt angry or you may be able to remember the inner feeling of anger without attaching it to a particular incident. In whatever way works best for you, remind yourself of the experience of anger vividly enough so that you can remember how anger feels in your body.

Let go of any inclination to rehash events, conversations and negative messages that may be going through your head. Instead, give your full attention to your body. Notice where in your body you have the most feeling. Where does anger seem to be strongest as a sensation in your body? What do you feel in your head, your chest, your shoulders, your gut, the muscles in your arms and legs? What does anger make your body want to do? What body posture best fits this sensation? You don't need to think too hard about this. Just see what feels right in your body. What is your awareness of temperature in your body when you are angry? Does anger feel hot or cold? If you were to assign a shape, a color, a vibration and movement (or lack of movement) to this sensation in your body, what would they be? Finally, ask yourself, "When I feel this way, what do I most want?"

When you have noticed all you can about how your body experiences the emotion of anger as a physical sensation, take some deep breaths and exhale all the angry feeling out of your body. You may want to shake your hands and body to help you feel that all the anger has moved out of you. When you are ready, open your eyes and write down everything you noticed about how anger registers as a physical sensation in your body and what you want when you feel angry.

In asking yourself what you most want, you may become aware of different levels of wants. For example, with anger, your first response might be to get even or to do violence. As you go deeper into this, you might go past the interpersonal dynamic to feel the pure desire in your body to perform some powerful physical act — to break something, to make a lot of noise, to beat on something. As you go deeper still, you may experience the fear or despair underlying your anger, and these feelings may be calling out for something very different. Perhaps you yearn for safety, acceptance or love. What started out in your body as an explosive feeling may become a feeling of wanting to curl up and cry.

Repeat this exercise for the emotions sadness, fear and joy. Some people have no difficulty doing this in one sitting and others need to break it up into two or more sittings. At each sitting, finish by imagining the emotion of joy, and instead of breathing it out at the end, breathe it in deeper and more completely, so that you come back feeling uplifted.

Step Two

After completing your meditation on each of the four emotions, spend the next week keeping an emotions journal. At least once or twice a day stop what you are doing and pay attention to the sensations in your body. See if the sensations you are aware of best match the sensations of anger, sadness, fear or joy. Ask yourself, "What does this feeling most want?" Do this check-in at times of high emotion as well as at those times when you don't think you are feeling anything in particular. Often when we think we feel nothing, it's because we have disconnected from our feelings. The more we "reconnect," the more sensitive we become to subtle messages from our inner guidance, to the hunches and gut feelings that can avert danger or assist us in being in the right place at the right time. We also become more aware of what we really want, a necessary step in having it.

The four emotions of anger, sadness, fear and joy are primary emotions in the same way blue, yellow and red are primary colors. All emotional experiences can be broken down into some combination of these primary emotions. For example, the emotional state of shame generally has a large component of anger (though it is anger directed at the self rather than another) mixed with fear and/or sadness. If you want to continue to develop your sensitivity to emotions, do this exercise focusing on feelings beyond the four primary ones. See if you can detect what combination of emotions are present and what each feeling wants.

Grief

In 1988 my mother died, and several months thereafter the mother of my close friend, Deb, also died. I received news of my mother's death near the end of a 5-day intensive workshop I was leading. At that time I was not a person who cried readily in public. In the years since my mother's death I have become more comfortable with letting my emotions flow, but then I was not. For a short time after hearing the news, I thought I could stoically maintain my professional persona long enough to get through the last two hours of my seminar. As soon as I voiced the news out loud to others standing nearby, however, I broke down. I remember very little more of that evening besides my tears and many comforting hands on me. After a while, the participants who had been comforting me quietly and respectfully left me alone with Deb, my workshop co-leader. We had developed a deep bond through the shared experience of our mothers both being terminally ill.

For the next twenty hours I did little else but cry, more than I have ever cried before. I was given the space to do that by my lover and partner of that time who took the many calls of support that came in until the funeral the next afternoon.

Many friends, most of whom had never met my mother, met me at the funeral service. I continued to cry through the service and when the many relatives and friends of my mother had left, my community of friends remained behind with me. As we all walked toward the parked cars, someone suggested we do a short ceremony of our own. Through the blur of intense emotion I have little recollection of what that ceremony was, but I do remember standing in a circle holding hands and, as it ended, my grief lifted, as suddenly as a summer storm passing. Synchronistically, at the same moment, a near-by flock of crows lifted in flight. My tears stopped and I was overcome with a feeling of lightness and peace.

I realized that I had no desire to go home yet and invited everyone out to dinner. I talked a great deal about my mother and we laughed raucously about everything. In those hours I felt able to truly celebrate my mother's passing as deeply as I had been grieving it.

Several months later we were again gathered for a funeral, this time for Deb's mother. On this occasion, because I was not so much in the center of grief, I was more aware of the stark contrasts in grieving and comforting styles. Just after the service, a group of a dozen or so friends, many the same who showed up for my mother's funeral, all overtook Deb who was walking alone to her car. She looked frozen as she walked — stoic, armored, displaying no emotion, alone. She was, as she put it, in "warrior mode," defending herself from the full impact of her grief. As we all gathered around her, many of us in tears even though none of us had known Deb's mother, she broke down crying. We held her and each other and cried together, sharing the experience not just of grief, but of hearts breaking open to love.

When we disengaged from this embrace I, for the first time, truly saw the other family members and friends standing separate, no one touching, seldom talking, displaying little emotion. There was a stiffness about people, as though each individual was working very hard to hold him or herself because no one felt permission or knew how to hold each other.

Most of us have received little training in what to do with our feelings and how to support each other in times of deep emotion. Yet, as we wall ourselves off in our own little worlds of grief and pain, wounds take much longer to heal. As we armor ourselves against the full experience of grief, we never get to the other side of it. I have found that invariably on the other side of grieving lies joy, love and laughter.

The following steps for facilitating grief are helpful during times of loss or when generalized feelings of sadness come up, even if they aren't triggered by particular events. Anniversaries and holidays often precipitate melancholy moods. The winter holidays, in particular, often trigger the sadness of nostalgia or a painful contrast between the imperfect reality of life and the happy family images associated with Christmas. Instead of forcing yourself to rise to cheerfulness when you are not feeling it, experiment with allowing your own seasons of grief. Just as the cycle of darkness and winter gives rise to new birth in the spring, so does the experience of grief give birth to new love.

Exercise: Turning Sadness into Love

Set aside a week or several weeks to do this process. If you tend toward severe depression or suicidal thoughts, be sure you have the support of a therapist before intentionally initiating a grieving process.

Step One

Over the next days or weeks, give yourself permission to feel any sadness or pain that weighs upon your heart. Imagine that you are letting these "dark" feelings complete their season within you so that you will be ready for a new season of growth and love that is coming soon. Say good-bye to the hurts, sadness and disappoint-ments of the past. Acknowledge losses, endings and deaths. Let yourself cry. If crying doesn't come easily to you, spend an evening watching sad videos, looking at old photo albums or reading old letters. Let your heart break open so that love can flow in again. When you are in the shower imagine that the water is washing away pain and melting away a protective crust that has grown around your heart keeping you separate from love. Imagine that you are preparing yourself for new love to enter your life.

Step Two

Reach out to someone you trust and ask them to listen while you share whatever pain you now want to release from your heart. Explain to this person that your intention is to release stored pain and grief rather than to find solutions, so he or she can best assist you by simply listening and loving you rather than by offering advice. Consider inviting a small group of trusted friends together to do this, letting each person have a turn to be heard, to cry and to be held.

Step Three

As you feel the darkness flowing out of you, gradually let your attention shift to love. Acknowledge and give thanks for the love and joys that already exists in your life. Create a "Blessings Box." Every day for at least seven days, place notes in this box describing all the blessings you were aware of that day. Make a separate note for every blessing. After seven days, continue to add blessings to your box whenever you are moved to do so. Read through these blessings from time to time, especially when you are filled with doubts or pain.

Step Four

Send blessings to other people. Every day for at least seven days, share with at least one person what you love and appreciate about them.

Supporting Another Person through Grief

There are some kinds of support that assist a person in going deeper and moving through feelings to emotional healing, while other kinds distract people from their feeling experience and inhibit a full emotional release. For example, when someone cries, shows deep emotion and vulnerability, many of us typically react with embarrassment. We don't know what to do and just hope the person pulls it together soon, or we try to reach out and comfort their feelings away. If we immediately stuff tissues into a crying person's hands and begin to stroke, pat or massage, her attention will shift to all of these external actions and away from her internal state. We literally pet her feelings away. Women are more likely to over-comfort a person in grief while men are more apt to look away and give the person space to "pull themselves together."

While they may look different on the surface, both of these responses to emotion are rooted in a similar place of discomfort. Both encourage the person to stuff their feelings rather than release them. In our culture, grief is a dark murky place where we don't want to go. To see raw, undisguised grief in another reminds us of our own, and unless we are willing to be with our own experience of grief, we are naturally going to be uncomfortable with someone else's.

Thus, the first and most helpful thing we can do to support a person in grief is to simply be willing to be with it, without looking away, without trying to fix it, without needing to speak, or hold, or pat, or run for the tissues.

When someone first begins to cry, too much physical contact will cause him to lose his focus on his feelings. On the other hand, moving your seat a little closer and leaning forward to show that you are giving your full attention gives support without being disruptive. If the first few tears turn into a stream, then it is appropriate to give supportive, not smothering, touch — a hand on his shoulder or knee or a hand offered for him to hold. A firm touch without petting or massage will help a person go more deeply into the experience, which ultimately facilitates a healing release. Tissues can be offered when the absence of them becomes more distracting than their presence. When someone is in the midst of experiencing powerful emotions, often less is more, which can be a challenge for those of us who are caregivers and want to start fixing anything that looks broken.

As the person gives over completely to the experience of crying — no longer talking, possibly hunched over — then it is appropriate to offer more physical contact such as hugging and holding. Still avoid petting or patting; offer a firm embrace. (See Appendix 1 for a description of a "cocooning" technique for working with grief in a group setting.)

Stroking, soothing and massage are helpful when the person is beginning to wind down from the emotional experience, when tears are subsiding and the body is starting to relax, open and stretch rather than curl up and tighten. The person will begin to look up and become more aware of the surroundings. Now petting will help the person come back and feel more grounded.

If someone seems to be having difficulty coming out of a deep emotional experience — if he or she can't stop crying, or is very frightened — it may be that a traumatic childhood experience has resurfaced and the person is literally in the "body memory" of this experience. When this happens you might notice that the person's cries or voice has become like a very young child's or infant's. To assist a person in this state, simply remain calm and reassuring. Let the person know that he or she is safe and that you are present. Allowing the emotions to flow will eventually bring the experience to a peaceful completion. If the person wants to "come back" and feels that he or she can't, you can help by gently encouraging eye contact with you and any other supportive people present. Use gentle massage and stroking to help him or her stay connected to his or her body. Touch the feet and hands and ask the person to feel the sensations in these areas. Keep talking, reassuring the person that he or she is safe and returning to his or her body after releasing a lot of pain. Make sure the person keeps his or her eyes open and continue to encourage him or her to engage with the people present. Allow the person to share anything he or she wants to about what the experience was like. Continue physical contact and allow plenty of time for the person to come back gradually before leaving.

When we allow feelings to come up and run their course, sometimes an experience in the present will take us back to unreleased feelings from the past. This is why many of us instinctively fear and resist our grief. There is a sense that if we give in even a little, we will be sucked into a bottomless sea of sadness we will never emerge from. Of course, it is our very resistance that keeps the sea so big and any trip down into it so painful. As we open to our feelings, perhaps for the first time, there *will* be a lot of intensity and some of this is painful. However, the less we resist the tears and feelings, the less they will hurt. Afterward, we are rewarded with a lightness, a feeling of renewal and ultimately, a feeling of joy that we may not have known since early childhood.

Releasing Anger

It is cleansing and healthy to allow tears, laughter and loving touch to be expressed fully, and the same is true of anger. Just as grief makes us want to curl up and cry, and love makes us long to reach out for physical closeness, anger makes us want to scream, to beat on things, to use our physical strength in some way. If we restrict our expression to quiet conversation, we are likely to wind up with headaches, stomachaches or worse. What's more, there is a great deal of power in the physical expression of anger. If we continuously hold this energy back, we ultimately diminish our capacity for power, passion and vitality. In our relationships with others, repressed anger creates barriers to intimacy and trust. As we store anger, our whole body becomes "armored" with it and this armor creates illness, alienation and depression.

Because we have so little permission in our culture to express anger, when it does come out, it is often in a hurtful way. We learn that anger is dangerous, out of control, and fear it in ourselves and others. But anger is like fire — we need its warmth and energy, and, yes, we need to learn how to handle it safely.

Opening to our feelings doesn't mean hurting other people or becoming socially inappropriate. Especially in dealing with anger, it is never healing to aim the power of anger at another person with the intention of hurting them. Yet there are many safe ways to allow the physical release of anger. Beating on a stack of pillows, screaming into a pillow or doing some heavy form of physical exercise are a few examples. We can transform anger by letting the emotion of it come up fully and then imagining the hurt of it turning into power as we let it out through our body.

I know of a man who never lets his sons yell or talk back to him on the upper floors of his house, but when there is anger between them, they agree to go to the basement together where they both beat on pillows and scream as loud as they can. In the basement they are allowed to scream out anything at all. Father and son do this side by side rather than face to face and there is a feeling of mutual empowerment rather than of power struggling. After one of these sessions it is much easier to work out their differences. Similarly, a mother once told me of breaking a long stretch of tension with her teenage daughter by taking her out to the garage with a set of old dishes and not coming out until they had smashed every dish against the cinder block wall, screaming out everything they were mad about.

Most of us have been trained to stuff anger and, consequently, have a build-up of stored anger that was never released. This becomes especially noticeable when something in the present triggers these "body memories." A little conflict may trigger a bigger reaction than the situation warrants and suddenly you notice your body trembling, tensing, sweating or developing other stress symptoms. Feeling depressed, numb or lacking passion for life are other common symptoms of unreleased anger. Finding safe ways to allow a greater range of physical expression alleviates these symptoms and releases blocks that inhibit power, joy and spontaneity.

I have often seen amazing changes in people after a session of physical anger release work. At times I have even seen whole groups of people transformed at once as long-held barriers of anger were released. In one of my workshops, the focus was on anger related to issues of gender. The men were on one side of the room and women on the other. People were speaking of their experience of being male or female and many childhood wounds were being touched upon. The atmosphere was one of defensiveness and mistrust. The gap between the two groups seemed immense.

One of the men, Ted, spoke of his fear of his own anger. He equated anger with the abuse he witnessed his father perpetrate upon his mother. He felt ashamed of being a man and had often heard women friends speak their pain over sexual and other abuse received from fathers, brothers, uncles, men. Beneath his fear there was rage at being seen as a perpetrator just because he is male and that no matter how "nice" he is, it never seems to be enough to make the women in his life trust him. Most of all he was afraid that if the women present discovered how much rage he had, they would surely see him as no different from all the abusive men in their lives.

In response to what Ted shared, one woman said that she would feel less afraid of Ted's anger if he expressed it openly instead of hiding it. Several other women encouraged him to release his anger, saying it would help them to get over their fear of male rage.

With support from the women and encouragement from the other men, Ted picked up a sturdy pillow, but his whole affect was one of grief. The anger had disappeared, stuffed beneath a safer, softer emotion. Another man was feeling his own long-repressed rage and came forward to assist Ted. He picked up a pillow and started beating it against the floor, screaming out all the anger he had never felt permission to voice. Soon Ted was screaming, too, and beating a pillow against the floor in loud thumps. The other men gathered around yelling encouragement and when these two fell back in exhaustion, others stepped forward to allow their own anger to be seen and heard and ultimately released.

When the screaming and rage was done, for many there were tears. Emotions are like layers of an onion — as one layer of feeling is released, another one surfaces. As the men fell silent, with a layer of angry "armor" released, many held and comforted each other more intimately than they had ever felt permission to comfort another male before. As they looked up from their own experience, they saw almost all of the women crying profusely. Their faces no longer reflected defensiveness, fear and remembered abuse as they had in the earlier discussion. Now they radiated love, compassion and trust. As anger is released, so are barriers. What is left is intimacy and love.

Anger Expression, Suppression and Release

However, simply expressing anger doesn't necessarily release it. "Release" has occurred when people feel better, when there is less physical tension being held in the body, less emotional tension between individuals, a feeling of true forgiveness and empathy, and a willingness to negotiate behavioral changes so that anger will not build up over the same issue again. Escalating arguments that result when two people "express" their anger toward one another from a place of blame, going back and forth with no resolution, can leave everyone frustrated and fearful. I have seen much "dumping" happen in the name of open and honest communication.

Expression and suppression of anger often go hand-in-hand. As some people start "expressing," all those who are afraid of anger shut down and suppress their own lest they become a target. This dynamic goes something like this:

Expresser: (shouts angrily) "Why don't you ever listen to me? You make me sick!"

Suppresser: (cool and detached) "I can't talk to you when you get like this. I'm leaving."

No one gets much out of an interaction like this. The Expresser feels guilty for blowing up and frustrated to receive so little feeling back, and the Suppresser feels attacked and afraid to respond for fear of more attack. Sometimes this dynamic takes a much more civilized but equally frustrating form, as it did in an interaction that took place between two men in one of my groups:

Expresser: (with a polite smile) "Mark, there's something about you that makes me feel very uncomfortable. I can't explain what it is, but it has been a big block to my getting close to you."

Suppresser: (also with polite smile) "Thank you for letting me know how you feel."

Neither person came away from this exchange feeling better. The Expresser seemed to have a genuine desire to overcome his discomfort, yet without identifying anything specific about Mark that he is uncomfortable with, there is little Mark can do. Mark winds up feeling that there is something intrinsically "wrong" with him and does not know what to do about it. The two people feel even more alienated from one another than before.

What makes conflict so difficult is that we often experience more emotional intensity than the actual situation warrants. This is a result of unresolved anger from the past triggered by a current interaction. For example, the following interaction happened in one of my workshops between a man and a woman who barely knew each other. The woman had just done some very emotional sharing and asked for feedback from the man.

Woman: "What are you feeling?"
Man: "I don't know."
Woman: (with obvious pain and anger) " What do you mean you don't know? Why can't men ever say how they feel? I'm so sick of spilling my guts and then getting nothing back." (louder) "What are you feeling?!"
Man: (very quietly, little affect) "I feel kind of numb. I guess I'm scared."

I stopped these two at this point because it was clear that her anger and his fear and emotional shut-down were way out of proportion to the depth of their relationship and interaction. They were both acting from familiar, painful patterns. She had felt abandoned and enraged in the past by men who withdrew from her emotionally. He had felt afraid and inadequate around women who demanded that he be as articulate about his emotions as they are. Both felt frustrated and stuck. The angrier she became, the more afraid and shut down he became, which angered her more.

To help them move past their old patterns I asked each to share with one another how what was happening now was similar to other important relationships. They talked to each other about painful experiences in the past when they had not been able to get what they needed from a partner or a parent. This opened the door for mutual understanding and compassion, after which they were able to ask for what they wanted from one another without charging it with so much fear, anger and pain.

To truly work effectively with anger it is necessary to address it on several different levels. It is important to physically release built up tension in the body, to separate past history from the present situation and to learn ways to effectively listen, communicate and negotiate. The following steps speak to these essential components of turning the pain of anger into power and healing.

Steps for Working with Anger

I. Separate the Past from the Present

When emotions seem larger than the situation warrants, step back from the conflict and get in touch with who the other person reminds you of or how the situation echoes a familiar pattern from the past.

The following visualization is helpful in identifying and clearing past experiences that are muddying the present. Do this with eyes closed. You can read over the whole visualization before you begin, but it would work much better to record it on tape and play it back or have someone read it to you.

Visualization: Healing the Past

Close your eyes, take some deep breaths and let your attention turn inward. Take a moment to let your body relax and your mind become quiet and still....

Now bring to mind the conflict situation or repeating pattern that you want to heal. Recreate this experience vividly as though it is happening now. Picture it. Hear the voice or voices of people involved in this situation. Notice what emotions are present and how your body feels in this experience. Don't try to push the feelings away, let yourself feel them fully....

Next, let these feelings take you back into the past, to a time when you were very young and you needed something and didn't get it. Let a memory come clearly to mind. Don't force a memory or try to decide which is the right one, just let one pop into mind. Let yourself reexperience this scene as if it were happening now. Feel the emotions of it. Let tears come or let yourself rage in your imagination. As you let yourself feel the anger, sadness, fear or powerlessness, imagine that, as these feelings come up, they are leaving you.

What you are going to do next is change the past. To help you with this, you will be joined by a very powerful being. This being is your perfect nurturer. It is not your real parent or any person you have ever met, because all humans have imperfections. This is an inner nurturer who will be any way you create him or her to be. This being is strong enough to protect you, loving enough to accept you unconditionally, wise enough to know exactly what you most need, and willing and able to give it to you.

So let this being join you now. Notice what sex, age and physical appearance this being takes. Feel him or her close now, touching you, saying your name. If you don't feel completely safe, completely loved and accepted in just the way you most need to be, send this being away and call forth another. When you have found the right Inner Nurturer, take a moment to just be in his or her healing presence. Let yourself be filled up....

Now, with your nurturer, return to the scene from your past when you didn't get something you needed. Know that this scene you have carried in your memory has shaped your experiences for many years, setting limits on the joy and love you have allowed yourself. Also know that the past no longer exists. All that is real from the past is this scene you have held in your memory for so long. So, with the help of your nurturer, let this scene play through again, and this time change it so that you are able to get what you need. If you need protecting, imagine your nurturer keeping you safe. If you need to speak words, or cry tears, or express rage, imagine yourself doing so safely. If you need love, support, acknowledgment or respect, imagine having exactly what you need. Completely transform this scene until it feels better, until you feel full.

Now, picture the people who were not there for you when you needed them to be as frightened, hurting children also in need of protection and love. If you can give this to them, do so. If you are not yet able to give this, picture each of them also with a perfect nurturing being, giving them the love and protection they never received.

Keeping your Inner Nurturer with you, come fully into the power of your adult self. See the person or people from your childhood scene before you in your mind's eye. Hold the intention that healing and forgiveness now happen between you. Imagine that all bonds of pain are now released so there is nothing tying you together except love.

When the experience feels complete, let it go, but keep your Inner Nurturer with you. See the scene and people fading into light. Take some deep breaths to help you come back to the present and back into your body. Imagine breathing your Inner Nurturer into your heart so you know she or he is always with you. When you are ready, take another deep breath and open your eyes. Come back feeling refreshed, alert and at peace.

II. Own Your Limiting Beliefs

Owning our limiting beliefs means recognizing how the situation, the conflict and the other person are all reflecting our core beliefs about how life works. It means shifting from a belief that we are victims of other people's behavior to a more empowered awareness that we tend to attract people and evoke behavior in people that will affirm our core beliefs. As we begin to see what part of ourselves brought the conflict into being, we have the power to change it. The following exercise is a powerful one for two or more people in conflict to agree to do together. It is just as effective, however for one person to do alone.

Exercise: Owning Limiting Beliefs

1. Reflection

Step back from the interaction for a moment and close your eyes. Relax and take a couple of deep breaths.... Imagine that how you are treated by other people reflects something about how you treat yourself and how you have come to expect to be treated. In other words, the extent to which others are harsh toward you reflects the extent to which you are harsh with yourself and expect to be mistreated by others.... Focus now on how you feel treated by the person you are doing this exercise with or about. How is this similar to how you have felt in past relationships? How is it similar to how you treat yourself? What is this person reflecting to you about your beliefs and expectations? For example, "I'm never good enough so people are always going to be angry with me." or, "I'm too weak to protect myself so I will always be in danger of being victimized," or "Unless I do things perfectly, I will always have harsh critics."

2. Share Negative Beliefs

Open your eyes and share with each other what limiting beliefs are being reflected. Share anything else that feels important about what in you has created this conflict.

3. Healing Action

Share anything you would be willing to do to heal the negative belief within yourself that this conflict has brought to the surface.

III. Empathy

Being able to understand and empathize with the other person's side of a painful conflict is a big step in going beyond merely expressing anger to truly releasing it. Through empathy we can find forgiveness and shift our focus from "winning" to "healing."

Exercise: Reflective Listening

This is a simple reflective listening technique that is frequently used by family therapists. It makes space for people to express complaints and still hear and be heard by one another. In this process, one person is instructed to listen silently while the other person states her position. When Person A is finished, Person B states back to her what he heard. Person B does not give a response or share his feelings about what he heard. Rather, he states exactly what he heard Person A say so that she is sure he understood her. "A" then either confirms that "B" understood correctly or corrects anything that he misunderstood, and "B" again feeds back the corrected version of what "A" said. This continues until "A" is satisfied that "B" understands her position.

Then "B" takes a turn, repeating the same process. Next, both "A" and "B" each in turn, state, "What I want from you is…" and the other repeats back the request. Finally, both talk freely, addressing each other's requests and negotiating how or if they are willing to comply with each other's wishes

Exercise: Role Reversal

An exercise for cultivating empathy that can be practiced alone is to imagine yourself in the role of the other person. Hold your body as you imagine this person to hold his or hers, see the world as he or she does, think the thoughts you imagine he or she thinks, feel the feelings he or she feels. Use your imagination to make this as vivid and real as you can so that you have an experience of stepping into this other person's reality. See if you can sense how he or she is afraid, how his or her defensiveness, attacks, rigidity or other unpleasant behavior is an expression of fear and a calling out for help.

IV. Clear Communication and Negotiation

To create changes that will address the source of conflict in the present, it is necessary to identify and communicate what specific behavior is bothering you, what you want and to do this in a way that the other person will be able to take in. John Bradshaw suggests the following four-step formula for communicating feelings:

1. I see... (Describe objectively the external behavior that you observe.)

2. I imagine... (Give your interpretation of what you assume this behavior means.)

3. I feel... (Describe how you feel. Remember, mad, sad, glad and scared are feelings. "I feel sad," is a feeling statement. "I feel like you are not listening to me," is an interpretation, not a feeling.)

4. I want... (Say specifically what different behavior you would like from the other person.)

Using this formula, this communication: "I hate it when you ignore me! You never listen to me!" becomes: "*I see* you looking away from me and not responding to what I said. *I imagine* that you don't want to hear what I am saying and that you don't care about me. *I feel* hurt and angry. *I want* you to look at me when I speak and answer me."

V. Releasing the Build-up of Anger in the Body

Much physical anger release work is best done with the support of other people rather than alone. This is especially true if you have never done any such work before. Anger can be frightening territory when it is unknown. The presence of skilled support people not only adds safety, it also provides comfort for when the anger is gone and other emotions such as grief or fear or love surface. Sharing pain in the presence of loving support generally has more of a healing impact than releasing pain when we are alone. Going into painful emotions when we are alone can sometimes intensify our feeling of emptiness and separation, but when others are present and pain has a chance to turn into love, we come away feeling full and healed.

Sometimes anger work can be done with the help of a therapist or support group, although many therapists and groups do not go beyond talking about anger to the actual release of it. If you are looking for a therapist to help you with this kind of work, ask specifically if the therapist works with any physical anger release methods. Anger release work generally involves getting loud and sweaty. If the therapist practices only talk therapy or is in a thin-walled office that doesn't allow for noise, you may come to some understanding of your anger but you probably won't release it.

This isn't to say there is nothing you can do to release anger in your body without professional support. Begin to manage your own anger by noticing what it does to your body. Notice when your shoulders are tensing in irritation, your jaw clenching, your stomach knotting up. Sometimes anger symptoms manifest as self-destructive impulses — a desire to drink too much or binge eat, a desire to put a fist through something, or feelings of inertia and depression. As soon as you notice these symptoms, do something physical. Work out, run, scream into a pillow. Ask your body what kind of exertion would feel the best and find a way to do it. If you tend to turn anger inward and get depressed and sluggish rather than angry, you can access the feelings by performing the physical actions of anger. Because emotions are essentially body sensations, the emotional experience will often follow performing the activity of the emotion. Beating on a pillow and shouting a phrase of anger like, "NO!" over and over will help the feelings to surface. Foam bats that are made specifically for anger work are great tools for anger release and can be used to beat on the floor. Although these are designed for "safe" fighting between people, I do not recommend it. I have found that any physical contact that has anger behind it can feel violent, frightening and can easily get out of control. See Appendix Two for more on anger release work in a group setting.

Overcoming Inertia, Opening to Passion

Are there things in your life that you wish you were doing or working toward but you lack the motivation to pursue? Do you think, if only you were more disciplined you could achieve what you want in life, but the will to go for it never materializes? Discipline alone becomes a cruel task master when passion is not present.

Where we have passion, we have energy to create, to change, to heal and to manifest. Without passion, life becomes endless drudgery leading to depression, illness and despair. Passion can't be forced into being. We can uncover it and invite it back into our lives but the more we try to force it, the more elusive passion becomes.

There is a process that leads to a lack of passion. It begins when we live for the future, putting happiness off until later. Then we settle for an unsatisfying present and cope with our emptiness through addictions and repressing feelings. The more we numb ourselves, the less we are able to hear the intuitive guidance that leads us to our path of greatest fulfillment. The more we deny our desires and passions because they don't fit with our future-focused goals, the more unhealthy and out of balance our desires become and the more we need to control them. So we set up a lifestyle where we are routinely doing something other than what we want to do, repressing our desires and, consequently, having to cope with the resulting stress and unhappiness. The result is depression, inertia and sometimes illness.

Inertia is always there for a reason. Sometimes it is because our effort has gotten off track somehow and is no longer in alignment with our highest good. During the process of writing this book, I reached just such a point. I had little enthusiasm for writing at that time and the harder I worked, the more the book seemed to unravel instead of come together. Not only was my writing slowing down, but my workshop business in my home town of Baltimore had hit a lull. I felt stuck, in need of new direction and completely unmotivated to do any work toward creating something new. After spending a couple of months sitting in the library, shuffling papers around, trying unsuccessfully to make myself be productive, I finally gave in to what I really wanted to do, which was nothing.

At age 42 I had worked full time without even a pause since I was 17 years old. Even though I still had workshops scheduled to lead and was only cutting my work load back to part-time as opposed to taking off from work altogether, I had to fight my way through some powerful fears and "shoulds" to justify taking time off. I feared for my finances, even though I had plenty of money in the bank and money was not an issue. I feared that I would flounder and never find my way back to the career goals I had been pursuing. I feared losing my identity — if I'm not Lynn-who-has-worked-full-time-since-she-was-seventeen, who am I?

But as I settled into a new lifestyle of doing exactly what I wanted every day and living with the uncertainties and unanswered questions about my future, I found myself relaxing. Instead of feeling stuck and frustrated, I felt peaceful and happy. I went for long walks, spending hours in quiet contemplation, not figuring out my future so much as simply appreciating the life I had already created. I found myself in an interesting paradox of having many of my life goals unmet, no idea of how I would meet them, yet I felt incredibly happy all the same, in spite of what appeared on the outside to be a total lack of movement in my life.

After two months of this, I traveled to Minneapolis to lead some workshops. During my trip I felt clearly guided to move there. This felt like the new direction I had been searching for in my work and my life. What's more, when I returned home I was able to pick up my writing again and continue it with ease and enthusiasm. After a two month break I just naturally wanted to go back to work, and the answers I was seeking easily and effortlessly found me. Sometimes inertia is telling us we need a break in activity to dream, regroup and become reinspired.

Sometimes inertia is there to protect us from going forward when some part of us believes that our desired goal is not safe or somehow not in our best interest. In the early eighties when I worked with many people who had cancer and other serious illnesses, I met a therapist who specialized in teaching people with cancer to visualize their disease away. This therapist shared with me her great frustration over the fact that so few of her clients were motivated to continue their healing programs. She could not understand why these people would not do a few simple exercises to save their lives. Yet what she perceived to be a foolish lack of discipline on their part was actually an unconscious instinct not to let go of their disease too quickly. For many, the onset of a life-threatening disease causes a profound reevaluation of life priorities. It often forces them to give more attention to themselves than they ever have and to receive more attention from others than ever before. These hidden gains of an illness may be so vitally important to our well-being that we unconsciously choose them, even over healing the disease. In this way, inertia comes up, not as a weakness or lack of discipline, but because some instinctive part of us is not willing to give up the hidden gains of staying as we are.

Giving too much energy to what we feel we "should" do and not enough to what we want to do is a sure path to inertia. Following our heart's desire is the only path back to passion. Everything else will just lead back to stuckness. Many people believe this to be impossible to do, identifying all the things they "should" do, that they really "have" to do, that they can't abandon to go do what they love. Yet, in the end, the part of us that really doesn't want to do all these things often has a way of winning out in spite of our best efforts.

A woman in one of my groups came in looking very drained and depleted from a flu that she had been battling for weeks and just wouldn't go away. As she talked about what else was going on in her life, she described feeling "stuck." She felt torn between wanting to continue to work in her husband's business, for which she felt no affinity, and wanting to stay home and take care of their home and five children. As she talked about wanting to help her husband in his business, she became noticeably tense, sounded guilty and unhappy. It was clearly what she thought she "should" do rather than what her heart wanted. As she talked about taking care of her home and family, her face softened, she sounded relaxed and happy. By forcing herself to work in her husband's business she became so physically depleted that she had become virtually useless to everyone.

Exercise: Recovering Passion

Step One

Begin by identifying where you feel stuck. What are the really big things you have inertia around? (These are things that feel like they are for your highest good like taking care of your body, starting a project that excites you, writing a book, etc.) Write the one thing that feels most important to you.

Step Two

Look at what you have written and ask yourself if this is something you love and feel a heart-felt passion for, or something you think you should do. Is this goal part of your heart's desire? If not, pick a focus that is aligned with your highest passion at this time. For example, if you think you want to make more money, yet your passion is telling you to quit your job and travel, then making more money is going to be an impossible struggle unless you go about in an indirect way by quitting your job, traveling and letting synchronicity connect you with a more joyful way to make a lot of money.

Step Three

Reflect upon what benefit there is for you in staying stuck. How does it serve you? If you look closely enough there is always a gain. For example, maybe part of you wants to deal with the extra weight you have put on, but another part of you needs the feeling of protection it offers.

Step Four

Ask yourself if you are willing to do without the "gains" of staying stuck or to give yourself these gains in a new way that doesn't necessitate staying stuck. For example, the woman described earlier who created a never ending bout with the flu, would need to deal more directly with her husband. She needs to acknowledge that, although she wants to support him, she can not do it by taking on work that is so unfulfilling to her. When you are ready to live without the gains of your stuckness, go to the next step.

Step Five

Men tend to lose passion and sink into depression when they feel out of touch with their purpose. Being in touch with purpose means feeling useful, productive, needed and that they have repeated experiences of being successful and appreciated. Women tend to fall into depression when they feel unsupported and overwhelmed by having to deal with the burdens of life all alone. Therefore to get back in touch with joy and passion, men often need to experience their power to successfully meet a challenge while women often need to feel that life is not such a burden and they are not alone. The following exercises are designed with those differences in mind. The first one is especially for men and the second for women. However, regardless of your gender, choose the exercise that you feel most passionate about doing. This is the one that will work best for you. You may even feel drawn to doing both of them.

I. Recovering Purpose

a) Make a list of things you are afraid to do but think would be good for you to do or that you would like to be able to do. Include in this list very small, low-level fears, medium sized fears and very large, major-life-change type fears. For example, a low-level fear might be saying hello to strangers you meet during the day, a medium-level fear might be tithing some money to a worthy cause, a big fear might be to quit your job and start your own business. Add as many things to your list as you can. Keep them in categories of small fears, medium fears and big fears.

b) Commit to doing 3 to 6 things on your lists of small and medium fears over the next month. Pick the things you feel most excited about doing. Do these things as symbolic acts. As you do them, tell yourself that these courageous acts are rekindling your fire for life and removing all blocks to your heart's desire. After completing these 3 to 6 things, continue down your lists if it feels exciting and joyful to do so.

II. Self-Nurturing

Make a list of self-nurturing activities. Include the things you love to do that are in alignment with your highest good, and not an addiction — taking a walk around the park, meeting a friend for lunch or leaving time every day to meditate or read, for example, as opposed to eating half a chocolate cake or drinking a six pack in front of the TV. Make sure the things on your list are things you enjoy rather than things you think you *should* do. Make a commitment to practice one of these activities every day for a month. Make this exercise a symbolic act so that as you practice your self-nurturing activity you affirm that this self-loving act is rekindling your passion for life and bringing you closer and closer to your heart's desire.

For Both I and II:

If you find that you do not keep your commitment to these symbolic acts, take this as a message that you are not ready to achieve your desired outcome. Either it is not for your highest good and you may need to revise your goal, or there is some way that staying where you are is serving you. In this case, you will need to more fully address the secondary gains of staying stuck before your subconscious self will let you move forward.

4

"The opposite of love is fear,
but what is all-encompassing can have no opposite."
—*A Course in Miracles*

"...Evil can only be overcome by good.
We don't need to reach out and tear down the things that are evil
because nothing which is contrary to the law of love can endure."
—Peace Pilgrim

Discovering True Power

Love is the only true power there is. Therefore, our experience of safety, health, creativity and success increases as we give attention to love rather than fear.

What Is Love?

I recall sitting in my first class in metaphysics when I was just a teenager and hearing this concept: that we are love, that love is all that is. My young mind, eager for new ideas, thought this was a fascinating idea. In practice, however, I hadn't the faintest notion of what it meant. In New Age circles I so often heard the message, "just send love" or "fill yourself with love" but what exactly was I sending or filling with?

The word "love" is used so freely — it's how we feel about ice cream and our dearest friends and family. It's the answer to world problems, it's some lofty spiritual "energy." Turn on the radio and its "Baby, let me love you tonight!" I wondered what, if anything, all these forms of "love" could possibly have in common? Is love something we do, something we feel or something we are?

Some of my more meaningful lessons about love came not from my metaphysics classes but from noticing what I feel when I use the word "love." I started noticing what I attach the word "love" to and asked myself what do I feel when I "love"? I found that the experience of love is immediate. It pulls my attention out of the past or the future and into the present moment. It is pleasurable and expansive. It is a feeling of aliveness and well-being. It is awareness that I am not separate from others, from joy, from the world around me. Perhaps this is what we are all experiencing or seeking in the many different things we say we "love." Whether we are speaking of a pint of Ben and Jerry's, or what emanated from Mother Theresa, or even a one-night stand, love is all about finding joy, pleasure, release or transcendence in the present moment and letting everything else go.

Perhaps these moments when we have released the past and the future, released fear and pain, released everything but joy in the present are the times when we are closest to some essential truth. Perhaps all the ways the word "love" enters our vocabulary indicate those experiences when we feel closest to this essence or are at least seeking it.

Certainly, many paths to love are fraught with pain. Addictions result when we seek this experience of love where love is not to be found. Drugs, alcohol, food or sex may seem to take us "home" initially but then become a detour with painful consequences. Heart break and disappointment result when we believe that something or someone outside of us is responsible for our feelings of love. When we look to other people to give us the love experience we long for, we become relationship addicts, always feeling empty until we find that "perfect" lover, who never stays perfect for long.

When we shift from seeing love as something outside of ourselves that we must get to be complete to seeing love as what we are, and what we have to share with others, then love has the power to move mountains. A phrase comes to mind from Dan Millman's book, *Sacred Journey of the Peaceful Warrior,* which is about the author's own discoveries of love: "There is no way to happiness; Happiness is the Way. There is no way to love; Love is the Way."

This "Way of Love" (different from the way to love), can only be found in the present moment. We seldom give ourselves permission to experience the present in a way that is complete and fulfilling. We set goals and tell ourselves that we will be happy when these are fulfilled. When we begin to experience "The Way" rather than pursuing "the way to...," things change. A door opens, we see things as we never have before. We look at our family, friends and the world around us with a newfound gratitude. And this sense of completeness somehow changes everything around us. Inexplicable things happen because we are no longer limiting our range of experience. The tightness inside of us loosens and then suddenly the check we have been waiting for arrives. We find the new job, enter the new relationship or get the big break we've been hoping for. And it comes to us effortlessly as we make the experience of love in the moment our only goal. The power of love is the power of miracles.

Miracles are love in action. They send out ripples of healing to all who are touched by them. Miracles operate outside our system of belief about how life is supposed to work. It is when something wonderful happens by means of synchronistic coincidences, where time and steps get skipped.

There was once a woman, Janet, who came to one of my 5-day workshops with the goal of creating fulfilling employment for herself. The workshop had nothing to do with career counseling — it was a workshop about love. Over the 5 days she did nothing that directly related to her career.

What she did was open her heart. She participated, in love, on a higher level than she ever had before. She released fear, pain and self-judgment. She let herself give and receive in the biggest possible way. She ended the workshop with renewed optimism and self-confidence. The next logical step in addressing her issues would have been for Janet to apply her new sense of power and purpose to the job market. But that's not what happened.

At the end of the workshop, participants invited friends and family to attend the last session. Minutes before this session began there were many new faces in the room. A woman came in, presumably someone's guest but, as it turned out, she was looking for another meeting that was being held elsewhere and had stumbled into our group by accident. Janet, however, knew this woman from a year earlier when she had gone to her seeking employment. It had been just the kind of work Janet wanted, but unfortunately the woman didn't have anything available in her state. The two women greeted each other and shared a moment of conversation. As she was leaving, the woman said to Janet, "By the way, are you still interested in a job? I have something available in your area now."

So, Janet fulfilled her goal — without doing anything "practical," without doing anything other than creating love in the moment. The paradox here is that she created what she wanted for the future by letting the future go and living fully in the present. Is this an unusual story? A one in a million coincidence? No. I hear different variations of this story after every workshop I give. And, no, I don't believe it is the result of the workshop itself or of my marvelous talents. The workshop is simply a place where we give ourselves greater permission to love. Love is the power that gives rise to miracles. And this is something that is always available to us, anywhere, anytime. As *A Course in Miracles* states, "Miracles are natural. When they do not occur, something has gone wrong."

Love Is Power

Research has shown that the experience of love physically alters the functioning of our heart. In moments of love and compassion, the heart's rhythm becomes more regular and even, more in alignment with health. The heart is the regulator of the physical body. It acts as a powerful oscillator, setting a rhythm for the whole body. When the heart is beating in a healthy rhythm, it draws other organs and systems of the body into alignment with health. This is an autonomic process that happens outside of the realm of conscious control.

A similar process takes place on more subtle levels of our being when we feel "open hearted." Psychologically, in moments of love, our thoughts, motivations and life force all come into alignment with health. We stop fighting ourselves with unconscious fears and mixed intentions (as in, "I want to do this but I'm afraid to," or "I want this in my life but I don't deserve it, don't believe it's possible, will be punished if I get it..." etc.) As love brings us into alignment, we have more energy to create our highest good because all of our energy is going in the same direction.

Spiritually, in moments of love, we act as a giant heart oscillator, pulling the world around us into alignment with health. We naturally begin to draw to ourselves the people, circumstances and opportunities that are in alignment with our highest good. This process is effortless and unconscious in the same way a healthy heart draws other organs into healthy functioning. The results range from timely coincidences to occurrences that are truly miraculous. We also become a positive influence on the world around us, pulling other hearts into alignment with love. The state of love is a state of power.

When I worked as Director of the Baltimore Center for Attitudinal Healing, I learned a great deal about the power of love. As people came together at the Center with a simple intention to release fear and practice unconditional love, miracles happened — miracles of the body and miracles of the heart. I saw a teenage girl whose doctor told her she had little hope of recovery from her brain tumor go into remission soon after joining one of these attitudinal healing groups. Other children and adult participants at the Center also had powerful healing experiences. One of the most profound lessons for me was in seeing some of the most physically ill people being of incredible service and comfort to others in pain. I learned without a doubt that our ability to have an impact on the world around us has nothing to do with the condition of our physical body.

From the limited perspective of physical reality, the only power of love is in its ability to motivate us toward good actions. Even if you currently believe in love as a powerful force, do you believe it has power if you don't translate it into action? Do you believe that your love is valuable even when you don't express it in words, hugs, gifts or deeds? Many people are left feeling incomplete when a loved one dies because they did not have a chance to physically demonstrate their inner experience of love and therefore assume it could not have been received. Yet, as we begin to know ourselves as having power beyond that of our physical interventions, then it holds that love is intrinsically powerful, even if we never speak it out loud or do anything concrete with it.

Larry Dossey in his book, *Healing Words*, reviews numerous studies documenting the power of prayer to heal. These studies show irrefutable evidence that a loving intention held by one person can positively affect another even when they are separated by great distance and the recipient has no conscious knowledge of the act. Healing prayer is nothing more than the intrinsic power of love, separate from word, deed or even conscious knowledge of it by the recipient. It is the state of love itself that is powerful, not just the acts motivated by love.

Accounts of people who have had near-death experiences almost always include profound experiences of love. These people who have survived close calls with death and lived to tell about it typically report an experience of consciousness separating from the physical body, often viewing one's body from high above, a transcendental experience of well-being and peace, and a beautiful light, accompanied by a powerful experience of love.

Melvin Morse, a pediatrician and author of a number of books on near-death experiences, including *Closer to the Light*, became the first person to conduct scientifically valid research on NDE's (near-death experiences). Morse noticed that for many NDE'ers, the experience of love and light are virtually indistinguishable. In fact, the "Light" that is the quintessential element of the NDE experience is, according to Dr. Morse, most frequently described as "a pure light of unconditional love." As modern physics is teaching us, light is the basis of the physical world. Light is the substance and energy underlying all existence. All is light, and if light is love, then love is all that is. It is energy, it is substance, it is power. According to Morse, people who have experienced this "light of unconditional love" are measurably healthier physically and emotionally, have more psychic abilities and may even become more intelligent.

The power of love is the power of joining. In the language of physics it is the power of "wave" energy, as opposed to "particle" energy. As we attune to the energy of love we tap into a collective power source (wave energy) that is something much greater than that of an individual acting as a separate being (particle energy).

Self-love

Well known author and teacher Louise Hay stresses the importance of self-love and says that all problems can be traced to the lack of it. Her book *You Can Heal Your Life* is an excellent primer on beginning the habit of self-love.

The concept of self-love is often trivialized and reduced to New Age narcissism. Actor Al Franken does a brilliant parody of the whole self-esteem movement in his "Stuart Smalley" comedy routine, poking fun at the dark side of "personal growth," and highlighting the sad truth that spending time in front of a mirror saying affirmations does not guarantee that our lives will work. (The much ignored movie, *Stuart Saves his Family* is a must-see for anyone in danger of taking their "personal growth" too seriously.) True self-love, however, is neither narcissistic nor sentimental. In fact, self-love often happens when we cease to think about ourselves and simply become ourselves.

Self-love is not so much the thought we hold about ourselves, although self-love can flow from our positive thoughts and be restricted by our painful ones. Self-love is not just about appreciating our positive qualities or liking ourselves, though these things can grow out of self-love. Rather, it is a state of being. It is the inner experience of deep, profound safety, well-being, peace, acceptance, faith and a certainty that all is in order. It is the feeling of basking in golden sunlight on a perfect day, where the experience of the present moment supersedes all thought. It is the feeling of faith that we are all right even in the midst of crisis. It is the experience of being completely present with other people, seeing, hearing and accepting who they are without judging or wondering if we are being judged. When we have self-love, we automatically become less self-absorbed. We have confidence, joy and a radiance that ripples out to the world around us. We are full and have much to share with others. We have a calm, even center that doesn't get buffeted by the ups and downs of life. The experience of unconditional love and self-love are the same.

There are many paths to self-love. Some include addressing self-judgments and other thoughts that restrict the presence of self-love and consciously replacing them with affirmations of loving acceptance. As explained in Chapter Two, this type of affirmation work can be powerful and effective. For more on this approach I highly recommend the work of Louise Hay, including *You Can Heal Your Life*, and Sondra Ray's book, *I Deserve Love.*

Yet this is not the whole story in cultivating our inner power of love. It is not necessary to pamper and indulge ourselves to have self-love. We don't need to take ourselves to lunch, send ourselves a birthday card and talk to our inner child to practice self-love. We may find value in doing these things, but they will not guarantee the result of self-love. Self-love happens in any moment that we surrender to the gift of the present. It can happen when we stop thinking about whether or not we are good enough, whether we are loved and accepted by others or how we have been wronged. It happens when we simply stop to enjoy a fragrant summer breeze, feeling content and one with something greater than our "self" (small "s"). Self-love happens when we forget our own needs, pain and imperfections long enough to truly see another person through eyes of acceptance and compassion. Self-love happens in moments of peace when we remember to put aside our own personal struggle and invite a Higher Power to intervene. After enough of these peaceful moments of "self" forgetfulness, we suddenly discover that when we do think about ourselves we feel the same acceptance and well-being that we felt in other contexts. We find that we have come to like ourselves.

In other words, in coming to love ourselves, there is a certain amount of work that we can do. Yes, it can help to state our self-loving affirmations out loud, and yes, there is a place for loving our "inner child," or cultivating a relationship with our self as though we were relating to another person. And then there comes a point when we need to simply get over our "self." You are the only one who can discern when "self" work is helpful, and when it becomes yet another distraction from your "Self."

Healing Loneliness

In accessing the power of love it is, first and foremost, necessary to recognize that love is not something outside of ourselves. It is not something we need to get from other people. It is an ever-present energy that is always within us, around us and available to us without limit. Practitioners of meditation often have profound experiences of love, intimacy and oneness during meditation even though from all outward appearances they look separate, alone, lost in their own worlds. Love is not something we do or get, it is a state of being. It is who we are when we release the distractions of fear and separateness. To truly heal loneliness we need to expand our beliefs about reality to include this basic truth about love.

However, as we do the inner work of accessing love, it is also important to reach out to others and create a network of loving connections. Tapping into our spiritual power is not work to be done in isolation. Feeling connected to people is so essential to our well-being that it is one of the most reliable factors in determining our risk of physical illness. Dean Ornish, M.D. in his book, *Love and Survival,* cites numerous studies all showing a clear, undeniable link between physical health and the experience of being loved. People who have a network of support in their lives, through marriage, family connections, or even a therapeutic support group, are more likely to recover from life-threatening illnesses and are less likely to contract serious illnesses. These benefits hold true independent of other such factors as diet, exercise, smoking, cholesterol level and heredity. Dr. Ornish noted how seldom this aspect of health is addressed in treatment plans in spite of the overwhelming evidence of its curative effects — and the sad irony that any drug found to have an impact as statistically significant as love would be major news in every medical journal and news magazine.

Despite the prevalence and power of love, misunderstandings can make it seem elusive and scarce. One common belief that perpetuates loneliness is our attachment to special love relationships. While the opportunity for love is everywhere, many of us languish in self-created emotional deserts because we are only interested in sharing love with one or two specific individuals. We focus on a parent or romantic love object and believe that this person's love is the only love that can fill us and make our lives feel meaningful. And quite often we pick the very people who will not give us what we want of them. A man in one of my groups once described his frustrating relationship with his emotionally unresponsive parents as being like going to the hardware store for a quart of milk. No matter how many times he never got milk, he still kept trying!

This kind of relationship consumes our energy, leaving no room for love to grow. Remember, what we give attention to is what we perpetuate in our lives. Thus, the more attention we give to one person who is not giving us what we want, the more we perpetuate this relationship pattern. The following suggestions can show you how to break out of self-imposed limits to the limitless love there is for us to share with others.

Steps for Healing Loneliness

I. If you feel unloved, look at the ways you are unloving.

If you feel unloved, it is essential that you look honestly at yourself, without self-judgment, to see the ways you are unloving toward others. If you are not feeling loved, you are probably not freely giving love. I once knew a man who was so intently focused on finding a romantic partner that he had difficulty giving and receiving love with anyone who was not a romantic possibility. When people offered him love and kindness, he did not value it because they were not his beloved. He didn't seem to be present with people because so much of his energy was projected into this future fantasy relationship. Consequently, he was not a very attractive person and spent many years alone without his beloved or close companions.

Regardless of how much you think you do for people ("loving" and "doing" are not necessarily the same thing), take a look at your inner experience when you are with others. Are you quick to judge? Do you have difficulty finding people likable? Do you enjoy what you do for people or do you resent it? Do you find that you don't often enjoy the company of other people? Are your requirements for enjoying the company of others so specific that there are very few such people in your life? Feeling judgment, separateness and a general lack of interest in other people are all indications that you are not freely extending love.

Once you recognize this, you can reframe your experience of loneliness. It is no longer a problem of being unloved, which is a difficult one to deal with since it requires changing the feelings of others. It is now a matter of not loving enough, which is in your power to change.

II. See every encounter as an opportunity to love.

Play with the following two exercises for changing limiting beliefs about love and cultivating a state of unconditional love. People respond to our beliefs and expectations. If we believe that people have nothing we want, or that only one particular person or one type of relationship can give us what we want, then we are certain to find ourselves in a loveless desert. As we change this expectation and begin to see everyone as an opportunity to feel loved and enriched, life changes from a desert to a fertile valley. What's more, we become the type of person who brings out the best in people. By seeing people's gifts and worthiness, we help them to access and express their highest qualities. Our very state of being begins to affect others in a powerful way. As we radiate unconditional love and open to experience love everywhere, we attract more love into our lives including, paradoxically, the special love relationships that once seemed so elusive.

Exercise: Everyone Is a Teacher

Devote at least one week to practicing the following:

Imagine that every person you meet has been sent into your life purposefully by some Divine Plan and that he or she has a gift or lesson to share with you. This gift is something you vitally need for your well-being and will bring you one step closer to a deeper, more complete experience of love. Your challenge for the week is to see how many of these gifts and lessons you can recognize and to allow yourself to fully receive and appreciate them.

Exercise: Opening to Unconditional Love

Devote at least one full day to practicing the following:

Imagine that every person you encounter is filled with a radiant light, just like a miniature sun. Imagine that you receive the gift of soothing warmth and healing light from every person you meet simply by being in their presence. Feel this light softening your heart, filling you with feelings of well-being and empowering you to manifest your highest good.

Picture this light of unconditional love as a very real and tangible energy that is limitless in quantity and power. Imagine that the love you give and the love you receive are increasing your power to heal yourself, to create your heart's desire, to be at peace and to serve others.

Remind yourself with each encounter that the extent to which you are willing to release fear, judgments and feelings of separateness is the extent to which you are now allowing love, healing and new possibilities into your life.

Do not attempt to change your outward behavior toward people as you practice this exercise. Behave as you normally do and simply notice how you feel. Also notice how people's behavior toward you seems different and any changes in the flow of events during or following this practice.

III. Start loving now. Don't wait for a special relationship.

If you want to experience more love in your life and in particular, if you want to attract specific types of love relationships such as a romantic partner or close friendships, it is important to be more open to the love that is present in your life now and to radiate love now, as opposed to waiting for the special relationship to come along. Love attracts love. Practice one or all of the following to begin a new habit of gratitude and love.

1. Look at every person you meet for the purpose of seeing something lovable about them. Imagine that each person has been precious to someone. Imagine all the people who have cherished this person and see if you can imagine what they must see.

2. Tell at least one person every day something that you admire, appreciate or cherish about them. When anyone acknowledges or appreciates you, receive it fully, let it warm your heart and know that receiving someone's gift of love in a heartfelt way is in itself a gift.

3. Make a habit of gratitude. Count your blessings. Every day see how many things you can find to feel grateful for. Don't just keep these reflections to yourself. Speak them out loud. Begin a new way of talking about your life so that instead of describing everything wrong, you share everything that you feel grateful for. (You may even speak about the same events, but describe them from the perspective of what you have gained rather than what you have lost.)

IV. Reach out to people

This step involves the obvious. If you are lonely, take steps to be around people. The state of alienation and lack of community in our culture today can make it easy to feel lonely in a crowd. Making connections with other people doesn't come as naturally as it once did. The following are just a few of many possible ways to reach out to people in a loving way.

Volunteer. If you are lonely, reach out to some of the many other people in the world who are lonely. Visit a nursing home, help deliver meals to shut-ins or become a big brother or sister to a child. Become a volunteer buddy for an AIDS organization, hospice or Center for Attitudinal Healing.* Volunteering is good for the volunteer. One of the studies cited in Dean Ornish's book, *Love and Survival,* showed a correlation between volunteering and longevity. Volunteers live longer!

Become or reach out for a mentor. If you have skills, expertise or just life experience that someone else could benefit from, take on an apprentice. This could be a formal or informal arrangement of offering to teach your skills to someone or simply making yourself available to a younger person in need of caring attention. In an interview with Bill Moyer, poet Robert Bly spoke of how few young men have older men who take an interest, not just in their work, but in their souls. He pointed out how rare it is for older men to compliment and encourage younger men in a nonshaming way. He also spoke to the other side of this dynamic, relating a story of a renown European scientist living in America who, as a youth, found an older man he wanted to learn from and asked him to be his mentor. Now as an older experienced man himself, he was disheartened as he waited for young men to come to him to learn, but none did. There are rich rewards on both sides of the mentoring relationship. For those of us who are older, there are many who could benefit from what we have learned. It is satisfying to pass on the benefits of our knowledge and maturity. For those of us who are younger or in need of guidance (mentoring does not have to involve an age difference), it is important to realize how much help there is out there for the asking. It can be an honor and a gift to ask someone for mentoring.

Join a group. Many people avoid groups, thinking that they must have the temperament and social skills of an extrovert to fit in. Nowadays people are so hungry for ways to create connections and feeling of community that

---

*To locate a Center for Attitudinal Healing in your area contact the International Network of Attitudinal Healing: 1-888-222-7205.

groups are no longer for a select few. There is a multitude of different types of groups that all offer opportunities to meet and get to know people. There are support groups, interest groups, political groups, volunteer groups, discussion groups, social groups, spiritual groups and many more. Find something that appeals to you and dive in.

Find a therapist. If your experience of loneliness is a long-term chronic condition accompanied by depression and poor self-esteem, a therapist may be your best first step out of isolation. The therapeutic relationship can be a good place to practice relating skills and to develop trust over time with someone whose primary agenda is to help you. There is more in Chapter Five about deriving maximum benefit from a therapy experience.

V. Touch

Modern mainstream American society is not characterized by close-knit communities. In our culture it is easy to remain anonymous and not even know our neighbors. A correlation to this is that Americans touch far less than most other cultures of the world. While touch is not essential to love, and insincere or inappropriate touch does no one any good, true loving touch is a powerful healing tonic to body and spirit. There is a well-documented correlation between touch and physical health. Studies have shown that children who are not touched fail to thrive and that people who have pets are more likely to recover from heart attacks — the very act of petting an animal has a positive physiological affect on both the human and the pet. In his book, *The Broken Heart,* Dr. James Lynch describes studies showing that people in intensive care being monitored for irregular heartbeats showed far less abnormal rhythms when a doctor or nurse touched them to take their pulse. Leo Buscaglia, author of *Loving Each Other,* became well known for his insistence that we all need many hugs a day for our health and well-being.

While this prescription may feel extreme to many of us touch-phobic Americans, we don't have to jump into the deep end of the pool to start incorporating more health-giving touch into our lives. Begin where you are comfortable and look for opportunities to use touch as a way of communicating caring. You can even start with the socially acceptable hand shake. The next time you find yourself shaking hands, let it be more than a hollow ritual. As you shake, imagine that you are sending through your touch your heart-felt positive regard for this person. If you don't usually, try adding a hug to your greeting or departure from a friend or family member. I have know more than a few people who grew up in nontouching families who started a habit of hugging with their aging parents simply by being brave enough to make the first move. Experiment with adding touch to casual conversations. Add a light touch to someone's arm or hand when you say thank you for a message that will go more deeply to the other person's heart. Consider treating yourself to a professional massage with a trained massage therapist. If you have never had a massage before and feel uncomfortable with the idea of being touched by a stranger, find someone who comes highly recommended or ask to have a meeting so you can ask questions and become comfortable before the actual massage. A full body massage can be an incredibly nurturing experience and is worth overcoming any initial discomfort for.

Don't force touch if it doesn't feel right. If we are uncomfortable touching, the people we touch will probably feel just as uncomfortable receiving it and the experience will leave us not wanting to do it again. So begin with forms of touch that you can do fairly comfortably then gradually expand to include more.

Letting Go of Fear

A Course in Miracles teaches that healing is letting go of fear, that miracles happen in the absence of fear, and that when fear is gone, what remains is love. Fear is antithetical to love. To tap into the limitless power of unconditional love, we need to move beyond fear. Our greatest safety and power lie in our defenselessness.

To what extent, though, are we even fully aware of the presence and effects of fear? Certainly, we recognize panic and moments of acute fear. Nagging worry and doubts may also be easily recognized. But what about less obvious fears that we take so for granted they blend into our normal state of consciousness? What about the fear that makes us on guard and defended around strangers or even around friends? The fear that anticipates the worst possible outcome before there is any reason to do so? The fears that we are not good enough, that we will not be supported, that there is not enough for us?

I once had a dramatic lesson in the power of fear many years ago when I first started leading groups on attitudinal healing. The presentation I was leading was on a principle of attitudinal healing that says, "Health is inner peace, healing is letting go of fear."

This particular group consisted of about a dozen friends, all women, who had gotten together and contracted with me to lead a six-month training in attitudinal healing for them. As an approach to this principle, I asked them to think about what fears they had and, in particular, what they feel afraid of in this very group. These women were all intelligent, self-confident, all with families, most with careers, all apparently successful in their lives. The overwhelming response to the latter part of my question was that no one felt they had anything to fear here and now in this group, and in fact, some considered the question ridiculous.

I, on the other hand, was feeling quite a bit of fear, though I was much too fearful to admit it. I was the youngest woman there by ten or so years. As both an outsider and a "young upstart," I had been finding it difficult to work with the closed dynamic of this group of long-time friends, many of whom seemed to have come more for an afternoon social break away from the kids than to study the principles of attitudinal healing.

Just as I was sinking more deeply into fear because my planned presentation was failing (how could I teach these women how to let go of fear if they had none?), a wasp flew into the room. Suddenly, women who seconds before were a picture of strength, composure and invulnerability, were now cringing, running and shrieking. One had removed her shoe and was attempting to beat the wasp to death. The room dissolved into chaos.

Being much less afraid of wasps than of this particular group of women, I managed to regain my composure and call the group to silence. Everyone stopped except the wasp, which had been whacked once or twice and was now stumbling across the middle of the floor. I reached down to let the wasp crawl into my hand and we looked at the tiny creature that triggered such a large reaction. Suddenly we all realized how much fear lives quietly within us under the surface, and how easily it can erupt and shake our equilibrium.

This level of fear is ingrained and stifling, limiting our choices and possibilities in ways we don't even know. If we have lived a lifetime in a cramped closed space, we don't realize that a wide open space exists. We don't include it in our range of choices. We may not even notice that we are uncomfortable.

Sometimes I ask people in my workshops to imagine the feeling of safety and talk about what it is like. A surprising number of people have difficulty even imagining the experience of absolute safety. Those who can are often amazed at how different it feels from their "normal" state.

There is certainly an abundance of physical evidence to substantiate the "truth" of how dangerous the world is and how we need to be ever on guard to survive. Every now and then, however, someone comes along to demonstrate the extent to which our fearful reality is of our own creation, a result of fearful thinking rather than the cause of it.

One such person was a remarkable woman who, in middle age, in the 1950's, let go of her middle class life, took the name Peace Pilgrim and spent the rest of her years walking back and forth across the country talking to people about peace. She owned next to nothing, she ate only when she was offered food, slept indoors only when she was offered shelter and talked to people only when they approached her first. She claimed to have no fear whatsoever, in spite of the fact that she sought out the most populated and so-called "dangerous" areas to travel through on foot at all hours of the day and night. She believed that she was divinely protected and that her willingness to see the best in people called forth people's highest qualities and behavior. She surrendered every aspect of her life to her faith and, even under the most dangerous circumstances, consistently experienced love, generosity and miracles wherever she went.

I was fortunate as a young child to encounter Peace Pilgrim a couple of times as she passed through my part of the country. Hearing her speak about her life is one of the most vivid memories of my childhood. Even then I recognized something special about this woman. Something seemed to emanate from her that was contagious — serenity, joy, inner peace. She truly did create her own safety from within.

The following is a simple exercise for replacing the habit of fear with the habit of safety. It will help you develop a relaxed, peaceful state of mind so that your inner guidance can come through as you need it and you can begin to be a source of peace for those around you. Practice this for a week or even just a day and see what happens.

Exercise: Creating Inner Safety

Remind yourself many times each hour of the day that you are safe. Say to yourself, silently or aloud, over and over, the words, "I am safe." It is not necessary that you believe these words. "I am safe" is the belief you are creating, not necessarily the belief you hold.

From time to time, as you affirm these words, take several deep breaths, relax and imagine a safe feeling. Let it start in your stomach as a sooth-

ing, peaceful sensation and radiate through your entire body and then slightly beyond, forming a safe, comforting cocoon around you. Feel your stomach relax into deep safety and well-being.... Feel your shoulders relax as though you have just had a weight lifted from them.... Imagine a hard and heavy layer of protective armor now dissolving out of every part of your body because it is no longer needed.

Imagine that you are naturally protected by your feelings of safety and well-being. Picture this safety as a beautiful light that fills and surrounds you. See this light attracting to you everything that is for your highest good while it repels everything that is not. Also imagine that this light is in place around you all the time, working for you, even when you're not thinking about it. Put yourself to sleep this way at night.

Some years ago when I felt a particular need to affirm my safety, I began to practice this exercise intensively. After several days, it seemed to be working very well. Instead of feeling afraid, I felt deeply peaceful and protected. That evening as I was leaving the somewhat remote country retreat center where I held my weekly attitudinal healing group, I got a flat tire half way down the long, completely dark drive leading to the main road. Although I was often the last person to leave, this time there just happened to be one group member behind me who, in a matter of minutes, changed my tire and got me back on the road. As I drove the long way to my home in the country, I was filled with a sense of gratitude that my tire had gone flat when and where it did with help instantly available. My worst fear is to be stranded in the middle of nowhere with car problems.

I was reflecting on my good fortune, feeling protected and at peace, when I suddenly felt my car wobble and klunk. The other tire had gone flat. I had an instant of panic. Here was my worst fear — on the highway in the middle of nowhere late at night, a flat tire and not even a spare to put on! But then I realized that I was at the only exit for miles and miles that had a service station immediately off of it. So I klunked the short distance to the station where I had to leave my car to be serviced the next day. Before I even had time to consider how I would get home from there, a man who saw my situation offered me a ride. I felt intuitively that he was a Good Samaritan rather than a psycho killer and accepted his offer.

When I got home, I realized that all of my mishaps had only added an extra 35 minutes to my drive home. It turned out to be very convenient for my housemate to give me a ride to pick up my car the next day at exactly the time I needed to go out. Through this whole experience, except for those seconds of panic on the highway, I felt peaceful, protected, safe. What's more, I had been meaning to get my two bald tires replaced but kept putting it off for lack of time. The 35 minutes it took out of my life proved to be far more efficient than the hour or two it usually took at my tire dealer. And the process of getting two flat tires, in a strange way, not only got my tires changed, but it reinforced for me that I truly am safe, more so than if the whole thing hadn't happened. I saw that I could encounter one of my worst fears and still be completely protected.

Listening to Inner Guidance

The state of inner safety that Peace Pilgrim so beautifully demonstrated is accessible to all of us. We all have the potential to create an aura of safety that is powerful enough to impact the world around us. We don't need to be saints, and it doesn't require hard work so much as consistent attention. Neither is it a matter of testing our bravery by exposing ourselves to frightening situations. Walking down a dark alley late at night in spite of our fear, because we believe we "should" feel safe, will more likely attract fearful experiences to us. Learning to recognize and release the habit of fear, however, frees us to hear inner guidance about when and where we are safe and when we are not. Peace Pilgrim was a big proponent of listening to inner guidance and doing what is sensible. Looking both ways before crossing a street, she said, is sensible — fearing streets is not necessary.

Inner guidance about our safety is always there for us when we are willing to listen. There are subtle signals that come to us through our thoughts and feelings that guide us to be in the right place at the right time and out of harm. For a time, I was in the habit of taking long walks along a beautiful country trail. It was an isolated area far from main roads. I seldom encountered anyone other than a handful of retired people taking some mid-day exercise. I felt very safe there. It was a place I went for peace and solitude.

One day, from a distance, I saw a young man walking toward me on the trail. Something about him felt "wrong." The only young men I had seen here were invariably jogging, or biking or strolling with a girlfriend. This man was alone, walking slowly and unsteadily. My instincts sensed potential danger and the "safe" thing to do would have been to turn around immediately while there was still a distance between us and head quickly back to the main road, a couple of miles back. A thought came to me clearly, though, telling me that I would be safe and I was to continue forward. I asked this guidance why I should test myself this way when I felt afraid and it would be so simple to just turn around. The answer I received was that if I turned around now I would never feel safe walking here again. This felt true and I continued. The piece of trail that was between us went under a highway, supported by a large concrete abutment. He came to the underpass first and I saw him slip behind the large concrete wall, out of sight. My fear escalated as I envisioned being ambushed. Still I continued, reminding myself that I am safe. He didn't reappear and I passed through safely, never even encountering him directly. I walked about another mile down the trail, then started back. He was nowhere to be seen on my return walk.

I came back to this place many times after that. Never did I feel afraid. I truly believe that I was "protected" that day and the experience of following my inner guidance left me feeling safer in the world. I was more certain that I would know in other situations when it is appropriate to go forward in spite of my fear and when to retreat.

Exercise: Listening to Inner Guidance

Either read over the next few paragraphs before you begin or record them on tape and play them back or have a friend read them to you.

Become comfortable, close your eyes and relax yourself with some deep breaths.... Ask your body to let you know how it feels when it is giving you the message, "YES!" That is, when your timing is right, when you are in harmony with the people and circumstances around you and when what you are doing feels just "right," how does your body feel?

Now ask your body to let you know how it tells you "NO!" That is, when things don't feel quite right, when your timing is off, when things aren't flowing smoothly and when you make the wrong decisions, how does your body feel?

Bring your attention back to your breathing now and breathe out the feeling of NO. Recall the feeling of YES and breathe that feeling back into your body.... When your body feels relaxed and comfortable, take a deep breath and open your eyes.

Immediately after this meditation write in detail all the ways you experience your body giving you the messages "YES" and "NO." Begin paying attention to when you body is registering YES feelings and when your body is telling you NO. You will get YES signals when what you are doing or thinking is in alignment with your highest good. You will get NO signals when you are off track in some way. These body messages are a form of intuition. You can use them to help you make decisions. You will find yourself better able to save time, cut corners, be in the right place at the right time and avoid experiences that are not for your highest good.

Experiment in little ways at first. For example, the next time you are invited somewhere and aren't sure whether or not to go, check in with your body signals and see if you get a stronger YES or NO feeling. Or, before making an important phone call, check to see what messages your body gives you. A NO feeling could mean that now is not the best time to have your communication received by this person. Through practice you will gradually develop confidence in your ability to read your inner signals accurately. You will be more attuned to the voice of your intuition when it's time to make big decisions in you life.

Creating Inner Safety vs. Protection

There are many spiritual techniques for protecting oneself against harm. A well known one is to imagine a bubble of light surrounding you, sealing out all the things that are harmful. This bubble of light can be visualized surrounding your body, surrounding other people for whom you feel concern, your home, your car or anything that you fear is in danger. It is a good one to use when your attention is being absorbed by worry.

Yet, while this and other protection techniques are useful, ultimately the most powerful thing we can do to protect ourselves is to change our belief about the reality of harm. There is a potential trap in focusing too much attention on protection because, as we do, we automatically hold in mind a picture of danger and of our vulnerability. As we give energy to this paradigm of potential victims and abusers, we inadvertently root ourselves more firmly in this reality. In other words, the more we direct our creative thought toward protecting ourselves against harm, the more we perpetuate a reality in which there is always danger to ward off. At best we create the experience of escaping danger rather than that of experiencing safety.

However, as important as it is to shift our fundamental perception of reality, it is also important to listen to our fears and address them. This might sound contradictory, but in practice, no matter how much we may want to believe that our house will never be broken into, if we feel strongly afraid of it at a gut level, our fear may be so intense that it overrides our intention to believe we are safe. When a fear is very big, it is often more effective to take action to address it in a physical way at the same time that we work on changing it at the level of belief. For example, if you are very afraid that someone will break into your house, along with affirming your intrinsic safety, it is wise to install good locks and a security system. Without these practical steps, your fear may take up so much of your attention that you attract exactly what you fear, thus strengthening your belief in your vulnerability. After taking action to protect yourself, your attention will be freer to focus on the inner state of safety rather than danger.

Listen to your own level of comfort or fear in determining what you need to do to be safe. Then take whatever physical protection steps are necessary for you to put worry aside and focus your attention on safety. While Peace Pilgrim felt perfectly safe walking alone at night in the most dangerous inner city neighborhoods, if you feel afraid of this, then don't do it. Your fear would send out a broadcast that could attract harm to you.

At the same time, if you feel perfectly relaxed and at peace in a situation that others find frightening, you do not need to increase your level of protection in response to someone else's fear. Be careful not to let others talk you into believing you aren't safe. This puts a ripple in your peace of mind, and it is your peace of mind that keeps you safe in a situation that might be dangerous for someone else. As a fortyish adult, I sometimes recall in horror and amazement my teenage habit of jumping barefoot onto a city bus and spending all day walking around the inner city of Baltimore having adventures, skipping innocently and fearlessly through broken glass and God knows what else. I remember feeling joyful, unstoppable and full of life on those days. By evening the bottoms of my feet would be black with city dirt but never cut or bruised. Now I find that when I walk barefoot in my own back yard my feet seem to find every stone, splinter and glass sliver. Often our innocence of danger creates such an aura of safety that we easily avoid harm. As we become "wiser" and know more about potential dangers, we lose this protective shield.

Cultivating an attitude of safety is a very fine line that is neither a defense against danger nor a denial of it (as in "If I pretend it's not there, it will go away"). Pretending that danger will not find us is different from truly feeling safe. In denial, we tune out our feelings and instincts rather than listen to them. Whatever we ignore in this way tends to come back in a disowned form through a person or circumstance that feels outside of our control.

Cultivating a natural state of safety involves listening carefully to all of our instincts, feelings, thoughts and fleeting impressions rather than tuning them out. The following three steps all play an important part in creating an experience of safety. Each step is equally important and must not be left out.

Steps for Cultivating a State of Inner Safety

1. Identify your fearful thoughts and beliefs and consciously replace them with affirmations of safety. (Review Chapter Two, if needed, for more on affirmations.)

2. Create the inner feeling of safety with the earlier exercise on "Creating Inner Safety."

3. Pay attention to your level of fear in various life situations. Fear is a very specific physical sensation. Notice when you have even a little bit of a fear sensation in the pit of your stomach or when you are tensing up, or sweating or having any kind of ominous

or anxious feeling. These are signals of fear. Don't ignore these! When they are present, practice the above two steps and ask yourself what action would help to alleviate these physical sensations.

Sometimes when we experience a generalized feeling of anxiety that is not related to a specific event or circumstance or when a current event triggers a big fear response because it reminds us of something in the past, the first two steps may be all that is needed to eliminate the fear. When they aren't enough, it is important to listen to your fear and find appropriate action. Sometimes this may mean taking sensible safety precautions such as locking your door or not walking alone at night. Other times it may mean doing something or not doing something even though you can find no sensible reason behind it. Your gut feeling may be telling you not to attend an event or drive down a particular street. Even though you may not have any visible reason not to do these things, they may be important messages from your intuition, steering you away from harm. Take whatever action will best help you redirect your attention away from danger and protection and back to inner peace and well-being.

****

Forgiveness

Without forgiveness we can't love. From the perspective of spiritual reality, the statements "I love you but don't forgive you" and "I forgive you but I don't love you" are impossibilities. Love and forgiveness go hand in hand. We can't have one without the other.

True forgiveness is not something we do for another person. I often hear people speak of forgiveness as something we give to someone else, something that must be deserved or earned, and sometimes needs to be withheld. The spiritual purpose of forgiveness is self-healing. As long as we are holding anger, resentment and grudges against another person, we are poisoning our bodies with toxicity, lowering our immunity to disease and on subtler levels generating thoughts, expectations and attitudes that repel our highest good. As we hold on to the belief that someone has harmed us so badly that we cannot, will not, forgive, we give power to the part of us that feels vulnerable and susceptible to being harmed. Our lack of forgiveness actually draws more circumstances that will feed our anger and victimization. Lack of forgiveness has been related as a contributing factor to physical illness, excess weight, financial scarcity, failed relationships and a host of other problems. Lack of forgiveness inhibits love, which is the only true source of power. As we withhold forgiveness, we inhibit our power and our very life-force.

Medical intuitive, Caroline Myss, who, through her gift of intuitive sight, sees the energy patterns that lead to illness says that, "By far the strongest poison to the human spirit is the inability to forgive oneself or another person."

Now that we have established its importance, what exactly does it mean to forgive? What often makes forgiveness so difficult is that we tend to think of it as a sacrifice, as giving in, giving up, losing our "rightness." It's like giving up the chip that says "You owe me." It seems to discount the pain we felt. Forgiveness is sometimes experienced as letting someone who hurt us off the hook, no longer holding them accountable for their actions.

But forgiveness is not an act of negotiation between two people. It does not begin and end by speaking the words "I forgive you." Instead, it is an internal state, an ongoing process rather than an act. True forgiveness is not about excusing someone's hurtful actions. It goes much deeper than this. It is the inner awareness that no harm was done, thus there is, in truth, nothing to forgive.

Most of what passes for forgiveness is rooted in the belief that we are separate and vulnerable and have been harmed. In this way, the act of forgiveness directs the attention of both people to the hurtful act. The forgiver feels self-righteous, the forgiven, guilty. The whole process strengthens both people's belief in the reality of separateness and harm, and in this way is disempowering to both.

True forgiveness is a shifting of attention away from the hurtful act, not in denial, but in release. It means identifying with the higher part of ourselves that was never harmed so we can see past the illusion of separateness to the reality of Oneness. As we understand ourselves to be one with the person who hurt us, forgiveness becomes self-forgiveness. As we transcend our belief in ourselves as victims, we are able to see the other person differently. Instead of seeing his or her "wrongness" we see the pain that motivated his or her actions. Living from a belief that doing harm brings personal gain is a prison of separateness, powerlessness and pain. Anyone who acts intentionally to harm another is trapped in this painful prison, even if he or she doesn't recognize it as such. When we understand this, we can more easily feel compassion instead of rage.

As with the idea of "love," I have heard the concept of forgiveness promoted in spiritual, metaphysical and psychological circles for years as the spiritual thing, the healthy thing, the right thing to do. And, as with teachings on love, I have heard much more on the benefits and reasons to do it than on how to do it. How can we coax our hearts into forgiveness when they feel hardened or broken? Words of forgiveness are worth nothing without love behind them. The following steps offer some different paths into forgiveness. Begin with whatever steps feel "doable" and let the easier steps lead you to the harder ones as you are ready.

Steps toward Forgiving

I. Release Anger

If you are holding a great deal of rage toward someone, you may need to release these angry feelings from your body before you can take steps toward forgiveness. (Review the section on anger in Chapter Three for help with this.)

II. Aim for Moments of Forgiveness

Think of forgiveness as an ongoing process rather than a one-time act. When we have felt deeply hurt, the feeling of forgiveness may come and go for a while. Aim for moments of forgiveness. Trust that eventually these moments will come more frequently and begin to string together until forgiveness is continuous and complete.

III. See the Reflection of Your Core Beliefs

Instead of focusing attention on the wrong thing that has been done to you, look at the experience or relationship from the perspective of self-responsibility. Imagine that this painful experience reflects some belief or expectation you have about life. Remember, this doesn't mean you "asked" to be hurt. It means that you learned, probably when you were very young, to expect painful experiences. So release blame, shame and any idea that you have done something wrong. Review the "Transforming Painful Life Experiences" exercise in Chapter Two. Pray to God or your Higher Self for help in stepping out of the dance you have created with this other person. Pray for help in releasing the beliefs and expectations that call hurt into your life.

If you are working on forgiving a parent or other person from your early childhood who helped to instill your limiting core beliefs about life, you can still see your experience with this person as reflecting some deep level of choice. Imagine that your Higher Self called this relationship into your life for a purpose. For example, if I look at all the pain my father caused me in my childhood and early adulthood, I am tempted to feel rage and powerlessness. However when I think of the turns my life took as a direct result of this early pain, I realize that my whole life path with its focus of love and healing was because of my father. From this perspective, I see a higher purpose to our meeting and can actually feel gratitude for this painful experience in my life.

IV. Ask the Other Person's Higher Self for Assistance

You may or may not ever choose to speak to the person who hurt you face to face. You can, however, begin the process of forgiveness by talking to the person in spirit without them being physically present. (In Chapter Five there is an exercise for doing this entitled "Relating from Your Higher Self.") Begin by speaking out loud all your anger and hurt. When there is nothing left unsaid, thank the person for the role they have played in your life. Thank this person for enacting your negative beliefs so that you can see them more clearly and choose to release them. Ask this person's Higher Self for help in creating a new pattern between the two of you where there is no experience of hurt. Ask that there be nothing holding the two of you together other than unconditional love.

As you align with your Higher Self, let your vision of the situation expand until you can see the pain, fear or misunderstanding that motivated this person's hurtful actions. If you can, communicate your compassion in spirit. Let your heart break open to this person, say silently or out loud any words of compassion that are in your heart and picture him or her surrounded in healing light. If you are unable to feel compassion yourself, picture an image of God, the person's Higher Self or a Guardian Angel embracing the hurting, fearful part of this person, surrounding him or her with healing compassion.

If it is difficult to feel compassion and forgiveness, then speak out loud to the person, in spirit, and simply apologize for continuing to hold anger and judgment, for holding on to your "rightness," and for seeing your separateness instead of your Oneness. *Don't judge yourself* in doing this process. As you complete your apology, picture yourself being embraced in total compassion, acceptance and love by your Higher Self, God or guardian angel.

V. Self-forgiveness

If all approaches to forgiveness feel equally difficult, you probably have at least as much trouble forgiving yourself as you do others. In this case, begin the forgiveness process by forgiving yourself. Make a list of all the things you hold against yourself and begin to say out loud and as written affirmations, "I, (your name), forgive myself for _____." Louise Hay suggests looking at yourself in the mirror as you say affirmations of self-love. I find this mirror technique to be especially helpful in working on self-forgiveness.

VI. Get to the Root of Displaced Anger

When your anger is toward a group, an institution or society, rather than an individual, it is important to remember that anger is a much weaker power source than love. Many feel that anger is a necessary ingredient for creating change. While anger can motivate action, ultimately, when we give attention to victimization and abuse, we may achieve some sense of victory, but we also perpetuate a reality that includes victims and abusers. The more we motivate ourselves from a place of anger, the more we will continually have to fight victimization.

Being angry at a group often has a feeling of hopelessness built into it. While we may be able to create peace and resolution in relation to one person, doing so with all of society is obviously more difficult. When we often find ourselves angry at "the system" in one form or another, there is usually a person or people from early in our lives we need to forgive. This early hurt, usually related to one or both of our parents or other significant adult care-takers, imbedded within us feelings of anger and powerlessness that we project onto other situations in our lives. We may also find that we have anger toward one or more of the important people in our adult life(a spouse, friend or co-worker — and have displaced this anger onto an impersonal system because we fear the consequences of our anger. It may be easier to face the anger we have toward a faceless system than to deal with the true source of our feeling, which invariably comes back to personal relationships with individuals. However, it is far more manageable to forgive an individual than a system.

When you find yourself angry at a group, find the one individual you most need to forgive. If, for example you are angry at a company where you used to work, focus on the one person you feel the most anger toward. If you are angry at society or other such large institutions where there is no one single individual who stands out, then look to see who in your life you are holding anger toward. Also look to your past. Review the exercise on separating the past from the present in Chapter Three under the heading, "Steps for Working with Anger."

VII. Let Go of Victim Scenarios

Write a "victim" scenario. Describe everything that was done to you unjustly, all the ways you have been harmed, every way you are right and the other party is wrong. Next, describe the same scenario from the perspective that it was somehow a great lesson, gift or turning point in your life that served you in some important way. Write this even if you don't believe it. Take the first scenario of yourself as victim and symbolically release it: burn it, tear it up, bury it or flush it. As you let it go imagine that you are releasing the need to feel victimized. Keep the second scenario and read it every day for at least a week.

Forgiveness Meditation

Record the following meditation and listen to it every day for a month.

Become comfortable, close your eyes, take some deep breaths and take several moments to relax....

Bring to mind a person from your present or past you have difficulty forgiving. See that person before you. Be aware of memories and emotions that arise. As you reexperience this unhealed relationship, take a moment to forgive yourself. Let go of any judgments you may have toward yourself for the way you have dealt with this person in the past.

Turn your attention inward now. Find within yourself a center of beautiful light that represents the always healed, unconditionally loving essence of your being. Feel this essence growing brighter as you give it all of your attention. Know yourself to be a being of love and light who cannot be harmed or do harm. Feel your body melting away, no longer holding you in a prison of separateness and vulnerability. As a being of light, imagine that your only purpose in coming together with other beings is to teach and learn forgiveness and love....

Now, once again, bring to mind the image of the person you have difficulty forgiving. As you see this person before you, see layers begin to fall away — layers of past experiences together, familiar habits, personality traits, the sound of the person's voice.... See all of these fall away like layers of an onion. Allow even the person's physical appearance to fall away from your mind's eye until there is nothing left but the essence of this person, which is light and love. For this instant, know that there is no separation between the two of you, only light and love. Feel that you are of one mind, one heart, and your one purpose is to teach and learn forgiveness and love. In this instant of knowing you are One, realize also that there is nothing you can need or want from this person, there is nothing he or she can withhold from you. Sharing love and forgiveness with this being is the same as loving and forgiving yourself because there is no separation between you. From this perspective you can see that your anger, fear and lack of forgiveness hurt you deeply and you now release them to the light.

Gradually allow yourself to again see this person through the eyes of your physical body. Let the layers of appearance, voice, habits and mannerisms return. This time, however, see the physical manifestations of this person as being merely the vehicle for learning forgiveness. Say to this being, your teacher of forgiveness, "In this instant I forgive you totally for not meeting my expectations. I recognize your actions as a cry for help." Say to yourself now, "I am completely forgiven now and always for my unloving thoughts toward myself and others." Repeat to yourself, "You and I are One. There is nothing I need from you. There is nothing to forgive. As I love you, I heal myself."

Now release all thoughts of this person to the light. Let them go and gently bring your attention to the rhythm of your breath. Let your breath help you bring your awareness back to your body. Slowly and gently, as you are ready, come all the way back and open your eyes, feeling refreshed and alert.

Choosing the Way of Love — Letting Go of Judgment

Judgment is not to be confused with discernment. Through discernment we have clear vision. Through judgment we define the world as good or bad, right or wrong, and create separateness. It is discernment that guides us not to rely upon someone whose behavior is untrustworthy. It is judgment that declares this same person to be bad, ourselves to be superior and causes us to withhold compassion, forgiveness and love.

There is something compelling about being right that is hard to relinquish. We tend to choose the self-righteous satisfaction of being right when we lack faith that we deserve and can have true happiness. Instead we settle for what seems like the next best thing — being right. Yet being right (by proving someone else wrong) is, by its very nature, antithetical to well-being and inner peace. As we make someone else wrong, we affirm that we are separate, we strengthen our alienation and wind up expending more energy on executing our defense than on creating our joy. Judgment effectively separates us from the power of love.

Living life without judgment, without the filter of right and wrong, necessitates a shift in perspective. It requires a leap to a broader paradigm.

This is illustrated by the Complementarity principle of quantum physics that defines a reality where mutually exclusive opposites can coexist. Remember the wave-particle duality: matter can act like particles or it can act like energy waves. The logic of our physical senses would tell us that this is impossible. Matter must be one way or the other. Yet this perspective of Complementarity represents a paradigm shift in perception. It is an expansion of vision that includes duality and paradox as part of truth.

Another principle of quantum physics is that of Nonlocality. Nonlocality says that all things are so connected that one part of a system cannot be analyzed separately from the whole, that there is an unbroken wholeness to the universe and that the pieces cannot be understood individually. This is yet a further expansion of perception from Complementarity. It suggests that parts of reality appear contradictory because we are focusing on them singly, as separate elements, rather than in the context of the whole of existence. This perspective is illustrated in the story of the three blind men who encountered different parts of an elephant and came up with three very different and incomplete realities of what an elephant is.

When we are attached to a position and hold it to be "the truth" to the exclusion of other truths, we are just as blind. When we expand our vision to a broader paradigm, we find a perspective that can simultaneously hold different perspectives of truth, even perspectives that are so different, they seem to be describing mutually exclusive realities. As we expand our vision even further, these seeming paradoxes become understandable parts of a cohesive whole, just as radically different pieces combine to make a perfectly coherent elephant.

When we are attached to our position of rightness and to another's wrongness, we can be certain that there is a bigger perspective where we can find joining, commonality and healing instead of separateness. This doesn't mean giving in or letting go of being true to our own values. Shifting to a broader paradigm means expanding to include more than one view, not sacrificing a view.

The first step in making this paradigm shift is being willing to believe, especially in times of self-righteousness, that the other position and your own both have validity, that neither is wrong. The idea that nothing is "wrong" can bring out self-righteous indignation in the best of us. It's so easy to think of wrong things. What about children dying? What about abusive parents? What about murder? What about Hitler?

Shifting has to begin with drawing our attention away from the incomplete truths of our physical senses in order to frame reality in the context of spiritual truths. Remembering that we are more than our physical body and consequently are beyond physical harm puts many "wrong" acts into a new perspective. If tragic occurrences and abusive acts, even on the scale of Hitler, at the deepest level of truth, do no harm, then what do they do? Perhaps at a spiritual level, we agree to play certain roles in relation to one another, to help each other ultimately see through the illusions of fear to the truth of love.

I have heard more than one woman who lost a child through miscarriage or death in infancy share years after the event that, while the experience was heart-breaking at the time, it had a long-term effect of cementing a relationship with the spiritual being of that child in a way that was very powerful and comforting. Perhaps children die because they don't need the lessons of growing into adulthood. What if there is a spiritual agreement between parent and child to spend a short amount of time together in physical bodies and then part? Perhaps this brief coming together makes an eternal spiritual relationship more conscious to the parent than it would have otherwise been if the child's spirit had never come into a body. Perhaps the parting helps to turn that parent's life in a new and productive direction.

Suppose there is a similar spiritual agreement that happens even between victims and abusers in which each agrees to play a role to learn specific lessons, to develop strengths, to play out a hurtful scenario until it is no longer needed. Perhaps there is some essential purpose to these experiences that ultimately helps us transcend the limits and tragedy of physical reality and open to a spiritual reality where there are no victims and abusers. I offer these examples, not as "The Truth" but as an invitation to continually stretch to find new and expanded views of reality.

Of course, letting go of framing behavior and life experiences as wrong does not mean that we let go of our own standards of behavior. We don't need to call child abuse "good" because we have stopped focusing on its wrongness. We would still be just as adamant about protecting children from such experiences. What we would let go of, however, is our anger, our pain and our belief that one person is bad and another person has been damaged.

This expanded perspective need not diminish our capacity to change a painful situation. It could even make us more effective. In her book **Creating Miracles**, Carolyn Miller collected many true stories of people who managed to escape unharmed from various life-threatening situations. In a number of instances, people escaped potentially deadly attackers by refusing to believe themselves to be victims and by seeing their attacker through eyes of compassion rather than rage and fear. One example tells of a former army M.P. named John who stopped a man as he was rampaging through a bar, slashing at people with a metal pipe. Instead of resorting to force, "John gazed steadily into the madman's eyes and said with great compassion, 'You must be in terrible pain to do a thing like this'." In moments the attacker had surrendered his weapon and was weeping in the arms of this compassionate man.

As we stop believing that someone is bad and, instead, see them through the eyes of love, we help to call forth their Higher Self. As we stop believing that someone is damaged, we give energy to the part of them that is intact, and support their healing. As we stop believing ourselves to be victims, we stop receiving abusive treatment. Opening to a bigger picture of reality means juggling some mind-boggling paradoxes. It means having compassion for a person's pain, yet still having faith in the part of them that is whole and undamaged. It means seeing the good in someone while saying "no" to their abusive behavior. It means accepting our power to create our own reality at the same time we surrender to a Higher Power.

The importance of continually seeking a higher truth is, very simply, it makes our lives work better. We become able to see options that were invisible to us previously. We are better able to resolve conflicts in a way that serves the highest interest of all concerned. We are more at peace and physically healthier.

Being right takes an incredible amount of energy. It can be consuming. The more we make someone wrong, the less willing they become to negotiate, compromise or give us what we want. And when we shift from a fear-based reality to one that holds everyone's highest good as interconnected, miracles happen. Energy flows, creativity awakens, joy returns.

I had a powerful experience of this once when I was engaged in a horrible struggle with my lover. We both agreed that we loved one another and wanted our relationship to work but we agreed about nothing else. We had broken up and gotten back together more than once, and each of us felt wounded by the other. One day I was pouring out my feelings in a long letter to him. I poured out my anger and my pain and how wrong I thought he was being. It was a long letter. It felt as though it could go on forever. When I finished, I read it over and changed it a bit to make my position sound more "right." It was ready to send. I felt no relief, only despair, stuckness, pain. At this point, something came over me and before I knew it I found myself writing:

"I know you love me and that you wouldn't do anything to intentionally hurt me. Even though I don't understand some of the things you are doing right now, I trust that you are acting for your highest good and therefore for my highest good as well. I release you and trust that whatever happens between us will be the best thing for both of us."

As I wrote these words I had a visceral reaction against them. They felt stilted. They were lies, the opposite of what I really felt. As I wrote, I had no plan to send this letter. I was simply following some tiny voice inside that said, "Just write the words." When I finished, I felt strangely relieved.

I was struck by how few words it took, how little effort was needed to convey this message. I suddenly knew I was going to tear up my first letter and send this one. It still didn't feel "true" but that didn't seem to matter. It was like a guardian spirit happened by and said, "Put down your pen. I'll do this for you." and lifted a heavy load from my shoulders.

The most amazing thing about the letter is that after writing it, I stopped thinking about my relationship. I wasn't thinking about how my words would affect him, what he would do next, what I should do next, if I could ever get what I wanted from him. These thoughts had been my constant companions for several months. To be free of them was like an endless headache suddenly going away. I started finding joy in small things again. I started having a life apart from "should I or shouldn't I break up?".

Experiences like this have made me wonder what is so seductive about pain and being "right" that have so often compelled me to hold them. Time and time again, I have discovered that the tiniest willingness to surrender, to "Let go and let God," has lifted the greatest burdens and pain.

The next time you find yourself stuck in conflict, indecision or pain, when your brain has considered every option over and over, when you're tired, overwhelmed and confused, consider this small experiment in willingness. It can be done in less than five minutes.

Exercise: Creating Willingness

Step One

Stop. Stop running, stop thinking, stop talking, stop worrying, stop controlling.

Step Two

Close your eyes, take a few deep breaths. Relax. Let your shoulders drop. Let the muscles in your stomach relax. Feel your brow become smooth and free of worry lines.

Step Three

Say to yourself in whatever words feel like your own, "I am willing to let this burden be lifted. I am willing to let this conflict be resolved. I am willing to be at peace and let my highest good unfold. I am willing to turn this over to a Higher Power." If you are alone, say these words out loud. If you are stuck in conflict with someone who is present, consider saying to this person, "I am willing to let this conflict be healed." Don't worry about how. That is the part you have just turned over. Imagine a heavy weight being lifted from your shoulders.

Step Four

That's all there is. Now let it go. Be open to thoughts, feelings and inspirations that may come immediately, but don't expect answers to come right away. Turn your attention to something else for a while, something that will let you continue in a relaxed frame of mind. If conflict thoughts arise later, simply affirm to yourself again that you are willing to let this conflict be resolved.

In the book *Peace Pilgrim, Her Life and Her Work in Her Own Words*, Peace Pilgrim told of a man who was very upset to hear that she would be speaking at his church. He had seen her picture in the newspaper and was horrified by her poor and scruffy appearance. He complained to his minister and to congregation members. Someone told Peace Pilgrim about this man's distress and right away she called him. This is the conversation they had, in her words:

"'This is Peace Pilgrim calling,' I said. I could hear him gasp. Afterward he told me that he thought I had called to bawl him out. I said, 'I have called to apologize to you because evidently I must have done something to offend you, since

without even knowing me you have been apprehensive about my speaking at your church. Therefore I feel I must somehow owe you an apology and I have called to apologize!'

"Do you know that man was in tears before the conversation was over? And now we're friends — he corresponded with me afterward. Yes, the law of love works!"

Faced with a similar situation, how much more natural it would be for most of us to take offense with the complaining parishioner, to see him in the wrong, and respond in nearly any way other than to apologize. Yet how powerful these words were. How big an impact they had.

I once witnessed the power of the words "I'm sorry" to bring healing to the incredibly deep wounds of racism. In a 5-day seminar I led once where the racial balance was about 80% African American and 20% White, issues of racism became a hotly debated issue throughout the whole workshop. The Black members of the group voiced their anger, pain and bitterness toward White culture in a way that I had never seen in groups that were predominantly White.

On the last day of our time together, there was an emotional exchange between a Black and a White member of the group. Both were crying as they talked about how the wound of racism had affected them. Others in the room were crying, too, as they listened, and in the midst of this sharing, another Black woman suddenly began sobbing loudly and uncontrollably. When she could speak again, she told us what happened to trigger her outburst — the White woman sitting next to her had just turned, and with tears in her eyes whispered, "I'm sorry." The Black woman said she had been waiting her whole life to hear a White person say those words. As she spoke, others began to cry and fall into each other's arms. For that instant, we transcended the lines of racial separateness and were able to love one another, not in spite of our races, but including our racial differences.

The woman who apologized was not overtly racist, no more so than any of us who try to be "good" people. She could argue that she was not responsible for hundreds of years of slavery and racial oppression, and had nothing to apologize for. Yet, in that moment, she was able to speak in a voice that felt representative of the whole White race, by taking responsibility for her own shadow. Her apology did not say I am guilty, I'm bad, It's all my fault. It simply said, "I see in myself a piece of the Oppressor, and I am deeply sorry for the pain it has caused."

Our shadow is the dark, murky side of our nature that most of us find repugnant. It is so painful to look upon that we project it outward and see others as having these hated qualities but not ourselves. It is a part of us that we have disowned and deny. It is the pain of acknowledging our shadow that makes saying, "I'm sorry" so difficult. So instead, we defend ourselves and prove our rightness. But when we let this go and see the kernel of truth in any attack made against us, we suddenly have less to defend. We are no longer losing energy in hiding our deepest secret — that we are flawed — `and we gain incredible power to transform our situation.

When you feel stuck in a standoff of disagreement, see if you can find a kernel of truth and validity in the other person's position. You will be amazed at how quickly this takes the steam out of a fight and opens new possibilities for healing. All it takes is an ounce of willingness to heal the most seemingly unresolvable conflicts. As *A Course in Miracles* says:

> *"...the barrier of grievances is easily passed,*
> *and cannot stand between you and salvation.*
> *I will there be light.*
> *Let me behold the light*
> *That reflects God's Will and mine."*

5

"We who are one would recognize this day
the truth about ourselves.
We would come home, and rest in unity.
For there is peace,
and nowhere else can peace be sought and found."

—A Course in Miracles

Uniting in True Relationship

Our true relationship to one another is unity rather than separateness. Our power increases synergistically as we shift from "me" consciousness to "we" consciousness and replace competition with a paradigm of win/win.

Shifting from "Me" to "We" Consciousness

Accepting unconditional love as the only source of power shifts us into a whole new paradigm of power that is fueled by the synergy of collective energy, something much greater than our own personal strength and will.

Collective energy generates miracles. It is the shift from "particle" reality to "wave" reality.

Yet, the reality that fear would have us believe is that the world is a dangerous place where we must live from a stance of defense to survive. When we believe we are separate and vulnerable, we naturally fall into a way of living that is self-protective. We take on "me" consciousness. Fear convinces us that there is not enough of anything to go around and everyone cannot get their needs met at the same time. This fearful perspective that we must look out for ourselves and guard our own interests because no one else will is deeply ingrained in our culture.

Living from this paradigm means we use energy inefficiently. As each individual strives to look out for self and perhaps a few others identified as family, we direct large amounts of our energy into maintaining our separate fortresses. Look down any street and you will see rows of locked houses containing many of the same items that are seldom used, but rarely shared. Even our physical bodies carry the armor of our defensiveness; the fear we take for granted keeps us in a perpetual state of low level tension. All of this drains our energy. As we pour energy into protecting ourselves, we have less to give to what we truly want.

Years ago when I studied group process, I learned that a group is only as functional as it's weakest member and that group consciousness tends to sink to the lowest common denominator. These are the rules of how people in fear relate. You may have experienced this dynamic yourself if you have ever participated in a group decision making process where egos were clashing, conflicting opinions were flying and consensus seemed miles away. In such processes, there is not a synergy of joined energy so much as a wearing away of rough edges until finally compromises are reached. Rather than reaching a height of excellence, an inoffensive level of mediocrity is settled upon.

As we open to the power of unconditional love, we naturally understand that we are not separate. We become aware of our interconnectedness, our "Oneness." In Oneness we don't need to compete with each other. It is possible then to listen for the highest voice in a group, not just the loudest, and a pooling of strengths results instead of a series of compromises. A common example of this kind of synergy is experienced in prayer and meditation groups, where people tend to bring more of their faith and less of their fear. Participants in such groups notice how much easier it is to achieve a high level of meditation and spiritual consciousness in a group than it is alone. The joined energies lift everyone higher than they could go separately.

As we open to "we" consciousness, we discover that what best serves one, serves all. So, pursuing our heart's desire becomes our gift to the world, and serving the good of others becomes our heart's desire. Without sacrificing our personal desires we become a force of healing and positive change in the world around us. This is the nature of true empowerment.

I sometimes ask the people in my workshops to create this moment as full and rich as they would like the rest of their lives to become. I give no other instruction about how to do this. I even sit out of the resulting experience so people will know that whatever they create is their doing and not mine. Typically, groups go through a period of haggling about what to do. Sooner or later, individuals start to break off from the group to do their own thing with a feeling that they can't get their needs met any other way. Sometimes there will be an amazing array of competing pandemonium. In one corner several might be grouped around a piano singing show tunes. Somewhere else several others are having a quiet, serious conversation, while still others are doing an interpretive dance as someone drums. Then there are lost-looking individuals scattered about the room, one trying to meditate, others sitting alone looking frightened and alienated as they are completely ignored by everyone else.

After these experiences where all but a few look like they're having a wonderful time, I ask everyone to share how they were feeling. In spite of working so hard to have a good time, it is rare that anyone enjoys these chaotic sessions. Many wind up feeling angry, fearful and alienated. People get a very clear picture of the beliefs and assumptions they bring to life, including the belief that everyone in a group can't get what they need at the same time. As everyone separately strives to make their own little piece of the whole perfect for themselves, we all fail, ending up disappointed and angry.

Every once in a while, a group will make a shift from this place of "me" consciousness, leaping to a higher level of functioning. It might start as one person reaches out to someone sitting alone and in pain. Suddenly two people are speaking to each other from their hearts, with the facade of separateness torn away. One by one, others in the group are drawn in by the power of this interaction, and soon the separate, chaotic groupings come together to support the healing of one person. By the end of this type of experience, people have spontaneously moved closer to one another. Everyone is engaged and participating. There is a feeling of love and trust shared by all. When asked how they feel after such a session, most people report feeling very good, very full, even though there was less visible display of dancing, singing and celebrating, and only one person was the actual focus of attention.

Paradoxically, as people let go of their defensive stance of self-preservation (which I have noticed to be as deeply ingrained in those holding spiritual beliefs, liberal politics and alternative life styles as it is in anyone else) and join together to serve the good of all or the good of one, there is a paradigm shift. It suddenly becomes possible for everyone to come away feeling fulfilled even if group time, attention and energy are not divided up equally. Compassion is not just a selfless act — it is powerfully self-serving. As Shantideva, the eighth century Indian author of the classic Buddhist text, **The Way of the Bodhisattva**, wrote:

> *"All the joy the world contains*
> *Has come through wishing happiness for others.*
> *All the misery the world contains*
> *Has come through wanting pleasure for oneself."*

Carolyn Miller in her previously mentioned book, *Creating Miracles,* interviewed many people who had experienced miraculous escapes from what would ordinarily be certain death situations. Whether the situation was of driving off a cliff, maneuvering an out-of-control vehicle through speeding traffic or dealing with deadly rapists and attackers, many people shared a common experience just as death looked inevitable. All at once they were no longer afraid for themselves. Their perspective expanded to include an appreciation and concern for the good of all, whether this was the passenger in their car, the people in other cars or even their attackers. When their perspective shifted, a miracle happened. The attacker peacefully left or the maneuver aimed at sparing the lives of other motorists turned out to save the driver as well.

When we make this shift from "me" to "we" consciousness, we discover that everyone's highest good is interconnected. There is no me instead of you, or you instead of me, there is only We. "We" consciousness has nothing to do with a loss if individuality, as in tribal (or in its baser form, mob) consciousness. This lower form of group-mind is still rooted in separateness, and eventually results in one tribal group of minds allying against another group. In the new paradigm of We, each individual shines *and* is one with all other individuals.

When we look out for our own needs from a place of fear and scarcity, we may get what we go after but these rewards do not truly serve our highest good and the end results do not satisfy. This is why in my workshop sessions, when people work so ferociously to do exactly what they want, separate from everyone else, they are still dissatisfied. When one person is in pain, it is felt by all. No matter how hard we try to separate ourselves, deep down we know that we are One.

The quantum physics model for this "Oneness" is the principle of Nonlocality. A local connection is one that exists within the parameters of what we can observe and measure with our physical senses. A cat jumps on a table and knocks over a glass. There is a causal connection between the cat jumping and the glass falling. A nonlocal connection is when no such phys-ically discernible relationship exists between events. For example, experi-ments have demonstrated that once subatomic particles have interacted then, even when they are separated by a great distance, a change in one results in an immediate, spontaneous change in the other even though there is no causal connection between the two. This phenomenon supports a per-spective of reality in which all matter is part of an indivisible whole, rather than a collection of separate parts. Thus, seemingly separate elements are really linked and can instantaneously affect and be affected by other ele-ments, regardless of distance.

There is much evidence to suggest that consciousness, too, is nonlocal, that minds are joined and can affect each other regardless of distance. In the words of Erwin Schrodinger, one of the early pioneers of quantum physics in this century, "The overall number of minds is just one."

When we shift into an awareness of this oneness, we gain access to a synergy of energy that empowers each individual far beyond their individ-ual capacity. So, just as we feel the pain of one person who is left behind, we also experience the gains as one person heals. This is why a whole group of people can feel healed and fulfilled in joining together to support one single individual.

The very process of joining for the highest good of all is powerfully healing. We release tension from our bodies, we relax and feed each other energetically. There is an exponential increase in energy that happens on many levels when we shift from "me" to "we" consciousness. As we join our consciousness with others, we suddenly have access to the collective creativ-ity of all minds, so ideas come more easily, our intuition speaks to us more clearly. Through "we" consciousness, we far surpass the state of just "getting by." We become miracle makers.

Telling the Truth

The essential truth that we are all one mind means that at the spiritual level there is no such thing as a lie. A lie implies and requires separateness which doesn't exist. This concept may seem abstract and divorced from everyday reality as we know it. However, as we learn to listen a little more closely to gut feelings and inner knowing, it becomes surprisingly easy to know when someone is not being truthful. We know because something doesn't feel right, look right or sound right. We know because at the deepest core of our being we are aware of the oneness of all consciousness, therefore *we just know the truth.*

When we live as if we can hide the truth from others, we diminish our power. Dishonesty is antithetical to synergy in the same way that fear is antithetical to love. I once heard a well known healer speak about the health benefits of telling the truth. This man was able to see auras — the energy field surrounding the physical body that reflects our state of physical and emotional health. He noticed that whenever someone spoke an untruth, their energy field would contract and become less healthy. Their immune system would actually be depressed. Medical intuitive Caroline Myss says, "...the human energy system identifies lies as poison." Spirit and body alike require honesty and integrity to survive.

Honesty and our ability to keep our word comprise a major component of our integrity. Integrity is far more than our ability to be a good and moral person. One of the definitions of integrity listed in the dictionary is "The state of being whole, entire, or undiminished. A sound, unimpaired, or perfect condition." We are all conduits through which Universal energy flows. The soundness or "integrity" of our channel is diminished by intentional dishonesty as well as by unintentional untruths, as when we fail to keep our word. Imagine this channel as a waterline and each untruth creates a tiny leak, lessening the energy that can come to us and diffusing the power that can come from us. While we may have chosen to lie to protect ourselves or serve our own purposes somehow, the end result is that every lie comes back home, undermining our capacity for intimacy, our power and even our physical health.

While most of us don't consider ourselves liars, if you were to review last week, how many moments would you be able to count when you spoke something other than the truth? Perhaps you said "yes" when you really meant "no," or made a social excuse that wasn't altogether truthful. The more attention I give to honesty, the more complex it seems. I become aware of how easy it is to lie, how natural and ingrained. I had always thought of myself as a truthful person, yet some years ago, when I challenged myself to total honesty, I was astonished by all the little "innocent" lies I was tempted to tell. There were my excuses for why I didn't attend social events; I had to learn to be truthful about my quiet nature and admit that I'm often just not in the mood for parties. There were excuses designed to spare people's feelings. I had to become willing to admit I was screening calls and didn't feel like talking instead of saying I wasn't home. I became aware of how many times people ask me how I am and I say "Great!" without even considering whether or not I am speaking the truth.

While my "honesty" experiment raised many situations where honesty seemed unnecessary, hurtful or inappropriate, ultimately I concluded that there is always an appropriate way to handle a situation truthfully and in a way that is less hurtful than a lie.

As I vowed to speak only the truth, I often found myself drawn into a deeper level of interaction than I might have chosen if left to flow with the path of least resistance. And, while the energy I had to expend was greater, so were the rewards. When an old friend called after a long break in our communication, instead of slipping into an easy social lie for why we hadn't talked ("Oh, I've just been sooo busy...") I found myself explaining how our last conversation had hurt my feelings a little and that instead of saying so, I had just put off calling again. Then as time went by I started feeling guilty about not calling and so I put it off even more. We wound up talking for over an hour about what was really going on between us, mending the hurts instead of sweeping them aside, and becoming closer in the end.

I've heard people insist that others can't always handle the truth and it's better to lie to spare their feelings. The chink in this theory is that there is a level of interaction that goes on between us, all the time, where we can't lie or hide the truth. Even when we may have no physical evidence that someone is lying to us, our instincts and gut feelings know the truth. We may not fully acknowledge this level of knowing consciously but it's still there. We may believe a spouse who says he's not having an affair but if he is, on some level we know it. Something doesn't feel right. There's a distance between us. If we don't trust or even know how to listen to our intuitive awareness, we may turn these feelings in on ourselves and become self-critical or depressed.

Many years ago I dated a man who was not willing to make a monogamous commitment. I always seemed to know when he was with another woman because I dreamed about it. He finally stopped seeing other women, admitting to me much later that every time he had been with someone else, he had a spooky feeling of me being in the room with them! Whether we are conscious of our intuition or not, we all have it and it registers in some way. When there is a lack of truth between people, it has a separating impact on the relationship whether or not the lie is ever discovered. This separation denies us the benefits inherent in that relationship — the synergy, the healing, the joy and love. Even when we believe we are getting away with something, we are actually losing.

However, telling the truth doesn't mean it's necessary to share every mean, judgmental thought that goes through our heads ("What an ugly dress..., bad haircut..., stupid thing to say...," etc.). Much of this sort of thinking is not really about the other person. It stems from our own self-judgment that we then project onto the world around us. When we don't believe we are good enough or believe we must be perfect to be accepted, we tend to be harshly critical of others as well. Our critical thoughts toward others signal a need to love and accept ourselves more rather than broadcast our judgments to the world.

The difference between truth and judgment is that judgment always creates separation between people. Remember, judgment is not the same as discernment and objective evaluation. It is possible to evaluate someone's strengths and weaknesses and still feel acceptance and compassion for that person. Judgment always sets up a context of better and worse. Through eyes of judgment, we see others as better or worse than us. Either way, our attention is focused on what's wrong with the other or with ourselves. Because what we give attention to is what we grow in our lives, as we give attention to our own failings, we make them bigger. As we give attention to the failings of others, we call forth the worst behavior from people. In this way judgment always boomerangs and comes back to bite the one judging. Judgment needs to be healed rather than shared.

Truth, on the other hand, when it's free of judgment, is ultimately healing and frees energy that had been stuck in preserving the facade. Even when truth stirs up a lot of discord and doesn't seem to be healing at all, it's a necessary step for true healing to happen. You can comprehend this by imagining that the tension and conflict you fear will be stirred by the truth is all held within your body, affecting your immune system and your physical health, your inner peace and your creative energy. While this energy of conflict may be challenging to deal with as it comes into the open, it could be lethal if contained indefinitely. Many people find their health improving as they speak the truth more often.

So, what do we do if a friend asks how we like her new hair style, dress or boyfriend, and we hate it or him? In this instance we need to be attentive to what she really wants to know. Does she want to know if you accept her taste or does she want an honest reality check on her choices? If it's the latter, you need to give honest, albeit painful, feedback. If, on the other hand, it's more a matter of different personal preferences, you may be able to find something that you honestly appreciate about her choice even though her style is not yours. This can be an excellent exercise in releasing the filter of judgment from your perception. I have an old friend whose taste I have never shared. We've come a long way since our junior high school days when she wouldn't hesitate to tell me how much she hated my clothes. Now we have developed a mutual understanding and acceptance of each other's styles so when we go shopping together and one of us excitedly pulls something off the rack saying, "Isn't this beautiful!", the other will say, "Why, that really looks like you!"

The difference between using the truth to hurt and using it to heal has a lot to do with our agenda behind the truth-telling. If there is even the slightest edge of judgment, it becomes hurtful. Sometimes our judgment takes the form of believing we know what someone else needs better than they do themselves. For example, a terminally ill person who is accepting of death and wants to spend her remaining time as productively as possible might welcome honest talk about death. However, another terminally ill person who is still focused on fighting the disease and surviving, might not be served by a well-meaning person crashing through her denial and not honoring her timing in coming to terms with death.

Many times I have been asked whether or not to disclose the fact of an extramarital affair after the affair has ended. My answer again hinges around the question, what does the other person want to know? If a spouse asks directly whether or not you have had an affair, it is important to answer honestly and deal with the consequences. As I mentioned before, on some level we all know the truth about each other, especially about things that affect us as deeply as our partner's fidelity. If your partner asks, it's safe to assume that he(she) already senses the truth at a conscious level. Not to acknowledge the truth at this point would create more distrust and separateness in the long run even though it may seem to keep peace in the short run. What's more, it can cause a great deal of inner turmoil in your partner to tell him(her) that his(her) instincts are wrong. To believe your lie (and most people want to believe their partners) he(she) has to assume that he(she) can't trust him(her)self. This can be even more painful and confusing to bear than the truth.

On the other hand, if your partner doesn't ask or seem to want to know, it may be his(her) way of telling you he(she) is not yet ready to deal with the information. It's not necessarily helpful or fair to dump a guilty confession on someone before he(she) is ready for it, so that it becomes the other person's burden instead of yours.

Neither is it healthy to keep a secret indefinitely. One option in this situation is to have a conversation with your partner's Higher Self at a time when he(she) is not physically present and tell everything that you need to get out in the open. Often by conversing in this way, the opportunity will soon arise to speak face to face in a way that is healing rather than shattering.

Higher Self Communication

This powerful technique begins with the assumption that we all have an aspect of our being that is much greater than our conscious thoughts, feelings, histories and the limits of our physical body.

I think of the Higher Self as being wise beyond limit, thus able to know the truth about ourselves and others beyond what we can know with our physical senses. Being something greater than our physical body, it is a part of us that is always whole and beyond harm. This means that at the highest level of who we are, we can't be victimized by another. This doesn't mean we don't feel pain, but that a deeper part of us always survives, whole and intact. Finally, and most importantly, the basic nature of the Higher Self is that of unconditional love and Oneness with all other beings.

Because consciousness itself has power, a very real interaction occurs as we direct our thoughts and feelings toward another person. This interaction occurs whether or not we are consciously aware of it and whether or not we are in each other's physical presence.

Speaking directly to someone's Higher Self is a way to gently, and often miraculously, heal stubborn rifts between people, send protection and healing, or broach a conversation we have not yet found a way to have face to face. It's very powerful between lovers, parents and children and family members because there is such a strong psychic link in these intimate relationships. But it's also an effective way to deal with any kind of relationship: with a boss, co-workers or friends. It can also be used as a way to relate to people who are no longer living or to connect with people we haven't met yet, such as a future lover, teacher, or someone who may be able to offer help in some important way.

Of course, it's not a technique for secretly getting other people to do what we want. People respond to "in-spirit" manipulation about as poorly as they do to in-person manipulation. Many will instinctively sense your energy-grabbing attempts and be repelled. Others who are more susceptible to manipulation may succumb for a while, setting up a relationship pattern in which the manipulator is affirmed in her belief that she can only receive what she wants through devious means and the manipulated person is affirmed in his belief that he is powerless and vulnerable. Ultimately, both are disempowered and come out losers. To avoid having this process boomerang in an unpleasant way, it's important to begin any Higher Self communication by first connecting with your own Higher Self and speaking from the part of you that wants only the best for everyone involved.

Exercise: Relating from Your Higher Self

Step One

Sit quietly in front of an unlit candle with paper and pen close by. Take a few moments to relax and attune to your own Higher Self. Play music if you wish. Bring to mind the person you want to speak with.

Step Two

Light the candle and imagine the flame representing the highest qualities of this person. Spend a few moments looking into the flame, feeling her or his presence. Feel only the presence of this being's highest, most loving essence.

Step Three

Speak from your Higher Self to the other person's Higher Self. Speak out loud or silently and imagine the person hearing you as clearly as if he or she were physically present.

Step Four

After speaking your message, imagine the response that comes from this person's Higher Self and write it down.

Step Five

Continue to dialogue in this way until you feel complete. End your conversation by thanking the person, saying good-bye and extinguishing the candle.

Releasing Habits of Secretiveness and Manipulation

Honesty is much more than the avoidance of telling a lie. An important step in becoming honest has to do with releasing secrets. Even though it may seem like a passive act, it takes energy to keep a secret. Keeping many secrets drains energy. This affects all areas of life including health, intimacy and feelings of empowerment. Secrets create a barrier between ourselves and others. There is a facade we must keep in place because we believe that if people see who we really are through knowing our secrets, something terrible will happen.

"Withholds" are another less obvious form of secrets. A withhold is when we hold back from someone information that is important to our relationship with that person. My story of avoiding a friend because my feelings had been hurt in a previous conversation is an example of a withhold.

Secrets release their hold on us as we speak them and come out of hiding. It is powerfully therapeutic to share secrets in an atmosphere of trust, forgiveness and love. Do, however, go gently into this process! Showing up at work one day and telling all your deepest, darkest secrets may be a bad idea. Find caring, sensitive support for this cathartic work. A trusted friend or family member, a therapist or a support group is a good way to begin. Another person's input can help you discern how, when and if you want to share your secrets with more people in your life. Hearing the secrets of others, as in a support group setting, can be a very helpful way of putting your own in perspective. Sharing secrets is only helpful if it promotes deeper self-acceptance, so never share a secret because of an impulse to punish or humiliate yourself for something you feel guilty about. This will not serve you or anyone else.

A commitment to honesty often requires learning a whole new way to relate and communicate. Very few of us know how to communicate honestly and directly with one another. We learn many messages growing up about how we are supposed to be — girls are supposed to be nice, boys are supposed to be tough, for example. Many of us have been taught that it is not acceptable to express anger or vulnerability. Perhaps we learned that it's better to be humble, so we developed a habit of being self-effacing. Or maybe we learned not to ask for things or to appear needy. This means that when we feel or want something that we've been taught not to express, we devise indirect ways of manipulating the attention or response we want.

For example, a person who wants to be acknowledged but doesn't want to appear "stuck-up" might be self-effacing so that others will contradict him and give him praise. Some people who have learned to fear anger act sad when they are angry so that people will be soft and sympathetic with them instead of harsh and angry. Many women have learned that when we want to receive something, instead of asking for it, we should give more. We try to manipulate by giving more and more with the hope that if we give enough, eventually the other person will do the "nice" thing and reciprocate.

Even illness can be a way to get what we need in spite of limiting messages learned in childhood. For some people who learned not to take up too much attention, ask for help or take time for themselves, an illness can be triggered by a deep need to throw off this conditioning of the past. Sometimes these early childhood messages are so violating to our spirit that they literally begin to kill us.

At a time in my life when I was grieving the impending death of a close friend, I became very susceptible to colds and flu so there was rarely a time when I wasn't blowing my nose and looking and sounding pitiful. I continued with work, leading many workshops in this condition. Through these illnesses, my body forced me to feel the physical symptoms of grief — a constantly runny nose and puffy eyes — and to take more time off than I would have otherwise. While I often carried on with work in spite of being sick, my condition successfully manipulated nurturing attention from people without my ever having to be emotionally vulnerable. What might have served me more at the time would have been to speak openly of the grief I was feeling, to let myself cry and let people comfort my emotional pain rather than my physical malaise.

Our habits of manipulation grow out of messages taught to us at a very early age. Many of these messages are so ingrained they may not be fully conscious, and the manipulations we have developed also tend to be unconscious habits. You can become more conscious of your own patterns of indirect communication by paying more attention to your interactions with others. Keep asking yourself: *"What do I feel and what do I want?"* Notice what you do to elicit what you want without having to ask for it or say how you really feel. Beginning with people you trust, experiment with sharing more of how you feel and what you want. As you do this, remember the difference between thoughts and feelings. "I feel angry, frustrated, afraid, ashamed, sad, anxious, happy," etc. are statements of feeling. "I feel that no one ever takes me seriously" is a thought.

Exercise: Honesty Challenge

Starting now, be aware of every time you are tempted to speak an untruth. See if you can find a way to make the truth work for you instead. Make a promise to yourself that you will speak only truth for at least a week. Every time you tell a truth when you would have told a lie, imagine that your power level raises a notch, and with it your capacity to receive your highest good and create your life as you want it to be.

Gossip

Gossip is another form of communication that can strengthen walls of separateness and inhibit the synergy of joined energy. This doesn't, however, mean that all gossip is destructive. It is a natural part of community for people to talk about others who are not present. At best it is a sign of interest in one another, of caring concern and sometimes a way to process difficult feelings so they can be addressed and resolved in the highest possible way. I have a friend who often jokes about gossip saying, "I'll be more upset when people *stop* talking about me!" because she recognizes that most of the talk that goes on about her comes from a place of love. When she's being talked about, she knows she's being thought about by people who care about her.

Gossip becomes destructive when people say things they are not willing to say directly. It siphons off tension without addressing the cause of that tension and creates barriers between people. Even when it creates a feeling of alliance between the gossipers, it does so with the negative consequence of creating a general climate of distrust. In a community where hurtful gossiping is the norm, everyone is left wondering what is being said about them behind their backs. Because we are so connected, negative gossip is felt by the subject even when it is never openly heard. A powerful exercise for any group of people in community is to agree not to speak of a person not present unless they agree to speak with them directly within a week's time. Even doing this as a time-limited exercise for a week or two can make positive lasting changes in the interaction style among a group of people.

So what can you do if you are part of a community where everyone gossips about everyone else? How can one person cope with the habits of a whole community? It may seem impossibly frustrating yet it is amazing how much difference one person can make. I know a woman who transformed the mean, gossipy climate of her workplace by not only refusing to participate in the office pettiness, but by genuinely finding things to love about her co-workers, even the most unpleasant ones who everyone else loved to hate.

If you are surrounded by people who routinely gossip, it can be a tricky path out of the gossip morass. It may not be enough to merely refuse to participate. If people sense a disapproving attitude, you may simply become the new target of gossip. In a sense you will have called this negative attention to yourself by stooping to their level — not in your behavior, but in your thoughts. As you look at others harshly by judging their gossiping, you invariably attract harsh judgment to yourself.

You could choose to leave this community, but if the community is a workplace, family or neighborhood, leaving is not always desirable. Another option is to truly join your community. "Joining" begins with acceptance and love. Start by looking at other people's behavior as either an extension of love or a call for help. For many people, gossip is a way of connecting. The gossipers feel closer as they ally against someone else. Many people have never learned better ways to feel connected. You can begin to join with others by understanding that even gossiping is a call for love.

Instead of separating yourself from other people by focusing on their negative behavior, give attention to what you like about them. Make a practice of acknowledging at least one person every day for something you admire or appreciate. As you reach out to people in a positive way, you will model a more loving way of joining. You may see people soften and transform as their call for love is answered in a more satisfying way, and they may feel less need to gossip.

Even if you say nothing out loud and just practice appreciating people in your thoughts, you will see a difference. We are all so sensitive to each other, we can't keep our true feelings secret. Just as unspoken judgment poisons a relationship, so can heartfelt acceptance heal it, whether or not words are ever spoken.

If you are focusing on keeping your thoughts and interactions positive but find yourself angered and upset by the negativity and pettiness of others, consider that the people and circumstances you attract to yourself reflect the energy you are putting out in some way. If you are very critical of yourself or others, or if you don't believe you are good enough, then you are likely to attract judging people into your life. The more you heal your own issues with judgment by accepting yourself and others, the more you will receive acceptance and love from the people around you. Instead of focusing on other people's behavior that you can't change, ask yourself how you can let go of a piece of your own meanness. When you are free of pettiness, you won't get hooked by other peoples'. It will just pass by you. When you feel stuck in your own judgment and irritation, try repeating silently to yourself the affirmation, "I am willing to see only love here."

As you make these changes in yourself, you may be amazed at how much others around you shift as well. At the very least, you will be able to create an atmosphere of acceptance and peace around yourself so that the behavior of others doesn't have to spoil your day.

Exercise: Building Integrity

Part I of this exercise is a self-assessment that will give you an idea of how much psychic garbage you have accumulated in the form of broken promises, untruths, lack of forgiveness, etc. This accumulation diminishes the power of your integrity. The second part includes some action steps to strengthen areas of weakness.

Part I: Self Assessment

Step One

Write down any times in the last month when you gave your word and didn't keep it. List everything you can think of even if you feel you did the "right" thing or couldn't help it.

Step Two

List any times in the more distant past when you have broken a promise. Include broken financial agreements as well as interpersonal situations. Write down as many broken promises as you can remember.

Step Three

Write down all the lies you can remember telling.

Step Four

Add to this list any other experiences that you have left incomplete or messy in some way. Include the words you needed to say but withheld, the unpleasant situations you chose to leave instead of clean up, the times when your integrity broke down and the people you have hurt.

Step Five

Next, make a list of people and situations that have hurt you, especially those you have not fully forgiven. (If an experience comes to mind and you think you have forgiven but there is still an emotional charge to it, you have not fully forgiven.)

Part II: Cleaning Up the Past

Step One

Imagine that everything on this list is a leak in your connection to the Universal Source. As you tell a lie, you literally depress your energy field and your physical immune system. As you break your word you affirm the weakness of your intentions and diminish your creative power. As you feel guilt and regret about the past, your energy is directed into creating punishment and drawing more regretful experiences to you. As you withhold forgiveness, your fear and bitterness attract people and circumstances that will bring more victimization into your life.

Step Two

Of all the unfinished business you listed, ask your Higher Self to direct your attention to one particular circumstance. Don't think about it too hard or to try to control what comes up. Just let your mind open and see what pops into mind first.

Step Three

Let whatever came up be the starting place for cleaning up your past. Trust that this circumstance came to mind first because it is significantly blocking your energy and keeping you from manifesting your highest good. Ask your deepest, wisest self to show you at least one step you are willing to commit to toward healing this unfinished business. It may be to speak words that have been withheld, it may be to right a wrong you have done to someone, it may be to take responsibility for a financial commitment. It may take a more internal form. You may feel called to talk to someone's Higher Self or to work with an affirmation of forgiveness, such as, "I am now willing to forgive and see innocence in myself and this other person."

What comes to you may be a small step or a large one or several steps. Make sure you are willing to keep whatever commitment you make to yourself around this. Don't set a goal too big to keep. Picture yourself doing this clean-up work and that it is increasing the flow of creative energy you have to draw upon.

Step Four
When you complete these steps, go back to Step Two and ask your Higher Self to direct your attention to the next issue on your list that you are now ready to heal.

Giving and Receiving Help Taps into the Synergy of the Whole

As we begin to recognize how deeply we are all interconnected, giving and receiving help becomes a way to tap into the synergy of joined energy. As we give or reach out for help with the knowledge of our Oneness, we know that as we help one another we help ourselves, and that our willingness to receive from another gives energy back to the giver. Yet to allow these healing exchanges, we must first break familiar habits of isolation. *A Course in Miracles* holds isolation to be synonymous with sickness. It says:

> *"Sickness is a retreat from others, and a shutting off of joining.*
> *It becomes a door that closes on a separate self,*
> *and keeps it isolated and alone. Sickness is isolation."*

However, it is so easy in our world today to take isolation for granted. "Shutting off" becomes so ingrained and habitual that we cease to define it as such. We ask each other, "How are you?" seldom really wanting to know. We respond with, "I'm fine," but how often is this the truth? As we routinely numb ourselves to pain with medication, recreational drugs, food, TV and addictions of countless varieties, we often lose the knack of asking for help. For many of us, asking for help feels far more uncomfortable than bearing our pain alone. We are so much more likely to seek remedies for our pain and problems in isolation. These remedies don't involve reaching out for the love and comfort of others or reaching up for the healing of a Higher Power or reaching within for guidance.

Yet, I often see remarkable transformations in people who have broken through their armor of self-sufficiency to accept even the smallest bit of help from others. I knew a woman once who, after attending four days of a 5-day intensive, was at a point of exhaustion. She suffered from chronic fatigue syndrome and felt she had to go home to take care of herself. Being a health-care professional, she also suffered from "care-givers syndrome," that is, always giving, rarely receiving and eventually burning out. Upon announcing her intention to the group, several people suggested she stay and sleep in the room. Then, with her permission, the group proceeded to make a bed for her on a comfortable couch with many soft quilts, gave her about 15 minutes of intensive loving attention, including massage, verbal acknowledgment and hands-on nurturing, and tucked her in for a nap. She fell asleep for only about 30 minutes, after which she was a different person — more alive and full of energy than we had ever seen her. It wasn't just sleep she needed; it was to be on the receiving end of caring attention for a change. She was full of energy for the remaining day and a half of the workshop.

As we go about shutting off our pain and living the life of isolation that seems so normal, the tragedy is that we lose our link to ecstasy as well. A lack of ecstasy goes hand in hand with a belief in separateness. Ecstasy is antithetical to isolation. Ecstasy naturally reaches out and instinctively knows "joining" to be our natural state of being. There is a relationship between pain, ecstasy and joining with others. In my experience, there is something akin to an alchemical transmutation that occurs when we stop numbing ourselves to pain and coping with it in isolation, and instead, experience it fully in the presence of loving others. While pain experienced in isolation usually remains pain, pain shared in love becomes healing and subsequently ecstasy.

My friend, Cheryl, was a woman who had more experience with pain than most. Born with a degenerative bone disease and not expected to live beyond her teens, at age 30 she was wheelchair bound and lived with chronic pain. She related the following experience she had once in a workshop when she dared to come out of isolation.

"Coming home from the first night [of a three-day workshop], my wheelchair tipped over and I fell hard on the back of my head. I was in a lot of pain the next day and, to make matters worse, at the end of the second night the people lifting my wheelchair accidentally dropped me and I fell on the same part of my neck and head. By the next, day the pain was so bad I almost didn't go back. Once there I felt overwhelmed, not just by physical pain, but also by shame and frustration at needing so much more help than other people and feeling so out of control of my body.

"I was encouraged to share my feelings with the group. One man offered to do some healing work on me, which helped some, but I still felt very blocked in my throat and in pain. Lynn asked me to give a word to the feeling in my throat. The word 'help' came to me, but I could only whisper it. It's so hard for me to ask for help. I hated to burden other people with my pain. I felt hopeless and ashamed. It was a very familiar feeling that I had been struggling with for most of my life. All I could do was cry. As I was crying, everyone in the group gathered close to me and said the words I couldn't. A drum beat started and everyone shouted, 'help me' over and over until I, too, was able to shout with them. All this happened very spontaneously as though we had become one mind and everyone just knew what to do and how to best assist me. Afterward, not only was the block in my throat gone but my physical pain was gone as well. Even more important was feeling released from shame and knowing that I'm not a burden to people."

Cheryl was not aware of this because her eyes were closed, but I looked around as the group chanted with her and saw most faces streaked with tears and a depth of emotion that is hard to convey. It was clear that what started as an experience to help Cheryl had given everyone an opportunity to release a piece of old, locked away pain. There was a shared ecstasy in that moment; the boundaries between giving and receiving, healers and healed, blurred. In moments of unconditional love such as this, there is only healing.

I witnessed some of the after effects of this powerful experience. Cheryl was staying at my house while participating in the workshop. I was her attendant for that time, helping her with bathing, dressing and other personal care. Having done this for Cheryl a number of times before, I was all too aware of the physical pain she lived with every day and the effort it took for her to perform the simplest tasks. The bumps she took were to the most fragile part of her body, where she had had repeated surgical procedures. I worried that her recovery time from the accidents would be slow and painful. I was amazed the next morning to find Cheryl practically leaping out of bed with more energy and limberness than I had seen in her before.

She described an even more profound result of this experience: "In the past I was very afraid of dying, and not just of dying, but of dying in pain and isolation. Through experiences like this one I'm not afraid of dying anymore. I know that the love I have shared will always be with me and I can never be alone. This realization came through taking the risk to share my pain with people and finding that they were willing to love and accept me anyway. I had always thought that my pain and my physical disability were burdens to people and tried to keep them to myself as much as possible, but now I realize that sharing how I feel, even my pain, can be a gift to others."

And what of the other people who participated in this experience? One woman shared, "I've learned compassion. I've learned a lot about healing myself. Being able to be with someone who is in pain has taught me a lot about being able to accept what is. In being present with pain and accepting it, I find myself also embracing the joy and love that it holds as well."

Very simply, love transforms pain. It becomes a doorway opening to a depth and richness that can't be found in isolation. In love there ceases to be givers and receivers, and the healing that results touches everyone.

Unconditional Love as a Healing Force

If love is all that is, our one true power source, then unconditional love is the most powerful help we can give to another person. Many years ago when I worked as a mental health counselor, I began experimenting with this idea. I stopped trying so hard to find the right words, the right techniques, and focused more on simply loving and accepting my clients. Each client who came to me for help seemed to have something important to teach me as well. Whenever they shifted or healed in some way, I felt myself shift and heal, too. I developed a deeper appreciation for the sacredness of the role I played in my clients' lives and the gift each healing encounter had for me.

Around this time, I had a powerful experience with my most difficult client. Each week he would come into my office, complain about how hopeless his life was, how therapy wasn't working and would challenge me angrily for new and better therapies that would make his life work. Leaping to the challenge, with all my feelings of inadequacy and irritation embarrassingly close to the surface, I would try harder and urge him to do the same.

Nothing worked until the day I decided to experiment with unconditional love. I stopped "trying" for a day and just listened. As soon as I stopped trying to make him better, an amazing thing happened: I found myself caring about him more. As I relaxed the pressure I had put on myself to make him better and stopped seeing his behavior as a reflection of my competence or lack of it, I was better able to see him. So I sat there for an hour, not saying a word, just listening and letting my heart open, while he talked.

That day I witnessed a miracle. His monologue began as usual grim, cynical and angry. But as the hour progressed, little by little, something, everything, changed. He sat up instead of slumped. He looked up, even made eye contact instead of glaring at the floor. By the end of our session he was telling me about some new possibilities he had just imagined for himself and how he thought things really could work out for the better. He was positively brimming with hope and enthusiasm. Before he left he said, "You know, things felt different between us today...," he searched a moment for the right words, "more intimate." As an eager young therapist I had difficulty believing at first that my easiest session with this man, when I didn't trot out a parade of therapeutic techniques, was the most effective.

What's more, I received at least as much benefit from this session as he did. As I simply let him be, giving only my love and acceptance, I found peace that day, deep and profound, that lasted long after the session was over. Experiment with this approach yourself the next time you get caught up in trying to change someone, sure that their lives would work if only they would listen to you. See what a difference you can make simply by changing your own state of mind.

The reason our attempts to "help" someone through advice, especially unsolicited advice, frequently fail is that it so often masks the unspoken judgment that the recipient is doing his or her life "wrong" and the advice giver could do it better. To the extent that our helping efforts are based in judgment, they are devoid of love. Consequently, the most powerful form of support we can give to another person is the way we choose to perceive him or her. This has nothing to do with what we say or do. It is an internal experience that we communicate loudly no matter how hard we try to convey the opposite with our words. When we choose to see another person as empowered, whole, healed and on track, no matter how tumultuous his life experience may be, the more we help him to remember and connect with his power. This is not the same as turning a blind eye and pretending everything is all right in the face of obvious distress. We can acknowledge and address a person's pain and crisis or out of control behavior and still see beyond these things to a deeper Self who is whole and complete. The more we hold judgments and see a person as unable to manage his or her life, the more we feed his or her own sense of helplessness.

Changing your perception in this way may require expanding your own vision to see a bigger picture. As you open your mind to imagine that even the darkest life situations hold meaning and value, it becomes easier to replace worry and disapproval with compassion and acceptance.

The following exercises can help you experience the power of giving and receiving help. One focuses on the inner work of joining and one involves taking action.

Exercise: Healing with Unconditional Love

Step One

Bring to mind a relationship you would like, for any reason, to infuse with healing and love. It could be a problematic relationship or a loving friendship. It could be a relationship with a child or family member, someone you wish to help, even someone who has died or is not currently in your life.

Step Two

Sit in a comfortable position. Have some quiet music playing in the background if it helps you to feel at peace. Close your eyes, take some deep breaths and let your body relax. Create a feeling of deep peacefulness. Make this feeling as vivid and real as you can. Feel it as deep relaxation in your body and a profound sense of well-being. Picture it as a beautiful light filling you and radiating from you. Say silently to yourself any words that help you to experience peace such as, "I am deeply peaceful... I am love... I am safe...," etc.

Step Three

When the experience of well-being feels strong, bring to mind the person you chose for this exercise and imagine your inner peacefulness expanding to include him or her. Picture this as a light that radiates from you like sunlight, naturally and effortlessly shining on this other person. Feel it as warmth and love flowing from you to him or her. Make it as real and vivid as possible, and surrender completely to the inner experience of sharing a moment of peace with this person. For this instant, let go of your past with this individual, release any future outcome you want with him or her, let go of your opinions about what this person should do or be or give to you and simply be at peace while holding him or her in mind. Know that this is the essence of true healing.

Step Four

Practice this exercise every day for a week. You don't need to force any change in your behavior toward this person. Let go of any expectations about the external results you want to see. Make your only goal to simply experience peace in relation to this person as often as possible.

Exercise: Reach Out

Step One

Spend this week creating opportunities to join with people. Reach out to someone you know in need of support. Instead of giving advice and opinions, focus instead on simply listening. As you listen, imagine how it must feel to be in this person's place. Let go of any feeling that you need to do something and just give your love and acceptance. Know that this is the most powerful gift of healing you can give.

Step Two

This step is especially important if you tend to retreat from sharing your pain with others. Pick one person you trust and dare to share more of yourself than you have before. Talk about how you feel, what's important to you, what you fear, what hurts you, perhaps even ask for help. Do this as an exercise in sharing yourself rather than in getting the response you want. Let go of expectations about the other person's response.

Step Three

In every interaction you have, know that your willingness to come out of isolation to extend compassion to others or to let others extend their compassion to you is creating healing for both of you.

More on Giving and Receiving Help

1. See the section, "Reach out for Help" in Chapter Three under, "Steps for Healing Addictions."

2. Also see the section, "Reach out to People" in Chapter Four under, "Steps for Healing Loneliness."

3. Start a support group to work with this book. The exercises and other material here make an excellent catalyst for deep sharing, love, healing and spiritual growth. If you don't know enough people to start a group, ask a local New Age bookstore or metaphysically-based church, such as Unity, to sponsor it.

"And as you let yourself be healed, you see all those around you,
or who cross your mind, or whom you touch
or those who seem to have no contact with you,
healed along with you....
And legions upon legions will receive the gift
that you receive when you are healed."

—*A Course in Miracles*

A "Wounded" Society

As we delve into the power we have to heal one another and ourselves through joining in love, I feel it important to address the current fascination, even obsession, we have nowadays with our "woundedness." An entire industry of therapies, support groups, medications and seminars has emerged in recent years to assist us in our "recovery" and many of us are fast becoming therapy addicts. Where did this wide-scale woundedness come from?

When my mother was in her twenties, back in the 1940's, she did the unthinkable — she went to see a psychologist. This caused a great scandal in her family since only "crazy" people did that. She, however, was a forward thinker and did not let public opinion stop her from seeing a specialist for help with a bout of painful depression. She visited a Jungian analyst regularly for several months until he declared her "cured." She never went back or considered therapy again. When she was in her sixties and going through a difficult time I suggested therapy. Her response was that she had already done that 40 years ago and she was cured. It struck me how differently psychotherapy was viewed by my mother's generation.

People of my generation are more likely to have a therapist as substitute parent/mentor/best friend, someone with whom we establish an ongoing relationship over a long time. We may even have many therapists. There's

the psychotherapist, the acupuncturist, the chiropractor, the massage therapist and so on.

The need this growing therapy industry fills is one that didn't exist in
my mother's generation. It's a need that has as much to do with community
and connection as it does personal health. Community used to be something that was our birthright. We were less on the move and more likely to
live our lives in the same neighborhood, in touch with extended family,
knowing and being known over time by a relatively consistent group of
people. For better or worse, there was a sense of belonging and identity that
came from living in close proximity. Now people living in the same apartment building or on the same street often don't know each other or share
any sense of connection. It's possible to live amidst thousands of people and
be unknown, unseen and desperately lonely.

Whereas a generation or two ago, people consulted therapists only as
an extreme last resort when all other personal, family and community
resources had been exhausted, people today often don't have these other
resources. As a result, a growing collective sense that something is missing
has given birth to the endless stream of support groups, therapies and workshops. Through these we have found a new sense of connection and a desperately needed refuge from pain and separateness.

These many therapeutic options have the potential to do a great deal of
good. It's extremely difficult to recognize that our true relationship to one
another is unity when we feel so alone in the world. Bonding with others,
in itself, is powerfully healing, and support groups and therapeutic relationships offer an opportunity for this to happen. But, to the extent that
wound-focused treatment becomes a replacement for community, friendship and family, it is limiting, harmful even, because it can inadvertently
strengthen our sense of being damaged goods by insisting that we be sick in
order to join the family.

A proliferation of support groups organized around particular types of
wounding, such as adult children of alcoholics, incest survivors and twelve-

step programs of all sorts, have helped us come out of the closet with serious problems. Before there were so many support groups, it was much easier to believe we were the only one with a problem while the rest of the world was "normal." We were more likely to hold addictions and traumatic life experiences as shameful secrets that kept us locked in painful isolation. Support groups have helped us recognize that we are not alone. In fact, as various groups bond together around a particular form of victimization, there aren't very many people who don't fit into one group or another. On her daytime TV show, Oprah Winfrey once asked her audience, "How many people come from dysfunctional families?" Most raised their hands, and her comment to the rest was, "And you're the ones in denial!"

Unfortunately, the danger in such groups is that, while they do bring us out of isolation and shame, they often don't take us the next step through and beyond the experience of ourselves as victims. When we believe ourselves to be more damaged and more vulnerable than most people, the best we can hope for is to do a lot of painful work on ourselves to become almost as good as we once were. We "survive" and "recover" rather than thrive and heal. Then we live in fear, hoping that terrible circumstances beyond our control will not befall us again, starting another cycle of wounding and the need to "recover." Groups and therapies that emphasize woundedness keep us caught in a pattern of victimization.

I once saw a psychotherapist on a talk show discuss his client, a "survivor" of severe childhood abuse and also a member of the panel, describing her as being permanently damaged with a chance of recovering only some of her ability to function through many more years of therapy. I feel certain that this man wanted to help his client and she, herself, claimed that he had "saved" her. An ongoing, caring bond between a therapist and client has the potential to heal no matter what the focus and method of therapy simply because the caring bond is healing in and of itself. Unfortunately, the powerful role he played in her healing and in her life must surely have made it difficult for her not to comply with his diagnosis and prognosis.

It is a well-documented phenomenon that patients tend to live up or down to their therapists' expectations. The clients of Jungian analysts will obediently dream in Jungian symbols, patients with life-threatening illnesses will commonly deteriorate rapidly after being given a terminal prognosis by their doctors or miraculously heal after being given what they believe to be a new wonder drug. And people who are repeatedly told by their therapists that they are damaged are likely to live the limited life of a "damaged" person.

Many of us now find a sense of identity, even specialness, in our woundedness. When we find that we receive special attention, care, sympathy and community as a result of advertising our pain, it's no wonder we may not feel much incentive to give up our victim status. The rewards are too sweet. However, those rewards get in the way of accessing the true spiritual power that comes from recognizing who we are beyond the wounds.

Recovery Vs. Healing

In this age of therapy, recovery and "survivors," I see us already beginning to take a next step. We are moving beyond what has gone wrong and is wounded to a celebration of the resilient spirit that is always whole and undamaged. It's time to redefine wounding. Rather than being our personal crosses to bear that make us different, our wounds are a universal human experience. Through limiting, us they provide access to strength and resources we might never have found otherwise. By forcing us to transcend limitation, our wounds offer a doorway out of ordinary life into the extraordinary. They connect us with our genius in the same way a diamond is created through great stress and pressure. The moment we find the gift inherent in a wounding experience, we cease to identify ourselves as damaged victims and we no longer identify others as victimizers. Consequently, we become less vulnerable to being wounded again. We are no longer merely recovering from our wounds, we have transcended them.

I believe we are ready for a whole new model of healing — one that acknowledges we are all healers and all in the process of healing. This is different from the traditional medical model in which a "well" expert treats a "sick" patient. This new paradigm for healing must recognize that we do not simply pay a professional for curative techniques. Rather, we enter into a healing relationship that, if it is to be profoundly transformative to one, will not leave the other unchanged. This new model will be neither a healing through "treatment" nor through "recovery." Instead it will be a healing through joining in love and accessing the synergy that becomes available through this connection.

Increasingly, relationship is being defined as a context for healing. Harville Hendrix, well-known relationship therapist and author of the bestseller, *Getting the Love You Want*, goes so far as to say that, "... to feel whole, to feel fully alive, fully human, and to heal the wounds we carry from childhood, we've gotta have it," referring to committed long-term love relationships. A whole new purpose of marriage is evolving beyond the traditional one to raise a family and support economic survival. As gender roles become less pronounced, we no longer need the structure of marriage to raise children and survive materially. Fathers are proving to be perfectly good nurturers of children and mothers are able to support their families financially. The more modern purpose of marriage has become to pair up with someone who will meet our emotional needs. Judging by divorce statistics of recent generations, this approach to relationship is failing miserably. Harville Hendrix suggests that we instinctively choose the mate who will best reinjure our childhood wounds and thus provide an opportunity to heal and transcend them. Ideally then, the opportunity of marriage is not just to meet each other's needs, but to become partners and allies in growing beyond the wounds of our past. Again, it is the synergy of joining in love that allows this healing partnership to evolve.

I see not only marriage, but community and interpersonal connections of all kinds, taking on added importance in our pursuit of healing.

Increasingly we are discovering how much healing can happen as a natural part of being in relationship with other people. This is not to devalue the role of therapists and teachers. There will always be a place for healers. However, releasing pain, resolving childhood wounds and sharing dreams don't need to happen exclusively in artificial therapy situations with anonymous strangers and detached professionals.

Quite simply, we are whole and healed when we start to love each other. There is nothing more important to realize that this. What's more, this is not something we can only achieve through exclusive methods or techniques; it is who we truly are. We all are healers. We all have within us the ability to find our own answers. Everyone has the capacity to be of help to someone else. I've seen this demonstrated time and time again. Every relationship has the potential to be a vehicle for healing.

Life takes on a new depth and richness when healing becomes an integrated part of life. For example, a friend once invited me and several others to support her in a healing ritual to release the pain of an old relationship. It was set up spontaneously for the next day with little preparation. The process was simple, informal and intimate. Each of us took a turn to share what painful burden we were ready to release. During our turn, we received undivided attention from the other three. Without giving advice we simply listened to each other with our hearts open. Each of us cried and was held and comforted by the others. At the end we all felt lighter, more at peace, and there was an intimacy and love between us that wasn't there before. The more we can share this kind of experience with friends, family, even co-workers, the more we regain a feeling of community. And, as we rebuild the web of connection in our lives there becomes less to heal. We no longer feel the same need to hold on to our wounds, replaying them again and again.

I see us moving toward a time when, instead of there being so many people feeling damaged that we require an army of therapists, there will be so many of us who have discovered our natural capacity to heal and be healers that the "industry" of healing will become obsolete. Instead of being something we buy from strangers, healing will be something we share freely as an integral part of relating and loving.

A New Role for Therapists to Empower Rather than to Cure

Those of us offering therapeutic services to others can play an important role in this shift from recovering to healing. The new challenge for therapists now is to empower our clients to become healers to themselves and others. But in order to do this we must be willing to release the seductive role of being the one who holds the cure.

I discovered the power of this in my own experimentation with group work over the years. Early in my career, I became very good at facilitating group therapy. I could create a deep level of intensity and healing in my groups through my own "expert" interventions: by working with people individually, by actively guiding the group process and by being the pivot the group activity revolved around. Years later, however, I noticed that I could create an even more powerful group experience simply by getting out of the way and helping participants facilitate one another. This approach formed deeper bonds and a sense of community that didn't rely upon me to hold it together. The healing that happened in these groups was deeper and more lasting because the healing agent was love and synergy, not just a new insight or therapeutic technique. People came away from these experiences as empowered healers, not just as healed participants.

It became apparent to me that healing is not nearly so dependent upon the intervention of a trained expert as we trained experts are taught to believe — a humbling thought for a therapist. Playing the starring role in someone's healing process is a heady drug and hard to give up. What's more, many of us who choose therapist, teacher and healer roles do so, at least in part, because the role is a safe hiding place for our own vulnerability. It seems easier to have people look up to us than it is to have people see the wounded child we may sometimes feel ourselves to be.

Ultimately, this hiding gets very lonely. I experienced this loneliness when I began to receive a lot of positive attention for my work. The more people told me how wonderful I was, the more I felt they only loved me for what I do and not for who I am. It was through allowing more of my humanness to show in my professional role that I started to feel safe and accepted — less adored and more loved. This transition did not diminish my power as a leader. If anything, it enhanced it and raised the power level of the group as a whole. As I allowed people to see more of my vulnerability, others had more room to show their strengths.

For example, during one of my 5-day workshops, there were a number of people focused on a common theme of letting go of pain related to their fathers. I assisted several men in some very profound healing experiences. On the last day of the workshop something happened that brought my own pain about my alcoholic father to the surface. At one time I would have maintained my detached professionalism, said nothing about my strong feelings and probably have gone home with a splitting headache. But I have come to believe that my willingness to "take the plunge" in my own groups and face things that are scary for me is an important part of what assists others in going deeper. So, without quite knowing what was going to come out, I started talking about what I was feeling, and almost immediately I was crying too much to speak. The men who had been part of the most dramatic "father work" the day before spontaneously came over to me, held me, and said and did everything right to help me release my pain and open to a more healed relationship with my father and with men in general. There was no need for a group leader at that time. Healing happened. It was a powerful confirmation of my growing hunch that a good therapist is one who makes her role obsolete.

The following are some guidelines for using the experience of psychotherapy in an empowered way to release woundedness and open to the healing power of joining.

Guidelines for Deriving Maximum Healing from Therapy

1.   Keep the focus of therapy on improving life in the present.

Deal with the past when it inhibits your joy in the present. While it might be interesting to unravel all the threads of your past, it won't necessarily improve the quality of your life in the present and future. Give more attention to the life you want to create now than to what has gone wrong in the past.

2.   Periodically assess whether therapy is helping you to feel more in touch with your wellness or your woundedness.

Change the focus of your therapy if it doesn't leave you more aware of your strengths, progress and possibilities than your weaknesses, wounds and limitations.

3.   Seek a therapeutic process that includes both insight and feeling.

Too much emphasis on insight and understanding your emotions can become an avoidance of actually feeling your emotions. On the other hand, too much emphasis on catharsis can leave you in an emotional whirlwind without a context to give perspective and meaning to strong emotions. Find a therapist who is able to combine insight (that is, talk therapy) with experiential approaches (such as Gestalt therapy, Inner Dialogue work, art, music, or movement therapies, guided imagery, anger release work, body work, breath work, to name a few) in a balance that is right for you.

4.   Expect results.

Keep in mind that therapy does not always feel "good." It's important to feel a basic level of comfort and trust with your therapist but the therapy itself isn't necessarily meant to be comfortable. Growth invariably takes us out of our comfort zone from time to time. While everything in your life will not right itself overnight with therapy, if you have been in therapy for many months and haven't felt any degree of shift, not even a sense of renewed hope or excitement about the future, then question the effectiveness of your therapy. Or if you have been stuck on the same issues for years and your therapist says that you simply need more therapy, there may be something wrong with your therapy, not just with you. Your therapist will not necessarily be the one to tell you that your therapy isn't working. This is an assessment that you must make yourself.

5.   Take breaks from therapy.
If you have spent years with the same therapist and therapy has fallen into a routine, you may benefit from taking occasional breaks. The most productive therapy usually has an element of risk to it. When therapy becomes too predictable and comfortable, your therapist might be more of a companion than a healer. This isn't necessarily a bad thing; it simply means it's time for therapy to end or take a new direction, or for your relationship to take a new form. While both of you may have resistance to ending for a variety of reasons, taking the leap to end at the appropriate time can be as important to your healing as the step to begin therapy. If you wish to continue doing therapeutic work, consider choosing a different therapist. This is not a betrayal or rejection of your previous therapist. Different people have different things to teach you.

6.   Determine whether you need couple's therapy or individual therapy.
If your objective is to improve your relationship with a lover or spouse, couples counseling is usually a better way to go about this than individual counseling. Individual therapy can even be counter-productive because two people talking about problems with a mate who isn't present always has the potential to create a wedge in the relationship even when there are the best of intentions. The therapist hears only one side of the story and may inadvertently "side" with his or her client at the expense of the relationship. When you go for counseling as a couple, however, the therapist is clearly

there as an equal ally to both of you and is focused on the health of the relationship, not just the needs of one individual. Because of this dynamic, is it advisable to find a neutral therapist for couple's work rather than going to one person's individual therapist.

Working with two or more people is a very different process than individual therapy, requiring different skills. Make sure that your therapist is willing to work with your agenda and does not plug you into his or hers. In my opinion, approaches to couple's therapy like Harville Hendrix's Imago Therapy* that supports two people in becoming allies in healing are more effective than approaches that focus on problem solving and negotiating ways for people to better meet each other's needs.

7. If you want support for your child, find a therapist who is experienced in family therapy.

Keep in mind that individual therapy isn't necessarily the most effective form of treatment for children. It is well known that children with behavior problems are often acting out family problems. In creating a disturbance, they force their parents to become allies in dealing with the problem so that, at least temporarily, parents are relieved of having to deal with crises in their relationship and in their own lives. Many parents would prefer to send their child to therapy than to confront their own struggles and relationship problems, yet this approach often allows the underlying problems to go unaddressed, making it ultimately ineffective. What's more, too much therapy early in life can burden children with a belief that there is something wrong with them. I have known many people who were placed in therapy as children and grew into therapy-addicted adults, unable to get through the normal ups and downs of life without ongoing psychotherapy.

8. Understand the limits of therapy and therapists.

As psychotherapists move out of the role of all-knowing experts we consult on occasion to ongoing partners in healing, psychotherapy becomes one

---

*To find an Imago therapist in your area contact The Institute for Imago Relationship Therapy, 335 North Kowles Avenue, Winter Park, Florida. Phone: 800-729-1121, email: IIRT@aol.com.

more place where we encounter the various challenges that face intimate relationships of all sorts. And this is where problems can arise. The dysfunction we learned as children (which is generally what brings us to therapy) and the dysfunction our therapists learned as children both come into play.

That therapists are themselves wounded does not necessarily mean they are not helpful. The metaphor of the "wounded healer" suggests that the very experience of being wounded is what makes a healer. This is a common thread running through the many traditions of shamanism around the world — shamans must survive their own wounding and dark night of the soul to gain the power to heal. However, in our culture what defines a healer is a university degree. So keep in mind that the "healers" among us are at many different stages of their own healing journey. It is important to acknowledge that therapists are not infallible and, no matter how hard they try not to, they have personal agendas they bring into your healing work.

These agendas could include the fact that you pay their salary and fulfill their need to be of help. Therapists may have abandonment issues and not like it when you leave, or they may have control issues so they don't like admitting mistakes. They may even be sexually attracted to you. Being in therapy is the same as being in any relationship — eventually we are going to experience the weaknesses of this person as well as the strengths. The extent to which the therapist's role prohibits acknowledging those weaknesses is the extent to which the relationship becomes dysfunctional.

Dysfunction and abuse result whenever the therapist uses the client-therapist relationship to address his own personal agenda without acknowledging that this is what he is doing. This extends far beyond the most obvious forms of abuse, such as therapists who seduce their clients, to include subtleties that can be easy to overlook. An acknowledged agenda, for example, is that a therapist expects to be paid fairly for her services. A hidden agenda would be a therapist who extends treatment presumably for the client's good, when, in truth, she is motivated more by a need to maintain a certain number of clients to meet overhead expenses.

But the problem isn't only about therapy and therapists. Our expectations and willingness to surrender personal responsibility is also problematic. Only a generation ago, health care professionals were our gods. Over the course of the 20th century, as religion waned and science prevailed, it was natural to project our need for heroes and our unconditional trust onto scientists who held our lives and well-being in their hands. But in the last two decades, patients have become less and less willing to turn their healing entirely over to their health care professionals. A new model of healing is emerging, based on a partnership where the patient (now called "client") is ultimately responsible.

For those of us who were raised in an era of doctors-as-gods, it can be an awkward transition. To reap the full benefits of the many healing opportunities available and to avoid the well-publicized pitfalls, it is essential that we release expectations that a therapist will have the magic "cure" or be our perfect parent. We need to acknowledge that therapists, too, are human and perhaps no more "healed" than we are; they are simply in a different role. Feelings of betrayal are more likely to occur when we go to therapists in blind trust, as children to parents.

9. Follow your own counsel as well as your therapist's.

What is called for is understanding and awareness rather than paranoia and suspicion. Try putting yourself in your therapist's place and consider how you would feel in a therapeutic relationship with you. Can you image that your therapist is very fond of you and might have difficulty saying good-bye when therapy is complete? Can you imagine that working with you has been difficult and has challenged your therapist's feelings of competence? If you suspect a possible hidden agenda on the part of your therapist, talk about it in therapy. In my years as a therapist, I found it very helpful when clients were brave enough to question my fallibility and point out my issues. It accelerated our therapeutic process immensely, both for the client who took a step out of passivity and victimization, and for me as I was assisted in seeing my blind spots.

You are responsible for the final decisions about your healing. Stay aware of what feels right to you. Follow your own counsel as well as your therapist's. It is important to trust the person you choose to assist you in healing, and when you trust yourself first, you create a trust between equals that won't leave you feeling hurt or betrayed.

Serving the Greater Good Healing the World

The plight of the world can easily feel overwhelming. Certainly the vastness of pain and suffering in the world around us can make it easy to lose hope and awareness of our power to help. We may give in to the feeling that one person can't really change anything. The idea that one person can't make a difference is part of the deeper collective belief system that we are essentially separate and alone and must fend for ourselves to survive. It is this belief in separateness that has created the world's problems, and it is the same belief that can undermine our best intentions to help.

Ironically, there may be a hidden gift in the world's apparent falling apart in that it forces us to become aware of our connection to each other. We are increasingly confronted with the reality that as long as one person is left behind, a piece of each of us cannot go forward. We may for a time be lulled into thinking it's possible to lead a safe, comfortable, insular life separate from the problems of others. But then there is an incidence of violence in our neighborhood or our children's school, or we are approached by a different homeless person at every corner, or a loved one contracts AIDS. Inevitably, there is just too much pain too close to home to think that we are unaffected or that we don't need to help.

Traditionally, "helping" has been what people who have more do for people who have less. There is an assumed inequality in this relationship so that being the recipient of charity carries a burden of shame. The choice to help others has had an element of self-sacrifice — as if somehow my highest good and yours could be mutually exclusive. As we step into our spiritual power, helping can no longer be about giving to those less fortunate, with its air of smug superiority. It needs to become an act of seeing ourselves in everyone — seeing that we are the same, joined to each other, part of the planet, one with all living beings — so that to go forward, we must go together.

I once did an experiment with a group that turned into an unexpectedly powerful experience of joining. It was very simple. I asked everyone to make a wish-list of everything they could think of that they wanted, from the smallest material things to the deepest inner experiences. We made copies of our wish lists and gave them to everyone in the group. Then we meditated on our own lists, imagining that all of our requests or something better was coming into being. Immediately following this meditation, we looked over the stack of lists we had from the other group members and let our intuition guide us to one wish on one list that we felt drawn to, and to grant or assist in granting this wish. I told everyone to go home and spend the next week repeating this meditation and wish-granting exercise as often as they wanted.

What followed far surpassed my expectations. A flow of giving and receiving began that was easy, abundant and thoroughly joyous. People who had money flowed money to people who needed money, people who had skills shared them. We shared ideas, creative talents, support and love. While all of my energy was focused on serving, a steady stream of gifts flowed in. I have never felt so present and alive as that week I spent focused on giving to other people. I have also never felt so abundant and cared for. What was especially striking was that for a time we shifted out of our stance of separateness and self-sufficiency. We were able to temporarily suspend some of our deepest core beliefs that warn us to look out for ourselves because no one else will.

There is a limit to how much we can do for others and for the world around us if we believe ourselves to be separate. As we set about the practical work of helping, it is essential that we also change our heart, knowing that this, too, heals the planet. I once heard Native American teacher, Jamie Sams, author of the *Medicine Cards* and *Sacred Path Cards,* say that the earth doesn't need us to heal her, especially in the gloomy serious way we tend to go about it. What the earth needs from us is our joy.

The following exercise is about effecting inner change toward oneness and joy that will empower our helping actions so that we become world healers in all we do.

Exercise: Healing One, Healing All

Step One

Write down on paper 3 things wrong with the world that you want to see healed. Don't spend a lot of time analyzing this. Simply write whatever comes to mind first. Next write down 3 manifestations of peace, abundance and joy that you wish for the world. For this second list, think beyond the absence of a problem. For example, instead of "No more war" imagine what "no more war" would look like. This envisioning is important. It's difficult to create what we can't imagine and what we fill our minds with is what we bring into being. This is true collectively just as it is personally. Thanks to books, movies and media of all sorts, we have many pictures of the world getting worse but relatively few of what world peace would be like. The world needs for more of us to start imagining peace, not just wishing for it.

Step Two

Look over your list of what's wrong and think about how you manifest the same or similar problems in your own life. For example, if you are focused on violent crime, ask yourself how you, too, manifest violence. You may find violence in your thoughts toward others or in the way you talk about people. Your violence may be expressed passively through coldness or sarcasm. For each problem on your list, write next to it your own equivalent issue. Elizabeth Kubler Ross often said that we all have an inner "Hitler" and an inner "Mother Theresa." In this step, take an honest look to see how your "inner Hitler" manifests.

Step Three

Pick one of your own problem issues and commit to healing it. Come up with at least three steps you are willing to take toward your own healing. As you take these steps, imagine that your healing is a gift you are giving the world. Imagine that your healing is felt by all and makes the whole stronger.

Step Four

For each vision of healing you hold for the world, ask yourself how you would like this form of world good to manifest in your own personal life. For example, if you want all the homeless and hungry to be sheltered and fed, ask yourself how you need to feel sheltered and fed, either literally or metaphorically. Or, if you wish that all children be raised with love, ask if there is a wounded child part of you that is calling out for help.

Step Five

Imagine that all these things you want for yourself and the world (or something better) have now come into being. As you imagine this, let yourself fill with joy, knowing that your joy, too, is felt by all and is helping to heal the world. Now find a way to celebrate. Sing, dance, drum, go for a walk, do something that engages your body and your physical senses. Keeping in mind that your joy heals the earth, let your passion, excitement and love build.

Step Six

Spend one whole day silently blessing each person you meet, including both those people you know and strangers you encounter throughout the day. To bless someone, imagine sending a heart-felt wish that they become as abundant and joyful as you wish to be.

Step Seven

Last but not least, volunteer. Find a path of service that brings you joy. This may take a quiet and personal form, such as practicing daily "random acts of kindness," or you may wish to volunteer for an organization, or organize your friends or community toward a service project. Let your heart, not your guilt, guide you to this. Find a form of service that is wholly joyful to you.

6

"I am entitled to miracles"
—*A Course in Miracles*, Lesson 77

"Ask and it will be given to you;
seek and you will find;
knock and the door will be opened to you."
—*Matthew* 7:7

Accessing the Limitless Source

There is a limitless spiritual source of power, wisdom and love we always have access to. Therefore, we don't need to live in fear of scarcity, and we are never alone.

Letting Go and Letting God

Most of us are control freaks at heart. Living within the narrow parameters of physical reality, it's no wonder. As we perceive so many forces beyond our control, we feel endangered and powerless. We respond by exercising as much control over our surroundings as we can. As we recognize that we create our own reality, we begin to operate at a higher level of power. We feel less at the mercy of a random universe. Yet, there is still another step before our power is complete. To the extent that we feel alone in the creative process, we are still living from fear. I have seen people take on the concept of self-responsibility as a terrible burden, planning, visualizing and affirming every step of their lives, fearing that if they relax their discipline for a moment they will create the "wrong" reality.

At some point in the process of accepting our spiritual power, we need to open to a power greater than our own. There is a paradox here in that one aspect of spiritual empowerment is recognizing that we have more control over the seemingly random forces of the universe than we thought, that we truly do create our own reality. On the other hand, another aspect of spiritual empowerment is letting go and allowing a Higher Power to move through us. The key to resolving the paradox is to recognize that personal control is not the same as power. The more we release our attachment to our personal will and to specific outcomes, the more we naturally attract circumstances that support our highest good.

Creative visualization and affirmations are very useful, but they are only effective to the extent that we know what to affirm and visualize. Sometimes the limits of our imagination do not stretch enough to show us the true path of our highest good. If we use these methods to exercise rigid control over our lives, these practices can backfire. There comes a point when we need to surrender control and attachment to outcomes, trust in a Higher Power, and invite the hand of Spirit into the process to show us possibilities that we haven't yet imagined.

It doesn't matter how we choose to conceive of this Higher Power. I have heard many people claim not to believe in God because they have rejected the definition of God that was taught to them in their early religious training. Yet when I ask, these same people will profess to an active spiritual life and feel a connection to something greater than their small personal selves. This sense of something greater, a feeling that there is something beyond our physical senses, a mystery, a miracle — these are all perceptions of God. God doesn't need to wear the face of a personalized deity to be a potent force in our lives. God can be perceived as energy or found within as a transpersonal aspect of ourselves. God doesn't need to be called God at all. We can call it the Universe, Spirit, the Collective Unconscious, our Higher Self, our Guardian Angel. We can call it a state of consciousness. For the purpose of accessing our spiritual power, what is important is to envision ourselves connected to something greater than the collection of thoughts, feelings, physical characteristics and vulnerabilities that we think of as our "self."

As with everything, our expectations of God will affect our experience. If we expect a harsh, unforgiving God, we will feel guilt, shame and judgment. If we imagine the nonexistence of God, we will live in a fearful reality where we have only those limited resources that we believe a separate and vulnerable individual can have. Yet as we envision and begin to expect the reality of God as a limitless, benevolent source, we tap into resources beyond those we can access through our rational reasoning and physical power.

Trust is a key ingredient in accessing the power of God. When we're afraid to trust other people, we create a prison of self-sufficiency that leaves no opening for people to prove themselves worthy of our trust. Our distrust becomes self-perpetuating because we're too afraid and disillusioned to ask for help and aren't willing to live in the uncertainty that exists between the asking and the receiving. As we try to protect ourselves from let-downs and unpredictable outcomes, we also deny ourselves the possibility of unexpected gifts.

This principle holds true as we relate to God. If we control every step and refuse to make a move until we can see the next ten steps down the path, if we refuse to ever live in uncertainty, we leave little opening for Spirit to move and guide us.

Following the path of inner guidance and listening to Spirit seldom feels safe and certain at all times. It's not that Spirit directs us toward harm. On the contrary, Spirit directs us to our path of highest good which is often new, unfamiliar and, consequently, frightening. While the path of growth invariably takes us out of our comfort zone, it also offers richer rewards than the more familiar routes.

As we ask Spirit for help and listen for guidance, that guidance often comes only one step at a time. What's more, the step may not fit into our plans or make sense to us. It may not seem to have any direct relationship to our desired outcome. It just feels right. It seems impractical but for some reason it's what we want to do. Taking this step requires great courage and faith. We have to trust that we will be guided to the next step when the time comes. We have to have faith that what feels right will lead us to the highest possible outcome even though we don't yet see how. We have to accept that there truly is a guiding force leading the way and keeping us safe.

A metaphor comes to mind from the movie *Indiana Jones and the Last Crusade,* where Indy has to cross a bridge that's invisible until he steps on it. Once he crosses the bridge he can see it is solid and safe and it leads him to the Holy Grail, but the first step is a "leap of faith." Indy has to trust in the unseen and can't make progress without that first step of faith.

One time in my life when I felt called to follow my inner guidance even though it was in direct opposition to my common sense was when I first took up writing. For some time I had made my living by giving seminars. While I loved doing the group work, I didn't enjoy the never-ending marketing needed to make the workshops happen. There was a time when several people who had been working for me in different cities doing the promotional work all left or cut back at the same time. The voice of fear told me I'd better pick up the slack by taking on an extra load of marketing work if I wanted to continue to pay my rent! My spirit felt deadened at the prospect of this. My greatest desire at that time was to devote myself to writing. My inner guidance told me to go ahead and write, to forget about setting up more workshops for the time being and that everything would work out.

With great trepidation I followed this guidance and started writing, having no idea how I would make ends meet. One day when I felt especially fearful, I asked God for a sign that I was on track and that everything was going to be all right. I said, "Okay God, if you really want me to continue writing instead of marketing my workshops, give me a sign! Give me a sign *this week* and make it so obvious that I can't possibly miss it!"

Several days passed, then four days, five days, and my doubts grew. Each day I waited for my sign. Then on the sixth day, I received a card in the mail from an old friend I hadn't been in touch with in a couple of years. He hadn't heard anything about my situation. He also was dying of AIDS. Being so close to leaving his body had put him closely in touch with "his angels," he said. His angels told him to write to me and reassure me that everything is all right, that I am on track, that everything is going to turn out perfectly. He enclosed a check for $200.

I couldn't have received a clearer sign and, as predicted, everything did turn out perfectly. Although I was in love with my beautiful house in the country, I gave notice to my landlord that I would be moving soon because I couldn't pay the rent. My landlord was so upset that I was leaving that he came to me and asked if there was anything he could do to convince me to stay. I said jokingly, "Sure, lower the rent!" To my surprise, instead of laughing at my joke, he said, "By how much?" He wound up reducing my rent by hundreds of dollars, enabling me to stay.

Other money miracles happened during that time. I had only one intensive seminar scheduled over a six month period, which provided my sole source of income for those months. I offered this workshop on a self-determined fee basis so I never knew until the end how much money I would make. The people in this particular seminar, without knowing about my impoverished condition, chose to give unprecedented amounts of money, one gift being over $5000. Though my finances were tight and I had to budget every penny, the money from this one workshop was enough to carry me through the long months when I had no workshops scheduled.

Within months I started to see the results of my writing. The articles I had written were published in local papers all over the country. They created more demand for my workshops with much less marketing. Filling workshops became easier, my business grew and I began to make more money than I had before, doing work I enjoyed more. Ultimately, the writing that I started those years ago led me to the creation of this book. All this came about through my willingness, albeit reluctant at times, to surrender to a higher guiding force than my ego.

Prayer

One way to invite Spirit to be a more active participant in our life is through prayer. The very act of prayer, which essentially is a conversation with a Higher Spiritual Power, affirms that we are not alone with our burdens. However, to effectively use prayer it may first be necessary to expand our assumptions about it beyond limiting stereotypes. Prayer is more than a hollow recitation of religious prose. It is also more than reading a grocery list of requests to God or telling God what to do.

When we feel that our prayers go unanswered, it is invariably because we are praying from our fear-based need for control. Instead of praying for the highest possible outcome, trusting God to show us what that is, we come to God with our list of specific requests saying, in effect, "This, God, and only this will do." In so doing, we undermine the purpose and power of prayer. Sometimes our highest good is bigger than we have imagined, and what we are praying for is not what we truly need or want at the highest level of our being. Our prayer request may not be in alignment with our highest health and well being, so we set up a situation of conflicting intentions and lose the power of having all of our energy in alignment. An example of this would be praying for a relationship to continue because we are afraid of being alone even though we know deep down that the relationship isn't healthy. In this instance, we give energy to a conscious intention that stems from fear, while another part of us longs for something better. In this way, our conscious agenda and our higher agenda are at odds, one diffusing the power of the other.

The act of praying for and being invested in a specific outcome can easily draw our attention away from the present, which is where our greatest power lies. When we become future-focused as in, "I won't be happy until this outcome occurs," we step out of power and lose our natural ability to easily and effortlessly draw to ourselves what we need. Life becomes a struggle.

Prayer is about developing a relationship with God. It is a conversation, personal and intimate. As mentioned earlier, part of what makes prayer so powerful is that our conversation with God continually reminds us of the existence of this relationship and that we are not alone. So to pray, we need some sense of to whom or what we are directing our prayers. The act of prayer helps to personify God, giving a face and personality to the vastness and abstractness of Spirit, making God more accessible. God wears an infinite number of faces. Our Higher Self, the spiritual masters of all the world's great religions, the guardian angels and spirit guides that many feel protecting and guiding them, animals and elements of nature, Great Spirit, the Holy Spirit, The Universe and Gaia the earth spirit, are just some of the faces of God. For prayers to be effective, it does not matter what "face" of God we choose to honor with our prayers. We may even direct our prayers differently at different times. The face that has the most appeal to us is the one that will have the most power.

Certainly, the ineffable nature of Spirit is greater than any face we can put to it. However, there is still value in finding our own personal doorway to God. The inscription on a Chinese stone figure of Buddha, dated 746, puts it very succinctly: "The highest truth is without image. If there were

no image at all, however, there would be no way for truth to be manifested." If you are unsure what image of God has the most powerful message
for you, do the following exercise.

Exercise: The Face of God

*Relax, close your eyes and open your mind to all of your impressions of
Spirit. Let go of your intellectual thoughts and concepts and instead see
what images feel the most comforting and emotionally appealing to
you. Let your imagination play with different images of the Divine to
find what represents spirituality most purely and powerfully for you.
Let go of your concepts and stereotypes about God. See what feels right.
Is Spirit best pictured for you in a male or female form? Human form,
animal form, or pure energy? Does it feel external or within? As you
imagine the most appealing personification of God, do you envision
Jesus Christ or another well known spiritual Master, a Light being, the
Earth Goddess, a Guardian Angel, a beautiful Light or a feeling of
energy, a child being, an old wise figure, or something else altogether?
Let yourself be drawn to a representation rather than deciding upon
one. The "right" one is the one that has the most positive emotional
voltage to it, the one that gives you the biggest lift.*

*When a vision or sense of God comes to you and feels right, you can
begin to establish a relationship with it. A good starting place is to
imagine this aspect of God being present as you go about your day, at
night as you fall asleep and the first thing you think of as you wake up.*

A Four-fold Path into Prayer

For many years I had difficulty understanding prayer. Having had no
religious upbringing in my family, I had no childhood prayer ritual to draw

upon. When I discovered spirituality on my own, I had more exposure to meditation than to prayer. Prayer was something I just didn't get. Over the years I slowly developed an understanding of and deep appreciation for prayer from my longtime friend Deb Teramani. Raised Catholic, prayer has always been an important part of her life and she devotes much time to it every day. She sees prayer as a four-fold process that she has drawn from both her Catholic upbringing and her more spiritually eclectic adulthood. Forming the acronym ACTS, I have found the following steps to be a very helpful approach to prayer.

I. Adoration

Adoration is all about opening our hearts to loving and being loved by God. A prayer may, but does not have to contain words. The act of adoration is 100% feeling. To help you rise to this state of love, use whatever words, music, thoughts or images inspire your deepest heart-felt feelings of love for God. Some find it easier to adore God in nature or a spiritual sanctuary. Music, song, chanting, dancing or drumming are other ways of lifting the spirit to a place of adoration. The adoration of God also includes adoring the God in each person. Mother Theresa made a life's work of Adoration. Offering love to the poorest of the poor, she lived by the words of Jesus, "Whatever you did to the least of my brethren, you did it to me," and so saw the face of God in each person she served.

Mark, a close friend and member of a spiritual support group I led for many years, offered a touching demonstration of adoration one evening when, after leading the group in a meditation, he silently came to each of us and washed our feet. Such a simple act left everyone profoundly moved.

If the experience of adoration eludes you, instead of doing the adoring, imagine God adoring you. Feel yourself completely surrounded by the deepest, most unconditional love you can imagine. In the words of Mother Theresa, "When you know how much God is in love with you, then you can only live your life radiating that love."

II. Contrition

Contrition is the act of acknowledging any aspect of your perception that has become separate from God, for the purpose of releasing that separateness. Contrition is a heart-felt apology to self and others for seeing faults and failings rather than the Higher Self that we all are. It is about acknowledging the ways we have acted from fear rather than love and the hurtfulness of these acts. Contrition is not about self-blame and guilt. It is about rectifying hurtful perceptions and actions. It is not about punishment, it is about healing. It's an opportunity to let go of our self-righteous ego that holds on to being right in relation to other people or in relation to God. Contrition includes the heart-felt willingness to see and act from love instead of fear. The following practices are some examples of prayerful contrition:

1. Take a daily, monthly or life inventory of fearful perceptions and actions and then turn them over to God to be healed.

2. Look in a mirror, apologize to yourself for self-critical thoughts and for seeing anything less than your own perfection.

3. Talking in spirit (see the section on "Higher Self Communication" in Chapter Five) or in person, apologize to others for judgmental thoughts, words and hurtful actions. Take steps in whatever ways feel appropriate to rectify your hurtful actions toward other people.

4. Feel the complete, unconditional acceptance and forgiveness of God healing any lack of forgiveness that you are holding toward yourself or another.

III. Thanksgiving

Gratitude is a highly magnetic state of mind. It promotes healing in our physical body, it leaves us feeling happy and at peace, and it naturally attracts to us our highest good. Because what we give attention to is what multiplies in our life, the more we acknowledge our blessings, the more blessings we attract. Thanksgiving is about giving energy and attention to what we have received rather than to what we lack. To practice thanksgiving, thank God often for everything you have now. Give thanks for all of your successes and joys from the past, and give thanks for what you want to create in your life as though it has already happened. Begin to notice all the small moments in your day when circumstances conspire in your favor — a parking place opens up just as you need it, you almost slip on the ice but catch yourself just in time, an unexpected check shows up in the mail — and thank God for each of these small gifts. At the end of each day, take a moment to review the blessings you have received. Put yourself to sleep this way at night.

Give thanks even for the experiences and life lessons that feel painful. Remember the woman described in an earlier chapter who healed her melanoma by repeatedly affirming, "Thank you, God, for cancer." As we give thanks for situations that feel hurtful, we relax, let go of struggle and become more open to healing. We open to the lessons of these situations without needing the pain to catch our attention.

IV. Surrender

This last step, surrender, is about humility. It is an ego-deflating step requesting to know and do God's will instead of our own. It's when we admit our own powerlessness in the face of God's power. Humility is an integral part of the teachings of Alcoholics Anonymous and the twelve-step recovery movement. *Twelve Steps and Twelve Traditions*, a book published by Alcoholics Anonymous outlining the twelve-step philosophy, points to the lack of humility as being a crippling defect of our culture. The book describes how we attach much pride to our capacity to control our destiny solely through our own cleverness and hard work. The downfall to this is that "As long as we placed self-reliance first, a genuine reliance upon a

Higher Power [is] out of the question. That basic ingredient of all humility, a desire to seek and do God's will [is] missing." The absence of humility is synonymous with a belief in separateness. As we rigidly propel our lives forward solely on the power we have as separate "particles," we invite the stress, emptiness and desperation that lead to addiction. Not only is humility a step in the healing of addiction, addiction is an end product of its absence.

Just as Alcoholics Anonymous teaches the necessity of admitting powerlessness over alcohol before healing can begin, we all need at some point to admit our utter powerlessness over the fears and limited vision of our ego (our "particle" self). The minute we believe we are completely free of our ego is when we become stuck.

Surrender invites us to look at where our attachments lie. Wanting something, feeling desire to have, do or be something is powerful. Where we have passion and desire, we have creative energy. However, we lose our power when desire becomes attachment, in other words when the feeling of "I want this!" becomes the feeling of "I can't live (be happy, feel good about myself...) without this." Instead of being fueled by the excitement of creating what we want, we become controlled by the fear of not getting it. Then we stop being open to the highest possible outcome because we have become fixated on the only outcome our fearful ego self can imagine.

For example, once when I was looking for a house to rent, I got to a point of frustration, fearing that I would never find what I was looking for. I was moving in with my lover and it was a big step for us. Finally after much searching, we found a beautiful place in the country. Everything seemed perfect. Coincidentally, my partner even knew the current tenants who said they would put in a good word for us. I was sure this place was meant for us and was devastated when the landlord decided to rent to someone else. After all the meditating, visualizing and praying we had done to attract our perfect home, I couldn't understand why God had dangled it in front of us and then snatched it away! After spending a good day or so being unhappy, I decided instead to assume that God must have a better plan for us. Instead of regretting the loss, I began to affirm that an even better house must surely be on its way.

Several days later, my partner and I had a very intense discussion of our mutual fears of living together and of deepening our relationship. It was a healing talk that helped us both shed some layers of resistance to moving forward together. Afterward he said, "You know, I don't think we're going to have any more trouble finding a house." The next day we saw a house for rent listed in the paper that was far more beautiful and perfect than the house we lost or anything I had previously imagined. The landlord rented it to us with no hesitation, saying later that he just had a "feeling" we were the right people to be there. As it turned out, God did have the perfect plan for me, but I needed to let go of my attachment to the outcome I thought I wanted to let it in.

To practice surrender, try working with the simple prayer, "Thy will, God, not mine." Say this many times a day, especially when life is not going according to your ego's plan. As you say this prayer, breathe deeply, let your body relax and imagine that a better way is about to open up for you as you hand the reins over to God.

Mentally, or in writing, list all the things you are attached to. Include those things you currently have as well as future outcomes. Remember, attachment isn't just about what you love or what you want. Attachment exists wherever we feel, "I can't be okay (i.e. complete, happy, safe, fulfilled, etc.) without this." Your list might include people, jobs, material possessions, your health, aspects of you identity and life circumstances, just to name a few. As you identify each of these things, picture yourself letting them go, imagining that life could still be meaningful and joyful without them. Imagine turning your life path completely over to God in absolute trust that whatever plan Spirit has in mind for you is infinitely better than your own.

There are many ways to work with these four aspects of prayer. You could practice one step at a time, spending days, weeks or months focusing on only adoration, contrition, thanksgiving, or surrender. You could see which one has the most appeal and start there. Or, you could start with the one that feels the most difficult, trusting that there will be important lessons in the step that offers the greatest challenge. You even could incorporate all four steps into a daily prayer ritual, giving some attention to each.

Asking God for Help

Often, if we remember to turn to God for help at all, it's at the point of desperation when all other resources have failed. We forget to include God in the day to day details of our lives and wait until a crisis forces us to turn to a Higher Power. Or perhaps we feel guilty asking God for too much help and think we should only turn to Spirit for the big things. Yet, God's help is always there whenever we ask.

I was given a powerful reminder of this in my own life when I was experiencing a multitude of personal crises all at the same time. I became so distraught and absorbed in the drama of struggle that my energy for other things was drained. My creativity seemed to have died. I needed to write an article that I had promised but I was so absorbed in the struggle I could think of little else. I hadn't a single idea in mind and wondered if I would ever find the heart to write again. After distracting myself for a couple of hours with food, daytime TV and the newspaper, I found myself falling into a dark apathy. I finally gave up altogether and asked for help. Sitting on the couch, I closed my eyes and asked for guidance. I told God, "I give up. I don't know what to do. I'll do whatever you say."

A copy of an inspirational book was sitting on the coffee table in front of me and, without thinking, I picked it up and opened randomly to a page. My eyes instantly went to a passage that spoke of the depth of love between mothers and daughters. This immediately brought tears to my eyes because I had dreamed of my mother the night before and she had been on my mind. I had been missing her lately. Right away I started writing about my mother's death. I spent the next couple of hours writing a story that seemed to pour out of me. I cried the whole time I wrote — tears of love, rather than grief. I had a powerful feeling of my mother's presence, not only helping me to write, but comforting me through this difficult time of my life. Afterward I was emotionally renewed and I had a completed article that was one of the best things I had written in some time. Even more important, I felt healed and at peace for the first time in months.

What I realized from this experience is how available God's help is when I am willing to ask for and receive it. I began to make a practice of asking for help often, for small things as well as large ones. I have found that when I remember to ask God for a parking place, a car invariably seems to pull out right in front of where I want to be just as I am approaching. I find that when I ask for help it is there, not always in the form I expected or wanted, but in a form that truly helps.

Some people imagine that God will tire of our requests if they are too frequent and that we should only ask for God's help when it's really urgent. Certainly, if this is our expectation of God, this is the God we will experience. However, I choose to see God as limitless, therefore there is no inappropriate amount of God that we can have. The supply of God cannot run out. It is my experience that the more I ask Spirit for help, the more the channel seems to open. I imagine it's like blazing a trail through wilderness. The first time through is incredibly difficult, with much that needs to be cleared out of the way. The second time is easier. Eventually, after numerous trips, the path of spiritual supply becomes clear, wide and open.

Of course, receiving God's help requires faith, humility and surrender — faith that help will be there, a humbling of our egotistical insistence that we can go it alone, and a surrendering to God's plan for us even if this doesn't fit with our personal agenda.

Being Willing to Live in the Void

The "void" is the term I use to describe a state of not doing, not having and not knowing. The void is a place of emptiness and of stillness. It is a time of letting go rather than of acquiring. It's the point after we have sustained losses and before anything new has come along to take their place. The void is the place of restlessness that precedes change, when we are dissatisfied with what is but don't know where to go next. Most of us are terrified of the void and will do anything to avoid or fill it.

This fear of the void stems from our collective belief in scarcity. When we believe that there is not enough for us, we become afraid to let go because we don't trust that there will be anything more if we give up what we have. Emptiness is our worst fear. We hold on too long to jobs, relationships and material things, resisting the ebb and flow of change, even when what is has become unfulfilling, even stultifying. We cling to what we have, not because we love it, but just so we won't have to face emptiness.

Yet it is in the stillness, the silence, the open space that's left when all the clutter is removed, that we are best able to hear our inner guidance and see the bigger pictures that will lead us to a new, improved level of being, doing and having — one that will better suit who we have grown to become. It is through emptiness that we make room for our highest good. If we have our arms filled with garbage we may have "a lot," but we don't have what we need. And we are not able to embrace something better because our arms are full.

The void is an integral part of the cycle of life and can't be avoided. Just as fall has to come after summer and sleep has to come after activity, the void is essential to life. We tend to associate the void with pain, but it doesn't have to be painful. It is only our resistance and our attempts to protect ourselves from the void that make it painful. When, at the spiritual level, we have outgrown the circumstances of our lives yet continue to cling to them, we precipitate much unnecessary crisis and breakdown. The gap between what we need and what we are clinging to grows bigger and bigger.

It is as though we are outgrowing our shoes but refuse to take them off even though they make our feet hurt more and more. If we fight change and resist taking a leap into the unknown, we wind up feeling victimized by the change that continues regardless of our struggles against it. Instead of gently leaving a situation on our own initiative, we experience being forced out as circumstances erupt around us, seemingly out of our control.

I once shared a rented house with a close friend. The house was cramped, in poor condition and inconvenient in a variety of ways. Neither of us liked it but we stayed simply because we resisted the trouble it would be to move. Then came a weekend when my friend and I were both away attending transformative events. Hers was a seasonal equinox ritual, mine was a weekend workshop. Both of us had very powerful experiences that we felt deeply changed us in many positive ways. Each of us subsequently had the less blissful experience of coming home and immediately receiving word from our landlord that we were being evicted from our house in just thirty days. At first we panicked and felt rudely jolted out of our transcendental bliss. We went through a brief crisis time of feeling victimized by the forced move. But then we reframed the situation and recognized that circumstances were merely forcing us to do what we had been saying we wanted to do for some time. We believed that our weekend growth experiences had caused us to spiritually outgrow our surroundings and that there was something better awaiting us. So, even though we had very little time to find someplace new, we resisted the fear-based urge to settle for places that we didn't love just because they were available. We didn't let ourselves be discouraged by realtors who told us we would never find what we wanted in our price range. Finally, in the last week before we had to move, we found a wonderful place that was fully twice as big as our last house, in better condition, with a nicer yard and for less rent. It was a perfect home for us that, because of its unexpected size and beauty, encouraged us both to expand our vision of possibilities in a number of obvious and subtle ways.

Paradoxically, allowing, rather than resisting, the natural emptying cycles of life tends to shorten their duration and fuels the next stage of active growth. When we stop struggling against emptiness, the void becomes a fertile place of limitless possibilities. Instead of scrambling for something to fill the void, these empty times are best used for dreaming, listening, healing and building energy. They are an opportunity to get clear about what we really want before proceeding forward. Speeding through the void is a bit like a caterpillar emerging too soon from the cocoon, coming out a slimy, lumpy thing instead of a beautiful butterfly. There is no efficiency here. When we try to skip over the void, we tend to find ourselves suddenly back in it again. There is a process to the void that can't be hurried except, paradoxically, by surrendering to it whole-heatedly.

Making our time in the void productive includes much of the work already addressed in this book. It requires allowing feelings to surface rather than numbing them through addictions or activity. The void often takes us into grief because we are experiencing the ending of an old way of being. Even welcomed endings bring with them some degree of mourning as we let go of something familiar. When we allow ourselves to grieve, we don't bring the past with us into whatever new beginning is to come and, consequently, are less likely to stay stuck in limiting patterns of the past.

The void is a good place to do some dreaming — as opposed to planning. Dreaming is an open state of imagining possibilities before we have a clue as to how they might manifest. It is about exploring in our imagination what we might want rather than what we think we can have. Planning, on the other hand, involves working out the means to the end. While planning is a good thing at the right time, too much planning when we are in a void phase of life can actually limit rather than expand our possibilities. Imagine the caterpillar in the cocoon, desperately planning a way out. The truth of his condition is that he needs do nothing but dream beautiful butterfly dreams and let nature take its course. Planning doesn't serve us when it's rooted in fear.

The void calls for a leap of faith in an invisible process. It is a time to listen to inner guidance and trust what feels right even if it doesn't jive with what seems sensible. All of this requires letting the empty spaces in our lives stay empty for a bit — allowing time for inactivity, silence and introspection. In this way, we gently grow out of the void and emerge organically into a wonderful new way of life instead of struggling out, feeling beaten and battered, with nothing positive to show for our efforts, like the caterpillar who succeeds in breaking out of his cocoon too soon.

This empty phase is a good time for journaling, meditation, creative activities and all forms of inner work. It's a good time to engage in a more active dialogue with your inner guidance, which is often very loud and noticeable during these times.

Exercise: Dialoguing with Your Inner Guidance

Essentially this is an exercise in automatic writing. Holding the intention that a higher source of wisdom will now speak to you, sit quietly with pen and paper, or at your computer if you are comfortable and facile with a keyboard. Begin with a specific question or just a request to hear whatever you most need to know, and then imagine that a higher, wiser voice is answering you. Immediately, as you hear these imagined words, write them down. Don't wait until the message is complete because that may interrupt the flow or you may forget parts.

It may feel at first that you are making up the words yourself and they are not coming from a higher source. However, as you continue with this exercise you will probably notice that you are seeing perspectives of your situation that you have never considered before. You may even begin to have a sense that the voice speaking to you is much different than your own. The voice may go on to new topics and have quite a lot to say. Whether you believe this voice to be your own intuition or an external spiritual being is not so important as whether the information feels helpful and useful. After a session of writing, read over what you have written and see if it feels right, shows you new possibilities and helps you to feel more at peace. Keep what rings true and feels helpful. Disregard anything else.

You can focus this exercise a bit if you like by directing your communication to a specific spiritual source. You may imagine a particular spiritual being to whom you pray, or speak to the Higher Self of any person, living or dead, who is a role model or source of wisdom for you. If there is a well-known person whose words appear in writing you can incorporate their book in the process. Hold your request for guidance in mind and then open the book randomly and let the passage that first catches your eye speak to your situation. Don't stop with the written passage, however. Imagine that the book's author is now speaking to you directly, adding to and personalizing the message.

The following exercise is a way to begin the emptying out process that must always precede new growth. I have found that many people who have made major changes in their lives were instinctively guided to release many old and familiar things right before they felt called to initiated changes. It wasn't consciously planned that way. Rather, they found themselves just naturally wanting to be rid of the old. I have noticed that the bigger the change people underwent, the more dramatic their shedding phase was.

Exercise: Letting Go

Step One

Ask yourself, what are you holding on to because you are afraid there won't be anything to replace it rather than because it is something you love? Do some writing on this, listing everything, big and small, that you can think of.

Step Two

Out of all the things you hold on to out of fear, is there anything you are willing to release to make room for more of what you want? This is not necessarily a push to make major life changes. Focus on what you truly feel ready to release so there is a feeling of "stretching" beyond familiar behavior without pushing yourself so far out of your comfort zone that all you can feel is fear. For example, giving up nonproductive spare time activities to make room for doing something you truly love might be a step you are ready for whereas leaving your job might feel like too big a risk.

Sometimes we are truly ready to step out of our old lives in a big way and it is appropriate to make major life changes. To determine what is right for you, it is important to listen carefully to inner guidance and to honor both your feelings of excitement and eagerness as well as your feelings of fear and resistance. The idea is to stretch past what is old, familiar and limiting to experience something new, without leaping so far at once that you catapult yourself into a state of fear and crisis.

This is also not a suggestion to sacrifice something you love. "Letting go" means releasing from your life something you no longer appreciate, such as old clothes that no longer fit or that don't express your taste. "Sacrificing" is giving up something you love because you think you should, such as giving up your favorite foods because you think they are bad for you.

Step Three

Look around your physical space and see if there is an accumulation of material things that need to be released because they are no longer serving you (things that have been stored in boxes for years, clutter that needs to be thrown away, things that have piled up and are crowding your space, etc.). A cluttered physical environment is often a reflection of "stuff" we are clinging to on other levels: hurts from the past, fears, resentments, nonproductive patterns of thought, excess weight in our bodies, and so on. Spend some time letting go of unnecessary clutter in your physical space. As you do, imagine that you are releasing everything in your life that is not serving your highest good and making room for what will truly support your well-being.

The Power of Not Knowing

The Pathless Path
There is no answer.
There never has been an answer.
There never will be an answer.
That's the answer.

— Gertrude Stein

Another thing the void phase of life periodically asks us to release is all that we think we know. "Not knowing" means letting go of the idea of a graspable Absolute Truth and cultivating the state of mind expressed by Socrates when he said, "I know that I know nothing." As soon as we hold a truth to be The Truth, we automatically separate ourselves from all others who don't share our truth, and the disempowering cycle of judgment, separateness and fear begins. *A Course in Miracles* begins with the lesson,

"Nothing I see means anything." The second lesson is, "I have given everything I see all the meaning it has for me." The third is, "I do not understand anything I see." These exercises in deprogramming are an essential step in opening to an expanded paradigm of truth. The more rigidly we hold on to our interpretations of life, the more we close off to the multitude of options and possibilities that are beyond our current ability to imagine.

In the absence of one ultimate truth that our human minds can fathom, there are innumerable perspectives of truth that serve us until we outgrow them. (It is in this spirit that all the principles in this book are offered — as helpful perspectives rather than definitive truth.) An important factor in making use of our perspectives of truth is to see them for what they are: frames we choose to view reality through. We can choose any number of frames that will each show us something a little different, yet all of reality is too big to frame in an absolute way. We may have transcendental moments of experiencing "All That Is," but as soon as we try to define what we experienced, we simply construct another frame. What we see through a frame will never be the whole picture, so from time to time we must drop our frame, releasing our tight hold on one over another, and experiment with different perspectives of truth.

An important aspect of stepping into our spiritual power is to embrace paradox, to search for and find coherency in two diametrically opposed truths. Remember the physics paradox of matter being particles *and* waves. We are the same — one with All That Is, yet unique and individual at the same time. The element of paradox is ever-present as we increasingly open to spiritual reality. We can be the creator of our own experience at the same time that we deeply accept and surrender to what is. We can offer compassion and support to someone in pain while seeing past their pain to the Higher Self who is whole and unharmed. We can know ourselves to be powerful enough to affect every atom in the universe at the same time that we know we are powerless to change the Divine Order of All That Is. We can know more as we recognize that we know nothing.

It is only through *knowing* that we know nothing that our minds expand wide enough to embrace paradox, which ultimately leads us to new options. Without this, we become trapped by our attachment to our narrow view. Without this, we become the housefly, trying to fly through a screen window, unable to see that if we turn away from our goal and fly in the opposite direction, we will find an open door.

Whenever we feel stuck in life, we can be sure that we have become too attached to our particular interpretation of truth. No amount of problem-solving will help until we first shake our rigid way of perceiving. The following exercise will help you free your mind from its rigid grooves to find the open doors that lie just out of sight.

Exercise: Freeing Your Mind

Step One

Think of some area of your life where you feel stuck, at a stand still or up against a wall with no or only limited options.

Step Two

What are you *sure* is true about this situation? Write down everything that comes to mind.

Step Three

Review what you have written and ask yourself what "truths" about your situation would cause you to feel very defensive if challenged?

Step Four

These are exactly the perceptions that need shaking up. The truth that you feel most defensive of is showing you where you have become the most rigid and closed. Ask yourself, "What would happen if this were not true at all? What am I *afraid* would happen if this were not true?" Do some more writing on these questions.

Step Five

Imagine that all you thought you knew for certain about your situation is not true. You don't need to figure out exactly how this new reality would look. In other words, as you release your current definitions, don't immediately grasp for new ones. Simply let your mind open and allow yourself to be confused. This process is much like letting your eyes go out of focus so that you are seeing the color, form and the big picture of the world around you rather than the details. Imagine that, even in the midst of confusion and not knowing, you are safe and at peace. Practice this step for at least a day or two before going on to Step Six.

Step Six

Do some imagining, perhaps in writing, about what options become possible if all that you thought was true about your situation isn't. If nothing comes to you, then go back to Step Five and let yourself continue to live in the not knowing. As you do, give special attention to relaxing into this place of ambiguity. Cultivate a feeling of faith that new, unimagined possibilities are now coming to you. Let go and don't try to make anything happen.

Opening the Flow — Releasing Scarcity

In his best-selling novel, *The Celestine Prophecy*, James Redfield beautifully encapsulates complex spiritual truth by defining everything in the physical world as "a vast system of energy." He says much of the current interaction among humans involves trying to steal energy from each other because we feel weak and insecure. This is the root of all conflict, all wars, all greed.

This insecurity that Redfield speaks of is rooted in our belief in scarcity. We are so conditioned to believe there isn't enough to go around, that we go through life like containers, scooping up everything we can and holding on to it for fear that whatever we release may never be replaced. We do this not only with material possessions and money, but also with love and other intangibles. We give love with the expectation that it be returned in kind from the receiver, or else we feel cheated. We have little faith that what we give to one person will come back to us, possibly from a completely different source.

When we buy into the belief that there isn't enough of anything, any abundance that does come our way has guilt attached. We fear that if we have enough or more than enough, it must be at someone else's expense. It's no wonder that suicide rates tend to be higher in affluent communities. Our collective belief in scarcity is such that even people who are materially well off often have the same fears of not having enough as those who are very poor.

It simply isn't true that there isn't enough on our planet. The truth is that we direct vast amounts of energy and resources into protecting ourselves against each other rather than into human well-being. Imagine what might happen if all the energy that now goes into national defense budgets around the world was directed instead into raising the quality of life. Imagine what could happen if all the resources and creativity that now goes into competition, advertising and going after a "bigger piece of the pie," went instead into cooperating to produce the highest quality product and the highest good for all.

It's hard to imagine, isn't it? It's easier to envision a cataclysmic end of the world than it is to imagine universal peace and well-being. This is because we have devoted so much more energy to imagining the worst that could happen. What we call "news," and broadcast many times daily, is little more that a report of everything that has gone wrong. This is what we consider important to know, and these images are the ones that fill our consciousness.

War, greed, abusing the environment for profit, these things all come from a core level fear that there is not enough for us. This is not the fault of governments, corporations and large institutions. This is a fear shared and perpetuated by all of us, even the most politically correct. Consider your own "hoarding" tendencies. How many material things do you own that you haven't used in a year or more? Are there clothes in your closet that you don't wear, but don't release? Are there things in drawers, boxes, your attic, basement or garage that you don't use, perhaps don't even like, yet keep because they are "valuable," because you might need them some day, because they are worth money? How many of your material possessions are things you actively use and value and how many are not? How easily do you let go of money? Do you wait until the last minute, perhaps past the due date to pay your bills? Do you withhold love? Do you hold on to resentments and hurts? Do you hold on to weight in your body? There are many different ways to hoard and hold more than we need or want.

Now, picture your own stockpile and multiply it by the millions of other people on the planet who are also sitting on stockpiles of excess. Imagine what could happen if each of these individuals released everything they had that they didn't use or like. Our problem is not one of scarcity, it is one of fear and withholding.

The exciting thing about this dynamic is that one person can make a difference. One person can live from the certainty that there is enough, trusting that it is safe to let go of what we don't need and give unconditionally of what we have. In doing this, one individual can begin to experience an abundant flow as reality and become an inspiration to others to do the same.

When we start to recognize that there is a limitless spiritual source of energy that we can draw from we will no longer need to feed upon each other through control, greed and manipulation. What's more, we will discover that giving energy to each other is the most self-serving thing we can do, for as we send energy to another, we call forth the best in that person. At their best, every person just naturally begins to give back.

Money, Power and Scarcity

Money, in particular, has a way of triggering scarcity fears and bringing out the worst in us. Even many of us who believe ourselves to honest, upright and nonmaterialistic are tempted to cheat a little on our taxes or resent paying the phone or utility bills. Countless marriages have ended with fierce haggling over money, and families have been bitterly divided over the distribution of an inheritance. As Caroline Myss puts it, "Within each of our psyches lives an element of the prostitute — a part of ourselves that could possibly be commanded by the right financial figure."

But what exactly is money, anyway? It is so important that it must surely be something more than the slip of paper, bit of metal or piece of plastic that we call "money." When I was a young child, money was the big shiny silver dollars my grandfather gave me and the five dollar bills my other grandfather gave me on birthdays and holidays. The silver dollars I kept as precious possessions. The bills I turned into comic books and candy. I loved money. I thought it was just wonderful.

When I got a little older, money became something there never seemed to be enough of. As my father's alcoholism progressed and his business failed, money became tighter and tighter. As my father's abusiveness escalated, I begged my mother to move away from him. Money was the reason she gave for us not being able to leave. I grew up believing that my safety relied upon having enough money. I believed if only there had been enough money, I would have been saved from the fearful experiences of my childhood.

Money is one of the primary symbols of power on our planet today. In our minds we connect it with all the various qualities that represent empowerment. We think it is synonymous with security, love, happiness, vitality or self-worth. If we don't have enough of these intangibles, we are taught to believe that money will take us there. We all know the expression, "Money isn't everything," but deep down, wouldn't even the least materialistic among us secretly like to win the lottery? When we are in fear about not having enough of it, doesn't money seem like everything? We invest money with so much power that it sometimes seems like the only means to an end. Unfortunately, this fixation on money as the solution has a way of taking us further and further from the inner experiences we crave. It can become an addiction that distracts us from what we truly need.

I experienced this myself once when my business, which had always continued on in a fairly predictable steady way, took a financial nose-dive, forcing a reevaluation of the whole structure of my organization. I had a very wise business consultant helping me with this. Before he was willing to address the mundane matters of dollars and cents, advertising, budgeting and managing, he kept asking me the disconcerting question, "What's in it for you to have your business be in financial crisis?" I resisted this question as long as I could. "There's nothing in it for me!" I thought. I blamed the recession, poor managing, poor budgeting. I thought perhaps there is just no calling for my work any more. I considered everything other than the possibility that I might prefer it this way.

Then one day it hit me that my financial woes began very shortly after some problems surfaced in my relationship with my lover. In fact, since that time I hadn't really had time to be upset about these things in my relationship because I was too consumed with the crisis of my business. And, I had to admit, dealing with the prospect of my business falling apart, as difficult and painful as it was, was not nearly as frightening to me as dealing with the possibility of my relationship falling apart.

When faced with the fear of emotional loss, the message I received early in life kicked in — that money was safety, money was a way out of a frightening emotional situation. Of course, the truth was that the more consumed I became with my business at that time, the more estranged my partner and I became. As my focus on money protected me from having to look at my deeper fears, it also contributed to making everything worse.

It wasn't until I acknowledged that money was not going to take me where I wanted to go that things began to shift for the better. As I recognized that my problem wasn't about money, I found the courage to stop focusing on it as the solution, in spite of how frightening that was for me at the time. I let go of all my worries about paying the bills and instead gave attention to letting go of fear — my fear of being abandoned, my fear of not being able to take care of myself, fears that belonged more to a frightened four year old than a competent adult business woman.

I gently opened to the inner experience of safety. I felt it in my body, I imagined it with all of my senses, and slowly I began to unwind the knot of fear that had been driving me. Little by little, as I let go of fear, I found answers about how to deal with my business problems and how to deal with my relationship problems. These answers were ones that had never occurred to me before. They guided me into a new phase of emotional well-being, professional expansion and financial security.

I have looked to money primarily as a source of safety. Of course, money has nothing to do with my safety and when I feel safe I know this. But when I am afraid, I shift into automatic pilot. I focus on money, thinking that it's somehow what I need to feel better, and the flow of money invariably reflects this by contracting. Other circumstances in my life plunge into greater chaos as well when I fearfully fixate on money as the solution.

We all have different expectations of money. A gambler I knew once got in touch with his belief that the "big win" was the only way for him to achieve the self-worth he had not been able to experience in his numerous failed careers. Sadly, each time he won, he affirmed his belief that he had to rely on "winning" what he wanted because he could not "earn" it. With each win he felt more inadequate, more of a failure, further away from what he truly wanted, but it was easy not to notice because the pursuit of the "big win" was so consuming.

Sometimes we think money will buy us the opportunity to do what we want. A woman once attended one of my workshops with a strong wish to make more money. She felt she needed more money to pursue her creative interests. Many months after completing the workshop, she shared that money had ceased to be a problem for her. She went on to say that nothing about her actual finances had changed dramatically, they simply were not an issue anymore. During the workshop, she had shifted her attention off money and onto the experience of joy and creativity in the present. As she did this, she suddenly found many opportunities opening up for her to do the creative work that she loved, and money was no longer an obstacle. Money always seemed to show up when she needed it. If she had followed the voice of fear, which insisted that she needed money before she could have what she wanted, she would probably still be plugging away at some unfulfilling job and ignoring her true creative callings.

Money is nothing in and of itself. It is only a symbolic representation of energy. If we make money our goal, without being clear about what we really want from it, we may succeed in creating more money but still not have the experience of safety, self-worth, love and joy that are our deeper desires. In fact, amassing energy without giving it a clear purpose or direction can ultimately do us more harm than good.

The inner experience we crave is always accessible to us, often much more so than we imagine, and doesn't hinge upon the manifestation of external changes. Instead of waiting to be happy until you have achieved certain external goals (as in, "I will be happy when I have more money..."), experiment with creating happiness now with the assumption that building into your life, now, the inner experience that you want is actually the quickest route to all the external outcomes that will best support this inner experience. The following is a simple exercise for clearing away nonproductive beliefs about money to find the real path to fulfillment.

Exercise: Cultivating the Inner State of Prosperity

Step One

Write down what it is that you want from money (such as, I want a new car, I want more time, I want a vacation, I want to pay all my bills, I want to start my own business, etc.).

Step Two

Identify 5 "essence experiences" related to having these things you want. An essence experience is the inner feeling you believe these things will give you. It could be, for example, security, freedom, joy, self-worth, relaxation, love, creativity, fun or power.

Step Three

Now, imagine that creating the money and other external circumstances you want begins with allowing yourself to experience the essence of what you want right now, rather than later. Start by creating within yourself the inner experiences that you seek. To do this take some quiet time, close your eyes, relax and let yourself imagine the inner feelings of safety, love, freedom or whatever you think you need money to feel. Feel the pleasure and fulfillment of it as a sensation in your body. Picture yourself having all the things you want as though it is now a part of your present reality. Tell yourself that you have already succeeded. Open to the emotions of joy and well-being that go along with having your dream.

Step Four

Do this inner work regularly and also take external action. Come up with some concrete actions that will incorporate more of the inner experiences you desire into your life now. For example, if you want money so that you can have more time for activities that you enjoy, build into your life now, even in a small way, more enjoyable activity. If you want money to give you a feeling of security, look to how you can create more experiences of emotional and physical security in your life now. Cultivate emotional security by spending time with friends or family who help you feel safe and nurtured or by joining a support group. Give attention to any small details of your life that will add to your experience of physical safety and security: check the tires on your car, start a savings account if you don't already have one, or attend to your health in some way. If you want money to be able to give yourself more luxury items and beautiful things, begin now to give yourself small things of superior quality. You don't need to live beyond your means to give yourself an expensive chocolate or a perfect flower or other item that will allow you to feel prosperous now.

Step Five

Most importantly, if you feel trapped and driven in your pursuit of money, if you deeply believe that you must have money to be safe, happy, worthy, etc., stop and recognize that money is not the problem or the solution. As with any addiction, the money addiction is a powerful one that will dull our awareness of what we truly need. Ask yourself, "What am I really afraid of? If I did not feel stuck around the issue of money, where else in my life would I feel stuck? What is it that I want even more than money?" Let the answers to these questions direct you to solutions that will truly heal and fulfill you.

The Power of Unconditional Giving

Years ago, when I was Director of the Baltimore Center for Attitudinal Healing, I plummeted to the depths of my scarcity fears. The Center reached a financial crisis point where our funding wasn't stretching to meet our needs. As Director I was the head fund-raiser and agonized over the burden of this responsibility and scarcity. I worked harder and harder to make ends meet. I whined to the Universe about the unfairness of there being insufficient funds for the work that felt like my highest calling. And, since my salary was not getting paid, I panicked and frequently lost sleep worrying.

In my clearer moments, I did a great deal of meditation and thinking about why this was happening. What was the lesson in it? My reflections led me face to face with an enormous, and previously overlooked, double standard I held about money. I thought I believed in the principles of attitudinal healing — that everything is love and that giving and receiving are the same — but I lived as though these principles did not apply to the "real" world of finances. In my meditations, I kept getting the message that if I wanted to create more of something, I needed to start giving it away unconditionally.

The specific suggestions that came from my inner guidance were to eliminate all fees for the Center's workshops, which provided the organization's only revenue, and to instead ask people to give whatever amount felt right, as a voluntary love offering rather than a mandatory fee. My guidance told me this would result in the givers prospering as well as the Center. I was also directed to tithe 10% of my personal income to whatever I felt to be my source of highest inspiration and to tithe 10% of the Center's income, as well.

At the time, this guidance was startling and frightening. It brought up a host of "rational" reasons why it wouldn't work. Yet, there was something about it that just felt right. When I presented my ideas to the Center's board of directors, I was met with even more "real world" resistance.

Somehow, though, in spite of virtually zero support for my plan, they allowed me to implement it.

What happened was truly miraculous. Not only did people who attended the Center's programs give generously even when they didn't have to, the amount of people coming for courses doubled. While some people didn't give as much as the full fee we used to charge, some people gave more, so the average per person collection remained about the same. As I gave away my own money in the form of tithes, for the first time in my life I began to receive large and unexpected gifts of money from other people. They often shared with me later that they had felt a strong inner guidance to give me the money. The gifts I gave frequently opened doors to new opportunities and linked me with people who helped me in many ways. As the Center began to give tithing gifts it, too, began to receive large donations of money.

The people who had stepped beyond their money fears in the process of giving to the Center started having equally miraculous experiences. Many shared feeling an initial discomfort with having to determine their own fee and fear when their inner guidance directed them to give a larger amount than they believed they should. But their doubts were quickly transformed into blessings. One man almost didn't attend a workshop because he had no job and felt so badly about not having anything to give. At the end, his inner guidance directed him to give an amount much larger than he could immediately pay as an unemployed person so he promised to pay it at a future date. Two days later, he found a job at a much higher salary than he had expected and was able to pay his promised gift very quickly.

Then there was a couple who attended a workshop together. Neither of them had very much money, but at the end of the workshop when they consulted their inner guidance about what to give, each received the same very large amount, which was about double the average contribution for this workshop. Neither knew what the other had come up with and when they conferred immediately after, they were horrified by the amount they had been guided to give as a couple. They debated for a few moments about what to do and finally decided to trust their initial guidance. As soon as they committed to giving, a friend of theirs who was also attending the workshop came over to them and, not knowing anything of the private debate they had just had, said his inner guidance had directed him to pay for both of them. Not only was their workshop paid for, but prosperity seemed to follow them home. Shortly thereafter, the man was given many thousands of dollars worth of equipment and grants for a community service project he was starting. The woman found ways to quit her job and pursue her creative interests full-time and found that money was no longer an obstacle to her doing what she wanted.

This principle of giving works on all levels. Whatever feels most scarce is invariably what we most need to give (and give lovingly rather than grudgingly) if we want to experience increase. The limited perspective of physical reality tells us that to have something we must hold it and not let it go. It's so easy to debate with the inner voice of guidance that urges us to give. We try to bargain and promise to give more as soon as we have more: "I will start tithing just as soon as I get out of debt," "I will start loving more just as soon as he(she) does." It is, however, just at these times of greatest poverty that we need to let go, to open our hearts and trust; to give and thereby start love and abundance flowing again.

But how does this spiritual principle of increase fit with lessons learned in therapy and codependency groups about the importance of boundaries? What if we feel empty? What if it seems that we give constantly but never receive back? Isn't it sometimes necessary to stop giving?

I believe not. Stopping the flow of giving invariably stops the flow of receiving. What is called for, rather, is to look at how we direct our giving and how we block our receiving. If we find ourselves measuring how much we give against how much is given to us, we need to measure instead how much we give to others against how much we give to ourselves. If the scales are out of balance and we find ourselves falling short, it is time to direct our flow of loving attention toward ourselves. What is it that you give so readily to others but not to yourself? Is it time, material things, pampering, respect, acceptance, love? Giving doesn't mean sacrifice. Loving doesn't mean loving others instead of yourself. As you balance the scales by making yourself the recipient of at least as much love as you give to other people, you may find that some of your outer-directed activities naturally fall away, yet you haven't stopped giving or stopped loving.

Opening the flow of giving means opening to the flow of receiving as well. No easy task for many of us who have deeply ingrained habits of denying what the Universe has to give us. Receiving doesn't simply mean saying "Yes!" to winning the lottery or to finding our perfect mate. Spirit will not give us more than we can bear to receive, and until we can tolerate the small gifts that come our way, we will not be burdened with bigger ones. So ask yourself, when someone compliments you, do you truly let it in or do you look away, make a joke and say something disparaging about yourself? When someone offers to help you, do you receive it or insist that you can manage alone? When you see a nickel in the street do you pick it up and feel richer or do you pass it by, wishing it were a $100 bill? And, when someone loves you, do you feel grateful for this most precious gift or do you retreat in fear? As you open to the power of giving, be sure that you also notice the many gifts, small and large, that are there for you everywhere and let them in.

Exercise: Becoming an Open Channel

Step One
Sit quietly in meditation and imagine yourself as an open channel, giving and receiving freely. Feel the absolute certainty that many gifts are now coming to you. You don't need to guess what form they will take. Just feel a pleasant sense of anticipation and excite-

ment. Know that whatever you most need for your happiness and well-being is now on its way. Imagine yourself "stretching open" to receive all of these wonderful gifts.

Step Two
This is the more important part of the exercise: For the next 24 hours, recognize all the gifts that come to you and receive them fully. Keep a written account of these. Receive each gift as gratefully and openly as you can, letting go of any of your usual methods of deflecting God's gifts to you.

Exercise: Giving and Receiving

This is a gift-giving ritual best done with six or more other people. It makes a good alternative to Christmas present giving for those who are tired of holiday materialism and the shopping rat race. I have also known people to do this ritual on their birthday for a different kind of giving experience.

Step One
Prior to meeting, each of you is to choose something of yours that is of great value to you, and that you are willing to release unconditionally as an experiment in giving. This thing may or may not have great material value. It may or may not be something you think would be of value to someone else. The important point here is that it's something precious to you, something that is not easily replaceable, something that feels like a "stretch" to release. Wrap it up as a gift and include a note with it saying a bit about why it's important to you.

Step Two

Come together in a circle with your gifts and begin your giving rit-ual with some quiet meditation time to relax and open to the flow of Universal Abundance. As people feel "open," they place their gifts in the center of the circle, releasing them unconditionally as gifts of love.

Step Three

Next, one person (or several people if the group is large) volunteers to act as the spirit of Universal Abundance by distributing the gifts in whatever random fashion feels right. There are no rules about how this should be done. It is only important to keep in mind that it can't be done "wrong." Before beginning the distribution, this person is to tell everyone, "Trust that whatever you receive will be the perfect gift for you, and this gift will hold a message about what you need to incorporate into your life for your highest good at this time." Trust in the synchronicity of this experience and assume there is some divine order at work even if someone gets their own gift back or if someone winds up with more that one gift while another receives none. Sometimes the absence of a material gift can be an important message about the need to live empty for a while or to look at scarcity beliefs that expect life to be about los-ing rather than gaining. Do the distribution and unwrapping of gifts in silence.

Step Four

When everyone has received and unwrapped their gift, take some time to share with one another anything that feels important about the gift you received, the message it holds for you and the whole process of giving and receiving.

Often, when we are in the grip of fear over financial scarcity, what we feel most inclined to do is exactly what will make the problem worse. When we are afraid, our first instinct is to freeze. When we freeze, we stop the flow of energy within us, physically, emotionally and spiritually. Our bodies become stiff and rigid (people frequently develop back pain and other ailments during times of money fear). We become less able to give and receive love and tend to feel more separate and alone, cutting ourselves off from sources of help. We close off to inner guidance and fail to see creative solutions. Consequently, we feel at the mercy of our lives instead of recognizing that we are the creators of them. All of this has a powerful impact upon our flow of money. Fear becomes a downward spiral that leads us to create our worst expectations. The following suggestions will help reopen the flow of healing, inspiration, assistance and money when fear begins to take hold.

Steps for Opening the Flow of Prosperity
I. Imagine

It has already been stressed that imagination is one of our most powerful creative tools. What we can't or won't imagine, we have difficulty creating, so let yourself dream! You are creating every moment. Instead of imagining all that you don't have, focus your imagination toward your prosperity in the following directions:

Imagine Safety. Take some deep breaths. Continuously remind yourself to relax and breathe. Affirm that you are safe and that you create your safety from within. Many times a day, stop and allow a feeling of relaxation and well-being to wash over you. Imagine that there is a Universal Source of Plenty that is ready to support your highest good as soon as you relax and let it.

Imagine Your Heart's Desire. What are your deepest heart's desires? Ask yourself what you want money for. Be specific and detailed. Write it all down and then imagine how it feels to already have these things. Fill yourself up with the good feelings of already having your heart's desire. You may find that what you long for the most has nothing to do with money. As you clarify what's really important, you may find money problems miraculously disappearing. Practice imagining your heart's desires regularly and update your list as needed.

Imagine Prosperity. Imagine that you are already prosperous. Imagine where you would live, what you would do, what kind of car you would drive, food you would eat, vacations you would take, clothes you would wear, etc. Go to expensive stores and decide what you would buy. Drive or walk through expensive neighborhoods and pick out "your" house. Imagine what you would create with your money and how you would serve others. Research charities and decide which ones you would give to. Practice thinking like a prosperous person.

II. Let Go

An abundance of mental, emotional and material clutter all take up space, making less room for what we truly want. An important part of opening the flow of prosperity involves making space for it by letting go of anything that is being held from a place of fear rather than love. Do some letting go in the following ways:

Clean House. Let go of clutter, excess and anything unwanted. Clean your living space, your working space or your car. Clean a closet, take out the garbage, empty out your purse or wallet, and as you do, imagine that you are making space for what you most want.

Change Your Thoughts. Let go of talking and thinking about poverty. Don't forget, what you think is what you create. Let go of thoughts and statements like, "I can't afford it." Let go of poverty as an excuse. Let go of poverty as an identity.

Surrender. Let go of trying to control everything. If you try too hard to do everything yourself, you will eventually break down and feel unable to do anything. Learn to ask for help before you get to that point. Let go of needing to be right. Surrender to a Higher Power and allow your Higher Self to take charge.

Live in the Present. Let go of the past and the future. We are creating our prosperity now by the thoughts we are choosing to think and the way we are choosing to live *in this moment.* Change begins *now!* Make the most of it.

Release Anger. Anger and resentment stop the flow of money in your life very quickly! Release anger from your body by finding a safe place to scream and beat on something. Release resentful and judgmental thoughts (toward yourself and others) by choosing to stop them as they arise and replacing them with a positive affirmation (such as, "I now choose compassion toward myself and others.") Work on forgiveness.

Pay Your Bills. Let go of money. Pay bills promptly and gratefully. Look at every bill as a reminder that you have received something. Never let a bill go unpaid. Energetically, stopping payment tends to freeze your incoming flow of money as well, so that while you may be spending less, you find yourself with less and less to spend. As you break promises, you set in motion the likelihood that you will also find yourself on the receiving end of broken promises, financially or in other areas of your life. As you break commitments, you disempower yourself and affirm your role as a victim rather than a creator. Declaring bankruptcy or otherwise refusing to pay bills isn't an easy out. Energetically, it leaves much unfinished business that will find you again one way or another. Once you shift your state of mind, you will actually find it less of a struggle to "clean up your act" and increase you financial in-flow than it is to walk away from a money mess. The following suggestions are helpful when bills feel out of control:

1. Rather than looking at what you can't pay and becoming overwhelmed, ask yourself what you can pay and give this amount regularly. When bills seem overwhelming, imagine that you are the Limitless Source of Spirit and your creditors are you. Imagine that you are establishing the kind of relationship with your creditors that you want the Limitless Source to have with you. In other words, if it feels that the that the Limitless Source has stopped delivering prosperity to you, begin to open the flow by paying your debts in the way you would like this Source to pay you. Begin with regularity. If you don't want Spirit to give to you in unpredictable fits and starts, begin a routine that establishes trust and good faith with your creditors. As you begin to make even small, regular payments, you are likely to find the incoming flow beginning to increase as well. As this happens, you can increase the amount of your regular payments to creditors, just as you want the Limitless Source to continue to increase payments to you.

   If you feel burdened or victimized by financial commitments that you wish you hadn't made, find ways to transform the burden of these so they work for you rather than against you. Turn paying your bills into a symbolic act by giving it a deeper significance, as in the preceding paragraph. For more on symbolic acts, see the last exercise in Chapter Two, "Using the Power of Commitment." Know that your finances can and will change the moment you change inwardly. As you stop feeling resentful, fearful and victimized, your outer circumstances will no longer burden you.

2. To strengthen your power of prosperity, starting now, keep the commitments you make and make only commitments you are willing to keep. If you feel that you have made unwise financial decisions in the past, take a look at how you make commitments and think carefully before choosing to spend your money. Ask yourself, do you need to say no more often? Do you spend money to avoid your feelings? (When you're depressed, do you go to the mall?) Do you spend to impress others or to get love? Do you spend just to get rid of your money because you don't feel worthy of prosperity? If your spending feels out of control, make a practice with each purchase of asking yourself, "Is this something that is really important to me? Am I using my money to enhance the quality of my life?" If you can't answer yes to this question, don't buy it. See if the way you spend your money is similar to the way you spend your energy in other contexts and make any changes needed to avoid wasting your energy.

3. Regularly visualize your bills being paid in full. Do this at least as often as you pay bills. Imagine writing a final check to all creditors with the words "Paid in full" on each one. Picture a surplus of money still in your account.

III. Receive

Spirit will only give to us as much as we are willing to receive. As you create the intention to receive greater prosperity in your life and make space for it by letting go, you *will* begin to attract gifts on many levels. Now comes the challenge to overcome learned patterns of fear, unworthiness, doubt or guilt that prevent you from receiving your highest good. If you reject gifts that begin to come your way, you strengthen these old thoughts that tell you

you're unworthy or that the gifts are unworthy or that nothing good can last or that you shouldn't take more than your "share," etc. Stretch open to receive, not only the big gifts that you have asked for, but also the smaller, less obvious gifts that you didn't even know you wanted. As you allow in the small gifts, you create the readiness for larger and larger gifts.

Receive Gifts. Look for gifts everywhere. The more you look, the more you will find. Eliminate statements like, "You shouldn't have," "I can't accept that," "You don't need to," "I can do it myself," "I don't really need it," and replace them with, "Thank you!".

Receive Compliments. Pay attention any time someone gives you a compliment of any sort. Listen to it, take it in and imagine that your willingness to receive this gift appreciatively is making you magnetic to prosperity.

Receive Help. If you are not accustomed to asking for and receiving help, you may be stuck in a pattern of trying to do everything yourself until your affairs are near a point of collapse. Then when you finally reach out for assistance, it is a desperate plea to be rescued. Since most people say no or give grudgingly to such extreme requests, every time you do ask for help, experience confirms your belief that you can't get it.

To start, learn to differentiate between help and rescuing. For example, asking a creditor for extra time to make a payment is a request for help. Expecting to be released from all financial responsibility is asking to be rescued. Learn to ask for help before you become desperate for it. You can ask for help just because you want it. You don't have to be in dire need to deserve assistance.

Learn to appreciate help in the form it is given. People may not be willing or able to give you exactly what you want the way you want it, but they still may have something of value they are willing and able to give. Let go of an "all or nothing" stance so that you don't deny yourself potential gifts and assistance.

Receive Love. Let love flow in your life. Love makes you magnetic to financial prosperity as well as all other forms of good. How we let money flow and how we let love flow are often very similar. To discover how deeply love and money are connected for you, try the following exercise:

1. Write down 5 assumptions you learned about money as a child.
2. Next, write down 5 assumptions you hold about money now.
3. Go over your list and replace the word or concept of money with the word or concept of love. See how much of it still holds truth for you.

Receive Money. Learn to receive gratefully and deservingly gifts of money that come your way. This includes everything from gifts of financial support from friends or relatives to saying "Yes!" when a friend offers to buy you lunch to stopping and picking up a penny you see on the sidewalk. Acknowledge each gift as a sign of bigger gifts to come.

IV. Give Unconditionally

Giving unconditionally means living from a belief in our abundance. It means trusting that there is so much for us that we are willing to share what we have unconditionally with others. Unconditional giving is when the act of giving is its own joy and we do not need anything back to feel fulfilled. When we give unconditionally, we always receive back, often in surprising ways that surpass our expectations. Unconditional giving truly connects us to the miraculous. However, the moment we begin to give with the agenda of God rewarding us for our good deeds, our giving is no longer unconditional and we don't attract the same abundance back. It is the *joy* of giving, not the *act* of giving that makes us magnetic to our highest good.

Give Thanks, regularly and often. Pay more attention to what you have than what you lack and give thanks. Give thanks for other people's prosperity and good fortune because they show you what you can have, do or become. Rather than feeling jealous of what someone else has, see that person as a role model and know that if he or she can have it, so can you! Give thanks for your bills. Each bill reflects something you wanted and received. Speak your gratitude out loud. Share more of your blessings than your complaints.

Give to Yourself. First of all, give yourself your own self-acceptance and love. Recognize that you are exactly where you need to be, doing exactly what you need to be doing, and that you have done your life exactly right. The more you accept and honor where you've been and who you are right now, the more you expand the possibilities for who you can become in the future.

Also give to yourself materially and in all the ways you give to other people. This is especially important if you tend to be a big giver but have difficulty receiving from others or caring for yourself. Give yourself time, give yourself attention, give yourself gifts. Put aside a percentage of your money to be used purely for personal enjoyment.

Give Unconditionally to Others. Give as much of your time, energy and material resources as you can give joyfully and unconditionally. The minute you have conditions and expectations attached to your gift, it's no longer a gift (it's a "sale." Stop giving your time, energy and material resources *before* you reach the point of resentment and burn out.

Give love without limit. As we let love flow unconditionally, we release blocks on other levels as well. It's important to note that conditional love (that is, "I'll love you as long as you love me back in equal measure") does not open the flow of prosperity because it is rooted in fear and holding on.

Truly, love is the only real gift we have to give and giving it does not require words, actions, energy, time or material resources. Love is an inner experience that is always healing to the giver and the receiver. When you feel it, it has already been given and received. Recognize that sometimes you need to do less to feel love more. If you feel burned out, or that your boundaries have been violated, or that your actions and material gifts have not been appreciated, you will be less able to love. Sometimes you may need to step back from the actions of giving to reconnect with the true essence of giving, which is the inner experience of unconditional love.

Give Toward a Higher Good. No matter how small or large your income, allocate a percentage to give to the individuals or groups you derive your greatest spiritual inspiration from. Giving 10% of all you receive is an ancient tradition called "tithing" and, if practiced as an unconditional spiritual act, is as beneficial to the prosperity of the giver as to the religious institutions that are the usual recipients of tithes. Unconditional tithing helps to keep money flowing in your life.

Along with your money, find ways to give of your time, energy and other resources to help others. This could be as structured as volunteer service for an organization or as simple as practicing daily random acts of kindness as you go about your life. Give only as much as you can give joyfully, without expectations, regret or resentment.

7

"There is no death.
God made not death.
Whatever form it takes must therefore be an illusion....
And it is given to us to look past death, and see the life beyond."

—*A Course in Miracles*

Recognizing We Are More

*We are more than our physical body — we are spiritual beings.
Therefore, we don't need to be afraid of death, separation and illness.*

Evidence of an Eternal Spirit

While world religions have always taught the existence of an eternal essence, increasingly scientists and researchers are directing attention to these mysteries as well. The study of near-death experiences offers some of the most compelling evidence that consciousness exists separate from the body and that there is something beyond physical life as we know it. In *Life after Life* Raymond Moody, M.D. published a remarkable collection of stories from people who had gone to the brink of death and returned to tell experiences of leaving their bodies, being immersed in dazzling light, and having profound experiences of well-being and transcendence. People who had these experiences emerged with a deep faith in the continuity of life beyond the physical body. What's more, their many different stories described a similar experience, which Dr. Moody believes is the experience we all have at the point of death.

As mentioned in Chapter Four, Melvin Morse, M.D. continued this line of investigation begun by Moody and became the first person to conduct scientifically valid research on near-death experiences (NDE's). Working with children, who are less steeped in the religious images of our culture, Dr. Morse observed that children's NDE's have the same predictable elements as adults'. He was also able to prove that people must be on the brink of death to have an NDE, ascertaining that these powerful experiences of transcendence and light are, in fact, triggered by imminent death, and are not merely symptoms of heavy medication, oxygen depletion or serious but nonlife-threatening illness.

Morse identifies the "Light" as being the core of the near-death-experience. He says, "Although many of the NDE elements can be explained by our knowledge of the way the brain works, the one that remains a true mystery is the experience of light." In his research he was able to identify a specific part of the brain responsible for things experienced during an NDE and other paranormal experiences. But, he says, "The experience of the light has no known origin in the brain." He has come to believe that the Light is actually located outside of the physical body — something not of our own making, but something we return to. He concludes, "I would like to believe that the Light is where we go when we die. Like a birth into a bright new world, the Light of the NDE represents the beginning of a new beginning." Increasingly, evidence is mounting that human consciousness is not limited to the physical body and that there is a powerful and awesome reality that exists beyond what we know through our physical senses.

This essential spiritual truth — that we are something bigger than our biology, more than our thoughts, emotions and history, something that can't be harmed by the destruction of our physical body — is at the root of virtually every spiritual tradition, yet is one that we have great difficulty believing and living by. If we truly believed in our eternal nature, there could be no tragedy because we would know that we couldn't be harmed. There would be no victims or victimizers because by definition of who we are we could not abuse or be abused by another. We would not live in fear of death because we would know we are eternal.

As we become less identified with our physical body, our perspective of reality shifts dramatically. Life takes on a new purpose. No longer is it about surviving because we know that we are eternal. It is less about reaching an outcome because we are not so pressured by the passage of time. As we focus less on our destination, we become free to live in the moment and enjoy the ride. The journey becomes a process of discovery and learning. Life as we know it begins to look more like a classroom with lessons and opportunities that allow us to see the consequences of our choices. Death is no longer the ultimate fear and physical illness and other life-changing events become learning experiences rather than tragedies.

Transforming Physical Illness

To address the topic of physical illness from the perspective of our spiritual power it is, first of all, necessary to arrive at a definition of healing that encompasses more than physical reality. If there is more to us and more to reality than what we can perceive with our limited physical senses, then healing must be something more than the alleviation of physical symptoms. From the perspective of spiritual reality, healing has more to do with a paradigm shift, a change in consciousness. True healing occurs when we shift our sense of self-identification from the pain and vulnerability of our physical body to our Spiritual Self that is beyond harm. This is a shift from fear to inner peace. Often, physical healing will naturally result from this change in consciousness because the symptoms are no longer needed. But once this shift has occurred, physical healing or the absence of it becomes inconsequential. Death or physical symptoms are no longer something to be fought and avoided at all costs because our Spiritual Self has transcended the fragile impermanence of the physical body.

Illness results when we fight the flow of our highest good and highest purpose. It helps us to become aware of this fight going on within and forces us to redirect our lives. Since illness helps us to meet some need we haven't found another way to address, it won't go away until we find another way to get that need met. True healing means that we have come into alignment with our highest good and highest path. If we address the symptoms of an illness without supporting this realignment, true healing has not happened and we will probably not be able to sustain a state of physical health for long. We will need to manifest some new event to help us continue the deeper process of realignment that we need spiritually.

There are many proponents of mind-body healing who hold that we are responsible for the health or illness of our physical body only to a point and then heredity, circumstance and environmental factors kick in. This view of illness is a picture limited by the narrow frame of physical reality. As long as we are primarily identified with our physical body and the limited reality presented to us by our physical senses, we naturally see illness as the enemy because it threatens our very existence. As long as we define illness as bad, to accept personal responsibility for creating our physical circumstances, it follows that we must have done something wrong to become ill. Or, if we have done everything "right" in terms of taking care of our health and we're still sick, we must have somehow failed at healing.

Remember, "responsibility" is not the same as "control." We can only control those aspects of self that are within the range of our conscious awareness. Illness is often the way we bring something unconscious into view. This is, perhaps, one of its most important functions.

Rather than seeing illness as an indication that we have failed in our efforts to be responsible for our health, it is more useful to see it as a sign of our readiness to bring some heretofore hidden and nonintegrated aspect of self into awareness. At the level of spiritual reality, illness is a step toward wholeness. No one consciously chooses pain or illness, yet the experience of dealing with these challenges can lead us on a journey that ultimately delivers gifts and blessings. I have heard numerous people with cancer and other life threatening diseases describe their illness as one of the greatest blessings of their lives because it forced them to completely reshuffle priorities and pursue new paths that brought profound fulfillment. The illness gave them permission to explore options they would not have allowed themselves to consider otherwise.

Quite simply, illness signals our inner readiness for change, though not necessarily a conscious desire for change. The "self" that chooses illness is rarely the small part of self that fits into our conscious awareness. What chooses illness is the "Self" — with a capital S — the Spiritual Self that sees our highest good from an expanded paradigm that our limited conscious perceptions may not be able to fathom. Illness generally comes about when our life choices are not in alignment with our highest good and the parameters of our lives have become too small to accommodate growth.

When we get sick, change comes about through our willingly choosing new priorities and life styles. Or, if we resist change, the illness forces us, against our personal will, to submit to a life circumscribed by the symptoms of illness. Either way, our lives change dramatically. We may feel empowered by these changes or we may feel victimized by them, depending upon whether we let the experience of illness lead us somewhere or force it to push us into our next step. Even death can be viewed as a transition out of a state of being that we have outgrown.

However, there is no simple mind-body cookbook explanation that can be applied to every illness. There may be profound spiritual purposes to illness that are not readily visible. For example, my friend Cheryl, who was born with a crippling degenerative disease was occasionally accosted by over-eager healers who told her that if she only had enough faith, she could heal. She took offense at this, primarily because these individuals assumed that just because she lived life in a wheelchair and in a deformed body that she was not "healed." Cheryl believed very strongly that there was an important spiritual purpose to her physical disability — that her life lesson was not to change her physical body but to love life in spite of any pain and limitation her body created. A believer in reincarnation, she felt certain that she had committed suicide in a previous life and had "chosen" her current situation to help her learn to love life no matter what. By the end of her life, she unquestionably did.

In coming to an understanding of why we are sick, instead of rushing quickly to a neat and tidy theory about what an illness means, it is perhaps enough, at first, to simply trust that there is meaning, maybe many levels of meaning. While the next pages offer some insight into the "language" of physical symptoms, keep in mind that a dis-ease often speaks to us on many levels at once. Be mindful not to latch on to one explanation to the exclusion of all others. Keep listening and opening, letting the messages of your body take you deeper into Self understanding.

Illness as a Metaphor

Illness communicates to us in a language filled with obvious metaphors. If we are willing to listen, our physical symptoms can tell us a great deal about our needs, imbalances and our path of healing. The very metaphors we use in speaking often mirror the physical symptoms our body manifests. I became especially aware of this during my time with the Baltimore Center for Attitudinal Healing when I worked with people dealing with chronic and life-challenging illnesses. I noticed that people's pet expressions had a way of literally describing their illness. A woman with cancerous tumors in her leg frequently used the expression, "I can't stand it!" Someone with food allergies continually said, "I can't stomach it!" and a woman with skin cancer spoke of things "getting under her skin." (As I shared these examples in a workshop once, a woman spoke up and said, "I have difficulty receiving from people, and I just realized that my favorite expression is, 'I can't take it!'".)

To understand the language of your physical symptoms, consider the metaphorical meanings of the affected body parts and functions. For example, hands are for handling things. If you have pain in your hands ask yourself: Are you are holding on too tightly in some way? Are you trying to "handle" everything yourself? Do you have difficulty "reaching out" for love and support? Are you having difficulty "grasping" something? If your neck and shoulders hurt are you "shouldering" more than your share of responsibility? Are you being "stiff-necked," and overly rigid in how you are seeing things? If you are a woman with tumors or pain in your breasts, have you been suckling the world until there is nothing left for you? Do you feel in need of nurturing? Do you feel in some way inadequate about yourself as a woman? If you have heart problems, have you felt "heartbroken"? Have you closed your heart to warmth and love? Have you lost your joy and passion for life?

A woman in one of my workshops once could not see any link between the back injury she sustained in a car accident and her emotional needs until I asked how easy or difficult it was for her to feel supported in life and to allow others to support her. (Our spine is what provides "support".) She admitted that receiving support had always been extremely difficult for her. As a result of the injury, however, her life changed to included a regular routine of numerous types of therapy by caring professionals whose sole agenda was to "support" her.

Exercise: Working with Illness

The following exercise can help you understand the messages your body is sending through your physical symptoms. You will probably find that more information and insight come to you if you do this exercise in writing. Even more effective is to do it with one or several other people, sharing each question out loud and giving each other feedback and added input. Often the messages in our physical symptoms remain stubbornly invisible to us while they are glaringly obvious to an objective observer. Another viewpoint can be invaluable in bringing some of these dynamics to light.

Step One

Where in your body do you manifest physical symptoms? What chronic or recurring physical conditions do you have?

Step Two

What are all the physical functions of this part of the body and what metaphors come to mind related to these functions? Let these metaphors give you some insight into the emotional dynamics underlying the condition.

Step Three

Next, ask yourself how this condition is serving you. What is it helping you, allowing you, or forcing you to do, be or have that you wouldn't otherwise experience? Write down everything that comes to mind, even the things that you wouldn't define as positive. Specifically:

1. Is it forcing you to let others help you?

2. Is it causing you to spend your time differently?

3. Are you receiving attention (positive or negative) that you wouldn't otherwise get?

4. Are you developing strengths and resources that you didn't know you had?

5. Is it preserving a familiar identity?

6. It is allowing you to put off doing something that is burdensome or frightening?

7. Is it protecting you from failing by preventing you from beginning something?

8. Does it give you permission to say "No," to get angry, to be selfish, to grieve?

9. Have your relationships with others changed in any significant way as a consequence of your illness? Have they deepened? Has your illness created "space" interpersonally: fewer relationships, more privacy or more time alone?

Step Four

Review the information you've gathered so far and explore what secondary gains this physical condition is offering you.

Step Five

What would you need to do to receive the secondary gains without needing the physical condition? The true answer to this question invariably involves some degree of risk and stretching beyond your comfort zone. Keep exploring this question until you find where the risk is for you. This is where the greatest healing lies.

For example, I did this exercise with a woman who had breast cancer. For her, the secondary gains of her illness involved putting herself first for once. As an assignment I suggested she invite a group of her friends to form a healing committee for her. This committee would support her recovery in many different ways including practical assistance, prayer and emotional support. I suggested she make and distribute a wish list of a variety of ways her friends could help her. She was comfortable with all of these suggestions until I added that she ask her friends if they would be willing to continue to support her in this way if she released her illness. She could justify deserving so much attention when she was fighting for her life but she had difficulty feeling worthy of this much support without the illness. This last step was where the biggest risk lay, and also the biggest healing. To truly be ready to heal it is essential that we be willing to do whatever our illness motivates us to do without needing our symptoms to force us there.

Step Six
Create and act on a plan of things you are willing to do to give yourself the gains without the pain of your illness. Come up with at least three things you are willing to do without having to have illness as a motivator.

Healing with a Life-threatening Illness

In the event of a life-threatening illness we usually start with the question, "How can I get well?" Yet, if we redefine illness as an opportunity to change, a more useful line of questioning might be "Why do I want to get well? What do I have to live for? Do I feel complete with my life as it stands? If not, what is there left for me to do?" Wishing for physical healing because we are afraid of the alternative as in, "I want to get well because I am afraid to die" is not a healing frame of mind. Having witnessed a number of people in their final months, I believe that this attitude contributes to long lingering illnesses in people who are afraid to let go, yet have no reason to keep living.

Healing begins when we find our passion and purpose for living, when we complete whatever is unfinished, and when we begin to embrace the joy in each moment. The form healing takes may or may not include physical healing. When we pursue healing in this way, the outcome of the disease becomes less important. True healing brings a profound sense of peace to the transition of death or it speeds up the physical healing process, whichever best serves our highest good.

Preventive Health Care

I have often asked people what they would do if a chronic health condition became life-threatening. Without giving it much thought, many people can come up with a whole plan of major life changes, such as finally leaving a relationship that isn't working or a job that they don't like, taking time for projects or self-care that always gets back-burnered, or spending more time with family and loved ones. Clearly these are changes the person has been wanting to make for some time but under normal circumstances does not feel permission to implement.

What would you do if you were diagnosed with a life-threatening illness? If you find that you quickly and easily come up with a plan of changes that you have been wanting to make but have been putting off for one reason or another, you may be unconsciously setting the stage for a health crisis to enter your life to give you permission to change. The wider the gap between the life we are currently living and the life we would create if we knew we were seriously ill, the more we "need" illness to help us grow. Practice preventive health care by finding ways to implement your illness plan now instead of waiting for a crisis to give you permission. If this plan necessitates difficult choices, ask yourself would you do it if your life depended upon it? And act as if it truly does.

Illness and Children

Why do children get sick? Do the same principles apply? With children there is often a deep spiritual agreement between family members that is being enacted. While it may seem tragic for a child to become sick and die, if we look at this situation from a spiritual perspective, there may be many lessons and gifts that each family member is receiving through such a profound, life-changing experience. These lessons may not ever be apparent to an observer. A child who dies may be a highly evolved being who wants to engage with and influence a group of souls on a physical level but would not be served by a longer life in this physical reality. Elizabeth Kubler Ross noticed in her work with dying children that their spiritual development is far greater than that of healthy children.

Another way to view childhood illness is in terms of family dynamics. We know that children act out behaviorally to protect the family — they create a disturbance to take the parents attention away from their own problems and force them into alliance around solving the child's problem. A child's illness may serve the same purpose. While there may be many complex levels of meaning and purpose with no simple explanation, we can trust that even in the case of children there is some divine order in place when illness is present.

Moving Beyond the Illusion of Death

Many of us live in constant fear of endings. We cling to what is no longer serving us because we are afraid of the unknown and of living empty. We worry about loss that will turn our lives upside down and we resist change that forces growth and ultimately renewal. Most of all, we fear death. Even if we rarely give the subject a thought, the reality of this absolute ending and ultimate loss of control is always with us, affecting how we go about life. Deepak Chopra suggests that, "All fear is ultimately the fear of mortality in disguise — the fear of change."

The more we identify with the vulnerability of our physical bodies, the more fearful death becomes. We are bombarded by images of death on the news, in movies and TV, so much so that we become desensitized to the horror of violence. Yet amidst so much death, many of us give little thought to the meaning of this transition. We are both morbidly curious and in denial about it.

As I browsed through a bookstore shelf in the "death and dying" section once, I was struck by how many titles included the words grief, grieving, loss, surviving, coping. Words like "wonder" or "celebrating" were nowhere to be found. The very titles of these books seemed to shout out the pain and heaviness with which our culture shrouds the final stage of life. In many other cultures there is much more to death than grieving, coping and loss. People of other places and other times have been more open to seeing death as a transition to another phase of living and have felt enriched by their ongoing ties to the ancestors who preceded them to the next world.

In our culture, however, we have, to a large extent, turned to science as our religion of choice. We have had no sustaining vision of after-life because science, until very recently, has not offered us one. This makes death simply the end, the enemy, the ultimate force beyond the control of science. Consequently, death has become our greatest shadow. We fight it, fear it and often just deny it as long as possible. We keep it in the dark.

Yet there is a shift happening. Starting with the ground breaking work of Elizabeth Kubler Ross, M.D. in the 60s, we have, over the last few decades, started to bring death out the realm of taboo. We are more willing to think about it, talk about it, face it. We are learning how to assist the dying with greater compassion and honesty. As the titles in bookstores suggest, we are learning how to grieve.

A more recent and exciting trend in our coming to grips with death, is our growing fascination with "The Light." Again, a trip to the bookstore or library reveals such titles as *Transformed by the Light, Embraced by the Light, Saved by the Light,* all books describing experiences of people who have glimpsed "Light" after death and lived to tell about it.

Physics is showing us that at its most fundamental level, all matter is made of light. Those who experience the Light directly hold it synonymous with unconditional love. This is the substance of the universe — awesome, powerful, transforming — that our physical senses are blind to, yet is always there to heal and empower us. The brink of death frees us from our physical limitations and we become aware of our true nature. It is no new idea to think of birth as a connection to the miraculous. Many are transported out of mundane reality to a place of innocence and faith through the birth of a child. Death offers us an equally potent portal. Just as there is a shining of Light through the doorway of birth, we are now learning that the doorway of death holds just as much opportunity.

The experience of death, facing our own or dealing with the deaths of others, challenges us to step beyond all of the illusions of physical reality or else succumb to the pain, limitation and victimization of this paradigm. It challenges us to define ourselves as something more than flesh that dies. It confronts us with the ultimate loss of control so that we must either recognize that there is a divine order to death and that it is safe to surrender to this final transition, or else we go out as victims of a random and all-powerful force. Death challenges us to recognize the eternal nature of love and the reality of Oneness that transcends physical separation. Otherwise we are faced with countless heartbreaks that make love seem limited and futile. To the extent that we identify with our physical body we must fear death, and as we fear death, we cannot fully live in the present or use our power fully. To understand the impact of this, stop for a moment and imagine the following:

Exercise: Examining Beliefs about Death

Regardless of what you think about death, imagine for a moment what it feels like to believe beyond a shadow of a doubt that your existence will end totally with the death of your physical body. Everything that is precious to you will be gone, everyone who is precious to you will be gone, there will be no more love, no joy, no consciousness, nothing.... How does this way of looking at death affect your experience of life in the moment?

Imagine yourself getting older and watching your body age. What does it feel like to imagine your own aging process when you believe that your existence ends with your body? What would it be like for you if you were to contract a serious illness? And how does it feel as you imagine yourself coming in contact with someone else who is dying? As you imagine life from this perspective, how does your body feel? Where in your body do you feel tension or relaxation, comfort or discomfort? Close your eyes for a moment and imagine these things before going on to the next paragraphs.

Now, take a couple of deep breaths and release that view of reality.... Imagine this time, how it feels to believe beyond a shadow of a doubt that there is an essence within you that is not your physical body and can never be harmed. Imagine that this essence consists of only the loving, peaceful aspects of what you think of as your "self." Also imagine that this essence is your source of wisdom, understanding and joy. Feel what your life would be like if you truly believed that no matter what happens, the part of you that experiences love, peace and well-being could never be taken away....

Imagine how you now go through life with this belief. See yourself growing older and imagine what the experience is like when you know that you can't be harmed. How would you deal with the experience of a life-threatening illness? How does it feel to be with someone who is seriously ill or dying, knowing that the essence of this person is eternal and beyond harm, and that the loving relationship that exists between you is also eternal? How does your body feel as you look at life this way? Close your eyes for a moment and imagine life from this perspective....

Now take some time to reflect on the differences in these two ways of living life. Were you able to feel the pain and burden that the first perspective adds to life? And, how much energy it saps? This is what many of us carry around all the time, dimming our passion for life, our ability to feel joy, draining our physical health.

The growing body of research of people who have had near-death experiences offers not only powerful evidence for the existence of life beyond the physical reality, but also a model for how life can be lived when we are free of our fear-based identification with the body. In his study of adults who had experienced an NDE in childhood, Melvin Morse discovered that these people who had powerfully experienced themselves as more than their physical body have virtually no death anxiety, less depression, more sense of purpose and a greater zest for life than the general public. They also have more paranormal experiences, that is, their perception is not limited by their physical senses and physical body. They use more of their spiritual power.

As we are released from the fear of death, we begin to live more passionately in the moment. Psychologist Susan Blackmore, another NDE researcher, suggests that the NDE allows people to let go of a "false sense of self." She adds, "With this insight, fear is left behind and life can be lived more directly and fully."

Yet it takes more than simply ascribing to a spiritual philosophy to change our deepest beliefs about who we are. In his testing of control groups, Morse found that even "people who identify themselves as being intensely spiritual, have the same death anxiety as the general population." Even those of us who consider ourselves "believers" may still have a fear-based identification with our physical bodies that doesn't change in spite of our spiritual philosophy. Intellectual insight doesn't seem to be enough to shake off the grip of death fear.

But neither is it necessary to have a near-death experience to finally be free to live. There are many ways to experience the reality of life beyond the illusion of death: by listening with an open mind and heart to the visions and inner journeys of loved ones who are dying; by trusting our own visions and intuitions, by inviting messages and ongoing communication with those who have crossed over; and ultimately, by actively creating our own death experience through the way we choose to live life. It is not enough to have a doctrine of belief. The reality of life beyond death needs to be known in the heart, not just the mind, to give us the advantages of enhanced power, health and zest for life. As you read the stories and practice the exercises in this chapter, let them lead your heart past the fear of death into the mystery that lies beyond what our mind alone can understand.

Death and the Fear of Losing Control

Many of us fear terrible, painful deaths that we will have no control over. Perhaps one of the most fearsome aspects of death is that it can plunge us into pain or disability beyond our capacity to bear.

But the more acquainted I become with people at the end of their lives, the more I believe that we tend to die in much the same way as we have lived, according to our temperament and beliefs and much more in control of the process than we may know. Perhaps the suffering of death is more the result of our fear and struggle against the ultimate loss of control than a random cruel blow of fate.

Working as Director of a Center for Attitudinal Healing, I witnessed many people's final months of life. I noticed that the people who experienced the most pain and suffering were those who were filled with fear and bitterness. They were people who had been stuck between not wanting to live and not wanting to die before the onset of their illness, and their dying process reflected the same dilemma. I remember Emily, a woman filled with anger at her life, cancer being just one more reason for deep disappointment. Her ending months were spent in the hospital in pain and rage. Her rage became so difficult to be around that her family could barely tend her. Her illness stretched out longer and longer, past her doctor's prognosis. She just wouldn't die, until finally, in her very last days, she reached a place of peace. Her anger left her. She was no longer afraid or in pain, she was able to say good-bye to her family with love and soon she peacefully died.

I have come to believe that death is much more than just the necessary end to life. It is a powerful learning time when we have an opportunity to resolve and complete the deepest lessons of our lives. My close friend, Cheryl, who died in her thirties from a life-long degenerative disease, feared dying for most of her life because the course of her illness left people progressively more disabled and in pain. For many years, she held a suicide plan for taking her own life before she became too disabled to do so. She never resorted to this plan, however, even though her disease did cause increasing pain and disability, because she stopped fighting the pain. Instead of trying to control death from a place of fear, she allowed its mystery to unfold, trusting herself, trusting death. Toward the end she had many experiences of leaving her body and meeting with spiritual beings who gave her encouragement and instruction. She had many deepening experiences of love with the people in her life. She found that, in spite of growing pain and physical disability, she loved life more with every passing day. She once reflected in horror that her fear of pain and of the unknown had almost compelled her to end her life prematurely, denying her this richest time of all.

The more we fear being out of control, the more we enter into death as a victim. The push for the "right to die" saddens me because it seems to assume that dying is a terrible senseless thing so it's better to beat death to the punch and never have to look into our darkest fears. The more we tidy up death by making suicide an acceptable and readily available option, the less opportunity we will have to learn life's last and most powerful lesson: that there is nothing to fear.

As we acknowledge our power as creators of our experience in life, we must recognize the perfect order and rightness to the endings we "choose" even when they are long and disabling. Allen, the father of a friend of mine, worked hard throughout his life. He supported five children and devoted himself to a company that did not reciprocate his loyalty, firing him when he was nearing retirement age and had been "used up." Shortly into retirement, Allen developed Alzheimer's disease and became incapacitated to the point that his middle aged son had to take care of him like a child. His son, who often spent days taking his father along with him wherever he went, said that it was the first time he had ever felt close to the man. He described a time he had even taken Allen to his weekly therapy session, and was amazed by his father having a sudden and unusual moment of lucidity. When asked by the therapist if he understood why he had been invited to the session he responded, "To show my son that I love him," then he lapsed back into forgetfulness. Allen was a man who had never been demonstrative. He had put his energy into what he thought was his duty: working hard to support his children and his company. Perhaps Alzheimer's was his way of finally allowing some softness in his life, of receiving support and nurturing, for a change, instead of always being the provider. Perhaps in his "right mind" he could never have accepted such a different role.

Becoming a Healer in Dying

As we live by the rules and limits of physical reality, we believe that we become useless when our physical bodies lose their health and ability. Yet as we know ourselves to be spiritual beings with life and resources beyond the visible and the physical, our lives continue to have meaning no matter what the condition of our physical, and even mental, functioning.

I knew a woman named Maria, who lived with Alzheimer's well into her nineties. Her last two years were spent in a hospice where she was sent because everyone believed she had less than six months to live. She had little memory at all in the way we think of memory. She couldn't remember what happened the day before, five minutes before, or the last sentence she just finished speaking. She had only fuzzy recognition of family members and others, and she was bedridden. She lived many people's worst nightmare.

Yet there was something magical about her. The hospice attendants found themselves gravitating to her room when they felt bad because they always felt better in her presence. Family members of another hospice resident continued to visit her even after their own relative had died. She chattered happily in conversation that was cryptic — delusion, nonsensical, many would say — describing trips she had made up through the ceiling and into fantastic dream realms. Just when one was ready to write off her ramblings as meaningless she would say something startlingly mysterious, referring casually to specific details of something that was troubling one of her visitors, details she had no explainable way of knowing. She seemed to know when someone was upset and had comforting words and sage advice that went right to the heart.

Maria was the aunt of one of my childhood friends. I had known her since I was a teenager and I sometimes went to visit her in the hospice with my friend. Though she was friendly and personable in her early years, there was something different about her in these last years, a newfound ability to reach people. I will never forget a day I went to see her, feeling slightly down and not really in the mood to visit a hospice. As we walked in the door, her face lit up and she talked on and on about how beautiful we both were, how wonderful the day was and how "romantic" life is. Little by little I found myself drawn into her world, where each moment is fresh and new. The magic fully hit me as I watched my friend talking to Maria, a light transforming her face from the competent, pragmatic woman she has grown into over the years to the fresh innocence I hadn't seen in her since we were teenagers. I wondered if my face reflected the same light.

Maria's son says that witnessing his mother during this time of her life has changed his whole concept of death. He no longer looks upon death as frightening and unknown. It is as though Maria had taken little peeks into the next world and came back to reassure those around her that it's all right, that there's nothing to fear.

Toward the end she became more tired, less talkative, less understandable, but, in a most lucid moment she said, "My life now is about reconciliation and love. I am so glad I stayed to do this post-work."

Five years prior to her death, Maria had moved from her home town to another city half a continent away to be closer to her son. She was already severely disabled physically and with Alzheimer's at the time of her move, yet at her funeral there were more than 60 people present, most of whom had known Maria only in this latter part of her life. All had been touched, healed and changed by their contact with her.

How do you imagine doing your own "post work?" What do you believe about the end of your life? Do you see yourself as an old person? If so, how old? If you can't imagine yourself as a seventy, eighty, or ninety year old person, what is the oldest you can envision? Does this age match the age of death of your parents, grandparents, or other close members of your family? To some extent, we learn how to die from our family models, and start to envision (and create) our own deaths accordingly. Start creating the peaceful, fulfilled ending you want now through the following exercise.

Exercise: Creating Your Life and Your Death

Write a story about yourself as a very old person nearing the end of your life. Write this story as someone who has experienced much fulfillment in life. As you look back upon your experiences, you can see that even the failures and disappointments had a purpose, teaching you something you needed for your next step. As an older and wiser person, you can see the whole of your life. You can acknowledge yourself for your achievements and accept that some of what you achieved was not what you planned or expected. You can feel warmth and gratitude for the love you shared with people, and now that many of your loved ones have died, you look forward to being reunited with them.

Picture yourself as healthy and vital, even at an advanced age, and your life filled with love, meaning and serenity. Describe what you do in a day, what you think about, what gives you pleasure.

Go on to describe the event of your death. Picture it as you wish it to be. See who is with you, where you are, what the cause of death is and what the final moment of letting go is like. Describe the experience of releasing your body to a wonderful sense of freedom and joy. Finally, describe how the people who love you celebrate your passing on and imagine your funeral or memorial.

Our feelings about death deeply affect not only the way we will eventually go about dying, but the way we live. Very simply, the fear of death stifles our zest for life. If the idea of death holds fear for you and you tend to push it out of mind, don't wait until you are confronted in some way by your own mortality or that of a loved one. Melvin Morse found that people experienced a measurable decrease in death anxiety simply by reading about near-death experiences, and this is a good place to start. Most libraries and bookstores now have whole shelves devoted to NDE's and the "Light." These moving, true stories offer more than insight and awareness about death — they change how we feel about it. It is in the moment of being uplifted, moved to tears and powerful emotion, be it at the bedside of a dying friend or from a story in a book, that we become more powerful. We burst through fear and numbness. We unlock more of our capacity to experience ecstasy. We see past the limits of our physical perceptions.

As death breaks into your life as always it must in one way or another, let it be an opportunity to look at death differently. Learn to look past the terrible tragedy and fearful loss of control to find the powerful lessons in trust, surrender and deep peace.

It's Never Too Late for Healing

So often people in our lives die before we have said good-bye or made peace, leaving us with sadness and regret. At worst, these incompletions keep us tied in knots, unable to open our hearts to love again. I have seen people in my workshops ridden with guilt and remorse over the way they ended with a parent or loved one who died. Yet, as we shift our awareness to see beyond the illusion of death, we realize that love, healing and ongoing relationship aren't limited by the transitory nature of physical reality. If we can look past our imperfections — of not being the perfect son or daughter, of not saying the right thing or being there at the right time — we can find the divine order in even the most seemingly imperfect endings. As we come more deeply in touch with our eternal nature through the death of someone close to us, there is the potential for the most profound forgiveness possible because, as we glimpse the reality of ourselves as being beyond harm and beyond doing harm, we understand that there is truly nothing to forgive.

What's more, there is much communication, healing and resolution that can continue after the transition of death. I found this to be true in my relationship with my mother. Our relationship has felt just as active since her death as before. For the first year or so after she died, I had frequent dreams of her where she appeared progressively younger until she was about my age. No longer did she feel like my parent, with all the baggage of our mother-daughter relationship. Instead she became a beloved best friend. As I think of her now and sense her presence, I feel even more love than when she was living and we struggled through the clashing of our personalities.

My mother was diagnosed with terminal cancer in 1988. The five months between her diagnosis and her death was both a painful and remarkable time for me. An only child, I had a difficult, love-hate relationship with her. It either felt close to the point of suffocation or so distant that we stopped talking altogether for months at a time.

When my mother and I first learned of her illness and prognosis, our relationship underwent a honeymoon period. We delighted in each other's company, went out to lunch, took all the family heirlooms and photographs out and documented the history of each. My heart was open to her as it hadn't been in years.

I was completely unprepared for what came next when she let go of her apartment and moved in with me. The enmeshment that had suffocated me for much of my life flared up with a vengeance. It was as though we shared some unavoidable destiny to enact our worst dance, one last time, in the biggest possible way.

My mother didn't go about dying in the way I had seen many others do. There was no wasting away, no confinement to her bed, no disabling pain. She remained relatively able-bodied until the last week or so. She was constantly bored once she ran out of things to do, friends to have lunch with and affairs to put in order. She took to following me around the house, creating unnecessary tasks for me to do for her, even calling after me when I went into the bathroom. I felt trapped by her neediness — not her physical needs, which would have been easier for me to cater to, but her emotional needs, which had overwhelmed me since childhood. I found myself doing what I had always done with my mother when I felt overwhelmed. I pushed her away and shut down emotionally. It was a nightmare. I had wanted to provide a safe, nurturing haven for her to live out her life and I felt like a miserable failure. I was furious with myself for wasting my last time with my mother in this way.

One day, at my wits' end over how to help her and myself through this stuck place that was so familiar to us, I prayed for guidance. In my meditation, I saw my mother and myself both looking solely at what was ending about her life and finding cause only for depression and sadness. I saw her on a path looking back toward where she had been and unable to see any future. The path she was on wasn't at an end, however. It continued. Just a little further along this path, I saw my mother's father, who died when I was very young, and her grandmother, who I only knew from photographs. These two were standing ready to welcome her the moment she turned around to continue on the path. The message they gave to me was that the highest help I could give my mother and myself would be to see her path continuing, not ending, and this would help her to turn around and see how much she has to look forward to. This vision was so vivid and I was so at peace afterward, that I felt I had truly been visited by my ancestors and that I was not alone in caring for my mother.

That evening my mother excitedly called me into her room while she was watching television. I responded sluggishly, worn down by her calls coming so frequently during the day. I wasn't quick enough to see what had excited her. On the TV, as background to a list of public service announcements, the local station had flashed an historical postcard of our hometown as it appeared around the turn of the century. It was a post card my mother had seen many times in her youth because it depicted her grandmother and her father, then just a toddler, playing in the park. The experience brought tears to her eyes and she said that she had felt somehow "meant" to see this picture, that there was some special comfort meant for her in it.

I then shared with her my own experience with these two relatives earlier that day. In that moment it felt as though we broke through to something real and sustaining. It was a magical moment that seemed to ease some of the tension between us. We still had problems, but shortly thereafter, she decided to accept my aunt's invitation to stay at her house, which helped considerably.

My mother's dying didn't change us — she acted like her, I acted like me and we carried on our uneasy dance until the end. A day finally came, though, when I found peace with her. I was about to lead a 5-day intensive workshop for the first time and it was a very big deal to me. I had once or twice thought, half jokingly, that it would be just like my mother to die in the middle of this important event. She had often managed to stage life crises at the most important times of my life, forcing me to make difficult decisions about my priorities and boundaries. On more than one occasion I had chosen to say no to her and then struggled with her anger and my guilt, feeling that I could never be a good enough daughter to please her. It looked as though this pattern wasn't to repeat, however, since my mother had just gone into the hospital and was awaiting transfer to a hospice where she would spend the remaining five or so months her doctor expected her to live.

On this day I had very little time. In fact, I hadn't planned to see my mother at all. But, as I hurried to get ready for my big workshop, something compelled me to take time out to prepare a special treat of perfect berries and summer ripened fruits, beautifully arranged (one of the few things that could still tempt my mother's waning appetite), and take it to her. On my way into the hospital, I tripped and fell in the parking lot, skinning my knee and mashing the berries and fruit that I had arranged so perfectly. The gift I had wanted to give was once again flawed.

I didn't stay more than fifteen minutes with my mother that day. She received the squashed fruit as though it was something precious and for the first time in many weeks, perhaps many years, there was only love between us — simple, uncomplicated. Neither of us said anything profound. I had a sense that there was nothing more she needed from me. There would be no more difficult choices between being myself and being the daughter I thought she wanted. I left to go back to work, looking forward to the following week when my workshop would be over and I had the whole week set aside to spend with her.

I never got the chance. My mother died during the workshop. Due to hospital error, I wasn't informed immediately and didn't find out until my workshop was almost over. So, one last time my mother and I managed to stage major life events at the same time, and one more time we got to do this dance we had created between us. At the time I felt regret at not being with her, guilty relief at the hospital error that delayed the news of my mother's death long enough for me to complete my workshop, and sadness over not having more "quality" time with her, even though the quality of our last fifteen minutes seemed to surpass a lifetime of quantity. In retrospect, I wouldn't have my mother's passing any other way.

What has been powerfully moving for me since my mother's death is how deeply I feel she is still with me. Several months before my mother knew she was sick, I dreamed that she died and we continued to have an active relationship after her death and were able to heal aspects of our relationship that we could not heal during her lifetime. I now know this dream to be truth. Where there has been love, it is never too late to heal, to extend forgiveness, to share love and to receive guidance and comfort.

Group Exercise: Talking in Spirit

Having a conversation in spirit, as described in the exercise, "Relating from Your Higher Self" in Chapter Five is a wonderful way to transcend the illusion of death and draw strength, love and wisdom from our ancestors and loved ones who have passed out of physical existence. It is also a good way to heal relationships fraught with pain and lack of forgiveness at the time of death. In instances where the emotional voltage of an unhealed relationship is very high, it is particularly important to firmly hold the intention that you will be in your Higher Self and only open to an experience of the other person's Higher Self. If you are very fearful of encountering a particular person, even in spirit, wait until you feel more at peace with the prospect. Or, you might consider doing the following group exercise with several supportive friends. This exercise is a variation of the "Relating from Your Higher Self" exercise and is meant to be done with two or more other people. If you are doing this in a group of six or more, it is best to break down into smaller groups of three or four. Have paper and pens ready for everyone.

Step One

Begin with some quiet meditation time or other means to become relaxed, peaceful and focused on the Light. This could include a guided visualization, some meditative music, chanting, an inspiring reading or any kind of preparatory ritual. It could simply be a period of silent meditation. Get in touch with your Higher Self — the part of you that is safe beyond all harm, wise beyond limit and exists only to give and receive unconditional love. Picture or sense the presence of beautiful light.

Step Two

At some point in this meditative time, focus inward and ask that the Higher Self of a deceased relative or loved one come to mind. Ask that this be someone who has important guidance or a gift for you. This may be the person you planned to contact today, but be open to someone else coming. Trust that whoever pops into mind first is the right person. It could be someone you know well or it could be an ancestor who died before you were born.

Hold the intention that you are inviting only the Highest Self — the part of this being that wishes you nothing but good and exists only to give and receive unconditional love. (Connecting with those who have passed out of physical existence is often associated with "spookiness." If you focus on the possibility of darkness and "spookiness" you are more likely to create such an experience. For a more meaningful experience, focus only on the Light. If you have concerns about the safety of this exercise, don't do it.)

Step Three

When someone comes to mind, let this person tell you or show you what they have come to give. Allow messages, images, feelings and thoughts to come to you. You may wish to ask your loved one to give you a signal that will alert you to their loving presence in the future, even at times when the "veil" seems thick and impermeable. For example, while she was still living, my friend Cheryl said she would signal her presence to us after her death by moving objects around. Since her death, many of her friends have had meaningful objects mysteriously appear or move. Now, when her picture falls off its shelf twice in the same week, I know that she is with me.

Though not everyone is able to work out such signals before death, it's never too late to ask for these signs that will let you know you are not alone. In this way you can begin to transcend the feeling that this person is "gone" so that he or she can become an ongoing source of loving guidance in your life. When your visit feels complete, say good-bye to this guide, see him or her fading into beautiful light, and gently bring your attention back to the room. Immediately write down everything you remember from your experience.

Step Four

Next, let one person share who came to them as a guide. Just share a few details about who this person is without mentioning the gifts or messages that the guide gave. A lot of information about this person and your relationship is not necessary and may even cloud the clarity of the following messages. Other group members are then to become quiet and relaxed and bring to mind the guide just described, opening to any messages, thoughts or feelings that spontaneously pop into mind. Just relax, don't censor and let your imagination play with this. Say whatever comes to you. Imagine yourself in the role of messenger, delivering the guide's message to the receiver. Even if you have never done anything like this before, you will be amazed at how quickly impressions will start coming to you and how appropriate these spontaneously channeled messages are.

Step Five
As the messages are spoken, the receiver is to write them down. When all messages have been given, allow some time for all of you to discuss what the experience was like. If the receiver wants to, she or he may then share the message she or he received in meditation. When everyone feels complete, repeat Step Four for each person in the group.

If you would like to make this experience into more of an event, invite friends together for the purpose of honoring deceased loved ones. Tell each person to come with one or two people in mind they wish to honor. Have them bring a picture, a candle and a dish of each loved one's favorite food. At the start of your gathering have guests place pictures of the dead in a special area, light candles by each one and say a little about the person they have chosen to honor.

After the exercise, hold a feast consisting of all your loved ones' favorite foods. Over the meal, share your favorite stories of these people. You may wish to include the ancient tradition of making a plate for the spirit guests of honor and later taking it outside as an offering to the animals and the earth.

I once had someone express concern that she was intruding upon her dead loved ones by pulling them away from wherever they were to be with her. When I asked her for more information, she explained that when she did the exercise she imagined herself reaching out and yanking them into her world! There need be no sense of invasiveness in this process as it operates on the assumption that we are all connected on some level, whether we are in physical bodies or not. At this spiritual level of being, we are always in relationship. So rather than calling a being to us, we are simply expanding our awareness to include this level of relationship that always exists.

Learning About the "Light" from Those Who Are Dying

We can learn a great deal from those who are nearing the bridge of death. If we step beyond our fear enough to let our hearts open to those in transition, we have an opportunity to glimpse the Light of true reality. One of the greatest teachers of my life was my much mentioned friend Cheryl Rhehovsky. When I first met Cheryl she was already beginning to talk openly about her death. Yet, at the time it seemed so unreal. She was so full of life and spirit, determined to try anything once, be it winter camping, fire-walking, skiing or learning to drive. Disabled from birth with a degenerative bone disease, doctors predicted that she wouldn't live beyond her teens. I met her when she was 27.

But gradually, over the years, Cheryl's physical limits became greater and greater. She lost her capacity to drive and was forced to give up her beloved van, specially equipped with wheelchair ramp and adaptations to her dwarfed limbs. This crushing blow of freedom lost proved to be a door opening. Fiercely independent and unwilling to be "needy," I saw her gradually soften, allowing others to help her. This loss of independence turned into a gain of friendship and support as she realized how many people were willing to go out of their way for her.

As the range of her physical capabilities narrowed, Cheryl directed her daredevil spirit into the new challenge of intimacy. She pursued the adventures and risks of opening her heart with the same courage that led her into her first vision quest (a night alone in the woods, propped against a tree, unable to move from her spot until someone came for her the next day). When Cheryl was forced to quit her job, she pursued being a friend and serving the people in her life, who were then quite numerous, as her life work. She became the hub of a whole community of people. Her home was a gathering place, always busy and full of life.

In spite of all the physical evidence, it was hard for those of us who knew her to believe that Cheryl was dying. How could such a warrior die? But then there came a time when every trip to town (we lived in different cities) meant I saw Cheryl with a new piece of medical equipment or a new tube running into her body. Toward the end of her life, I found myself arranging more frequent business trips to her home city and staying longer than work necessitated just to spend long days with her. Those were dreamy days. We would cuddle in her bed. Sometimes we would talk, sometimes Cheryl would doze, and I would feel strangely transported to a peaceful place where all is well, all is in order. I would leave Cheryl's house feeling open, peaceful, floating above the world's cares.

Then it would hit me — Cheryl was dying. She would leave me soon. Driving home from her house I would cry and cry, torn between wanting to be with her every minute I could and fearing the pain of loss that this attachment would bring.

Over the years of our friendship, Cheryl and I fell into a routine of talking on the phone regularly, keeping each other posted on life's events. But, during this later period, we spoke less frequently. For a long time neither of us commented on the change. It didn't seem entirely intentional or even conscious. One day, however, when we were together, we both shared the strange feeling we had been experiencing of late, of being in each other's presence, in spite of the miles separating us and the fact that we rarely talked on the phone. As we spoke this out loud for the first time we realized that this "together" feeling was the reason for our lack of phone calls.

Cheryl shared that she had omitted calling to tell me she was in the hospital recently because she had felt such a strong sense that I was with her. I had experienced something similar when I had written an article about Cheryl. I didn't bother to call her until it was finished because I had an odd sense of her speaking to me as I wrote, directing my words. When she read the article, she was amazed at how much the words I had written felt like her own. In fact, on the day I wrote this piece, she had been napping all afternoon, going in and out of dreams about being with me.

Cheryl and I had often talked about doing some collaborative writing. She had a message she wanted to give to the world but lacked the energy for such a project. For a time we both felt pressured to accomplish this task — time felt short. But the writing just wasn't happening, the inspiration wasn't quite there yet. Then somewhere along the way we both relaxed. We didn't speak about this change until long after it happened, just as with our lack of phone calls. When we did finally speak, it came out that, again, we were responding to a new and growing certainty about our connection. We both were beginning to feel that our work together would not be stopped by Cheryl's passing from her body. We even sensed that it might be enhanced. I thought that writing "with" Cheryl after her death might be very similar to my earlier experience of hearing Cheryl's words speaking in my head the day I wrote an article about her.

Because Love Is Eternal, We Don't Need to Fear Death

Some of my deepest fears and wounds have been related to people leaving. I was separated from my father for a year when I was four, my older half brother who I adored was always in and out of my life, going back and forth between his two parents, and my beloved grandfather who was a second father to me died suddenly when I was seven. I have had trouble trusting that love could last. As for Cheryl, one of her biggest struggles in coming to terms with dying was feeling that the love she shared with so many people would not be gone. These experiences we had of being together beyond our physical bodies were profoundly comforting to both of us.

The last time I saw Cheryl was the first time I didn't experience the usual pang of fear and grief that had accompanied my previous visits. Something felt healed in me and, as I know how close friends have a way of rubbing off on one another and changing together, I had a feeling that Cheryl was resolving her struggle as well. I wondered if I would see her again. Even as I wondered this I felt a sense of excitement and anticipation of what our relationship would grow into after she passed out of her body.

Several weeks later I received a call from her in the middle of the night. She had been in the hospital for the last week and was having a hard time, reacting poorly to her latest dose of pain medication. She could hardly breathe and apologetically asked if we could stay on the phone even if she couldn't speak. So, for a time, I did all the talking, filling her in on the events of my last few weeks. I'm happy to recall that I was able to share with her many wonderful changes that had been going on within me during those weeks — a renewal of faith and joy after a very difficult year of painful endings and failures.

When Cheryl could finally speak again, she was very excited, telling me in breathless gasps about how earlier in the day she had experienced one of her recurring episodes of suffocation. She had been having these for months and they always triggered panic. This time, however, instead of feeling frightened, she felt deeply peaceful. She said, "I had a feeling of being born. I was stuck but it was like being stuck in the birth canal. I felt that if I could just push a little harder, I'd be free. And, I saw my Uncle Bud [Cheryl's favorite Uncle who died just months earlier] waiting to catch me when I break through. I feel like I'm going home!"

Cheryl went on to tell me another experience she had earlier in the week, "I had a bad drug reaction and was really frightened, and then I felt like you were holding me. First I felt someone trying to get on my bed. The sheets and curtains were rustling, I kept hearing a faint whispering voice. Then it was you, and you scooped me up and kept whispering to me, telling me everything was all right. With you there, I knew I was okay and we went to sleep." More than ever before, Cheryl seemed clear that her connection to me and the other people she loved is not reliant upon the existence of our physical bodies.

We talked for hours, into the early morning. We both spoke of all that we had meant to each other over our years of friendship. I could feel a change in Cheryl and was excited for her. I said, "For the first time you sound like you are struggling toward something wonderful instead of against your pain."

When we hung up I felt happy and warm. I also cried because I could tell Cheryl was ready to go. I wasn't surprised when I received word the next day that she had died. I was happy to hear that her death came quickly and painlessly after a perfect day of seeing close friends, eating her favorite treats and receiving a much longed-for shower. She had been affirming that death could be like this — quick and easy, instead of the slow lingering end she had feared for much of her life.

I cried a great deal in the following week. No amount of faith and higher vision kept my heart from breaking. And then, one night as I lay in bed crying, missing my friend, it was I who felt her scoop me up and whisper to me that she loves me, that everything is all right. And I knew I was okay. I knew that our friendship isn't over, that Cheryl isn't gone.

It's cold winter as I write this and recall that summer's long dreamy days with Cheryl and the deep feeling of peace that came over me as I spent time in her presence. In thinking back, it seemed that Cheryl already had one foot in the Light as the other foot remained here in physical reality. Through her, an extra ray of Light found its way into my heart as well. It made the world seem more mysterious, less fixed, less harsh. Just as I know with certainty that the cold barren scene outside my window is destined to melt into summer again, so I am coming to know that the ending we call death is no more permanent than winter. Death is life distilling to its essence and becoming brighter because of its invisibility to the physical senses. I continue to learn, with Cheryl's help, that love continues, that we are never alone, that ultimately we are always safe.

APPENDIX I

Working with Grief in a Group Setting

Cocooning

"Cocooning" is a comforting way of holding a person who is experiencing deep grief and feeling regressed to a childlike state, such as when someone is wracked with sobs, perhaps in touch with childhood memories. In grief, there is a natural tendency for the body to curl up. People who are crying tend to cover their faces, hunch over and assume a caved in, protected body position. Cocooning intensifies this body posturing and gives a deep comforting feeling of safety that encourages the person to release emotion. Many people feel self-conscious about crying in a group and feel compelled to "pull it together" after a short cry rather than going as far as is needed for healing. Being cocooned makes it easier to let go of self-consciousness and stay with the feelings.

To cocoon someone, have him or her lie down on his or her side tightly curled up, in a fetal position. The person's knees should be pulled up and held as close to the chest as is comfortable. Have several people gather around and hold the person in this curled up position. Do this using your whole body, not just your hands, wrapping yourself around the person being cocooned. Create a tight, warm, protected cave all around the person. Of course, ask permission before cocooning someone and check in to make sure he or she is comfortable. Sometimes people will crave more pressure on their body, or need more air or a lighter touch. Remember not to give a lot of petting or massage while the person is sobbing deeply, saving this kind of touch for when the emotional wave has past.

Let the cocoon continue until it reaches a natural conclusion — when the strong emotion has passed, the person is talking and has his or her eyes open. End it with any verbal feedback that seems appropriate about how the experience touched other group members and any other relevant sharing of feelings. Help the cocooned person to come back very slowly. It's nice to sit the person up and support him or her in a seated position so that he or she does not have to do any of the work. This is a very hands-on process. Unless the person being cocooned asks people to stop touching, maintain physical contact at all times. Any sudden break in contact can be very disturbing to a person in such a deeply emotional state. Be especially aware of this during transition times, such as when the actual cocoon ends and the person is helped to a sitting position. People need to keep hands on and break contact very slowly and gently after he or she has come back from the young child state he or she was probably experiencing.

When offering touch to someone experiencing deep emotions it is very important to be respectful of boundaries. If you have any question about whether touch would be welcomed or feel invasive, ask before touching, especially before offering anything more than a hand. There are times when touch does more harm than good. Say, for example, a woman is speaking about her childhood abuse experiences and is crying. She grew up feeling that her physical boundaries were not respected. To reach out and hug her without asking permission may reinjure these wounds rather than give comfort.

Another time that touch becomes invasive is when it is motivated by hidden agendas. For example, many people are uncomfortable with strong emotions or grew up burdened with the family role of "fixer." People who fall into these categories may feel strongly compelled to give physical touch whenever anyone is crying to make them stop or to "fix" them. To the receiver of this touch there is a vague or acute awareness that it doesn't feel "right." This is because the giver is actually attempting to deal with his or her own discomfort by "comforting" the other person's feelings away. Other hidden agendas include sexual attraction or neediness. When a group is engaged in activities that involve a lot of physical contact, it is good to give frequent reminders that each person is responsible for stopping any contact that doesn't feel right. It is not necessary to understand why it doesn't feel right — just say no!

APPENDIX II

Facilitating Anger
Work in a Group

Safety

Safety is paramount when doing any healing work around anger. The reason we are all so afraid of anger is because of its potential to do harm. So it's essential to have clear and strictly adhered to safety rules that are spoken (or even written) rather than assumed. It's also important that these rules be unanimously agreed to by all member of the group, and enforced by immediately stopping any action outside of the rules or by asking someone to leave the group in the event of repeated violations.

Safety Rules for Anger Work

1. "Stop" means Stop!

It is important that anyone involved in anger release work can stop the experience if it feels too overwhelming or out of control. Before beginning an anger release process, agree on a designated word that means stop! It's good to have such a word because yelling exercises sometimes involve shouting "No!" or "Leave me alone!" and other things that could make it hard to tell if someone is wanting the process to stop or just "releasing." If someone is screaming and you are not sure if they mean "stop" or not, ask.

2. No touching other people in anger.

No pushing or hitting, even with "nonharmful" objects like pillows, not even in a semi-joking manner. When anger comes up, all spontaneous physical contact can feel dangerous and frightening and there needs to be clear boundaries. (This doesn't mean it's necessary to strictly prohibit all friendly pillow fights or other gentle roughhousing that happens in spontaneous play, separate from anger. Physical play can be fun when it is not an expression of anger and as long as people's boundaries are always respected. But keep in mind that what is play to one person may feel like abuse to another.)

3. No throwing things in anger, around the room or at another person.

There are more controlled ways of getting the same release, such as beating a pillow against the floor. Throwing things is often frightening to other people and feels out of control even if the thrower feels in control.

4. No hitting anything that could result in damage to the hitter or the object hit.

For example, stop someone from beating his or her fists repeatedly against a hard floor or kicking a wall, etc. People who are releasing anger often do not heed pain and need to be redirected to a pillow or other safe method of release.

5. No verbal battering.

Verbal battering includes name-calling, cursing, berating and otherwise dumping anger in a way that is meant to hurt rather than heal. (This rule applies only to people who are present and is not meant to censor the occasional "I hate you, Mom!" that may burst forth during release work.)

NO! (A Group Release Exercise)

This simple group exercise that I learned from Washington, D.C. healer, Prem Deben, Ph.D. is a good way to introduce anger work to a group that has never done anything loud. In this exercise, everyone stands up and screams all at once, *"No!"* as loud as possible. Then each person turns to face the person next to him or her and screams *"No!"* again. Everyone continues to scream "No!" over and over, screaming it in a different person's face each time. Do this for about five minutes or until the energy seems to be winding down.

This is a relatively low-risk way for everyone to break through the "polite" barrier and experience some physical release without anyone having to be "on the spot." Most groups have fun with this and it is guaranteed to raise the energy level of a sleepy group.

Facilitating an Individual Through Anger Release

In a group that has never dealt with anger before, one or more sessions may be needed to discuss release work before actually doing it. This discussion would address all the reasons why anger work would be beneficial and give ample opportunity for group members to talk about their fears and concerns, their feelings of safety and trust and, ultimately, their willingness.

Anger release work cannot be sprung on an unwilling group by an over-eager facilitator. It needs to be an organic process that arises to meet the need for it, and the group as a whole must be generally supportive. Assuming there is a readiness and willingness among the group, the following steps offer a structure for facilitating an individual who is in touch with angry feelings and would like some help releasing them. Never begin anger work unless you have sufficient time for it — at least an hour or more of group time left. Anger release work generally doesn't work well in groups that run for less than two hours. I usually schedule three hour sessions for any group that might include deep emotional catharsis work.

Step One: Set up the release area.
Stack a large pile of pillows up several feet high in front of the person (whom I will refer to as the protagonist, to borrow a term from psychodrama) who assumes a kneeling position to pound on them. Or, have the protagonist hold one sturdy (emphasis on "sturdy" — this pillow will take a beating!) pillow to beat against the floor. Even better than a pillow is to invest in a pair of foam bats designed specifically for anger release work. Clear a wide space around the protagonist. The facilitator will act as a safety monitor, remaining close enough to the protagonist to make sure that other group members do not get in "pounding range" and to protect the protagonist from getting dangerously near lamps or breakables, making sure the pillows stay arranged appropriately, etc.

Step Two: "Stop" means stop!
Before beginning, remind everyone that "stop" means stop! The facilitator or the protagonist can call "stop" at any time. This is important for the facilitator to remember as well as the protagonist. People who are in the midst of anger release work may look out of control, but they are not. If the protagonist's activities in any way get out of the safe release boundaries that were set up, call "stop" and set it up safely again. This could be something

as simple as taking a flimsy pillow that looks about to burst out of the protagonist's hands and substituting one that's sturdier, or keeping the person centered in the middle of the room away from furniture.

Step Three: Invite active group support.

The group can assist by adding some auditory volume to the protagonist's release. This can be done by screaming with the protagonist. Drums can also be used to provide added sound. In anger release work, sound is as important as the physical action and group support can dispel the protagonist's self-consciousness around screaming and being loud. It's important that the volume and intensity of this added sound match rather than outdo the protagonist. For example, as the protagonist gets started, the group can begin a soft drum beat, making it louder and faster as the protagonist rises in volume and intensity. If the protagonist is shouting, "No!" group members can shout out loud, too, the same or similar expletives. This gives everyone who needs it a chance to do some release work of their own as they help the protagonist warm up by adding their own emotional energy.

Step Four: Begin.

If the protagonist doesn't know how to begin, a simple phrase is a good start. "I'm angry!" or "No!" said over and over, each time accompanied by a pound on a pillow will usually start feelings flowing. It is not necessary to be feeling a high level of anger to start a release process. Sometimes people who were sufficiently in touch with angry feelings to want to do some release work, will have lost them by the time the process gets set up. They may feel self-conscious. Just the action of beating on pillows and vocalizing will bring back the feeling state. If not, the next step may help.

Step Five: Pick a support partner.

If the protagonist needs some added help to become warmed up to the release work, let him or her pick a support partner. Invite the protagonist to pick a person who is good at releasing anger. The person chosen is free to agree or decline to support in this way. (The person chosen is often someone who also needs to do some release work, and may be a little more ready than the protagonist.) If willing, this person joins the protagonist in the cleared release area. Sitting side by side, the support partner assists by screaming and pounding with the protagonist, giving encouragement and lending emotional energy.

Step Six: Afterward.

After the protagonist has done some release work and has stopped, encourage him or her to relax for a moment and see if there is more. The energy of emotional release tends to come in waves and after a brief pause another wave of feeling may arise. Doing emotional release work is like peeling an onion — as one emotion is discharged, another surfaces. Anger release often ends with tears and feelings of vulnerability. After yelling and pounding, the protagonist will often crumple, crying. Hands-on nurturing is needed at this point. (See the preceding Appendix on "Cocooning" for more on this.) The facilitator can encourage this if group members don't spontaneously come forward to hold and comfort the protagonist. Allow as much time as needed for the protagonist to cry and receive loving attention from group members. Verbal reassurance is helpful. Let the protagonist know that he or she did well. Share how you may have benefited from and were touched by the process. This will help the protagonist feel less exposed and to reintegrate into the group.

Step Seven: Support for the rest of the group.

There may be people other than the protagonist, the support partner in particular, who did so much release work in their support roles that they, too, need some special attention and support. Sometimes the protagonist merely serves to warm up other group members to do the deeper emotional release work and there will be a shift in focus, midstream, from the protagonist to another person. This is not complicated or hard to figure out. Simply give attention where it is most obviously needed. If the protagonist appears cool, calm and collected while another group member is sobbing hysterically, the latter person is the one in need of immediate attention. Catharsis has a way of being contagious and there may be more than one person at a time crying and experiencing strong emotion. Not everyone needs full group focus and appropriate care is usually given quite spontaneously. Someone begins to cry and those people close by just naturally embrace that person. This is all that's needed. The facilitator needs to be aware of anyone who is crying but not receiving any support. In this event ask that one or two people sit with that person as long as needed.

Step Eight: Resolution.

When one or more people have gone through an emotional catharsis, some time is needed afterward for talking about what happened. This helps the people who were most actively involved in the emotional catharsis to reintegrate into the group, and it helps the people who were watching to feel less alarmed by the process. Emotional release work can look very painful from the outside even when it feels good and empowering to the protagonist. An open sharing period helps everyone know that the protagonist was in control of the experience and is safe. This is also a time to care for anyone who feels uncomfortably open and vulnerable. In particular, see if anyone would like support calls during the week to help process feelings that may continue to come up.

REFERENCES

INTRODUCTION

p. 1 Richard Wilhelm, Cary F. Baynes, *The I Ching* (Princeton: Princeton University Press, 1990), 16.

CHAPTER ONE

p. 13 *A Course in Miracles* (Foundation for Inner Peace, 1975).

p. 14 Louise Hay, *You Can Heal Your Life* (Santa Monica: Hay House, 1984).

p. 17 Fred Alan Wolf, *Taking the Quantum Leap* (San Francisco: Harper & Row, 1981), 129,139.

p. 17-18 Helmut Schmitd, random events generator studies: see Larry Dossey, *Healing Words* (New York: HarperCollins, 1993) 120-121.

p. 18 Stephen Hawking, *Black Holes and Baby Universes and Other Essays* (New York: Bantam Books, 1993).

p. 22 Caroline Myss, *Anatomy of the Spirit* (New York: Three Rivers Press, 1966), 45.

p. 24 Price Pritchett, *you2* (Dallas, Texas. Pritchett and Associates, Inc., 1990).

CHAPTER TWO

p. 29 Erwin Schrodinger, *My View of the World* (Cambridge: The University Press, 1964).

p. 40 Shakti Gawain, *Creative Visualization* (San Rafael, CA: New World Library, 1995. Originally published 1978).

p. 40 Louise Hay, *You Can Heal Your Life* (Santa Monica: Hay House, 1984).

p. 42 Richard Bach, *Illusions: The Adventures of a Reluctant Messiah* (Delacorte Press, 1977).

CHAPTER THREE

p. 69 Hui-neng, quoted in Fritjof Capra, *The Tao of Physics* (Boston: Shambhala, 1991), 179.

p. 99 Stephen Levine, *Who Dies?* (New York: Anchor Books, 1982), 134.

CHAPTER FOUR

p. 131 Cheryl Canfield, *Peace Pilgrim's Wisdom* (Santa Fe, NM: Ocean Tree Books, 1996), 110.

p. 133 Dan Millman, *Sacred Journey of the Peaceful Warrior* (Tiburon, CA: H. J. Kramer, 1991).

p. 136 Larry Dossey, *Healing Words* (New York: HarperCollins, 1993).

p. 137 Melvin Morse, Paul Perry, *Closer to the Light* (New York: Villard Books, 1990), 116.

p. 138 Sondra Ray, *I Deserve Love* (Berkeley, CA: Celestial Arts, 1976).

p. 140 Dean Ornish, *Love and Survival* (New York: HarperCollins, 1997).

p. 145 *A Gathering of Men,* Robert Bly and Bill Moyer. To obtain video copies contact Mystic Fire Video, Inc., P.O. Box 1092, Cooper Station, New York, NY 10276, 1-800-727-8433.

p. 146 James Lynch, *The Broken Heart* (New York: Basic Books, 1977).

p. 146 Leo Buscaglia, *Loving Each Other* (New York, Fawcette Columbine, 1984).

p. 159 Caroline Myss, *Anatomy of an Illness* (New York: Three Rivers Press, 1996), 84.

p. 169 Carolyn Miller, *Creating Miracles* (Tiburon, CA: H. J. Kramer, 1995), 263.

p. 172 Friends of Peace *Pilgrim, Peace Pilgrim, Her Life and Work in her Own Words* (Santa Fe, NM: Ocean Tree Books, 1982), 38.

CHAPTER FIVE

p. 178 Shantideva, *The Way of the Bodhisattva* (Boston:Shambhala Publishers, 1997).

p. 180 Erwin Schrodinger, *What is Life? and Mind and Matter* (London: Cambridge University Press, 1969), 145.

p. 209 Harville Hendrix, *Getting the Love You Want* (New York: Harper & Row, 1988).

p. 220 Jamie Sams and David Carson, *Medicine Cards* (Santa Fe: Bear & Company, 1988).

p. 220 Jamie Sams, *Sacred Path Cards* (San Francisco: Harper Collins, 1991).

CHAPTER SIX

p. 231 Mother Theresa, *A Simple Path* (New York: Ballantine Books, 1995), 80.

p. 233 Alcoholics Anonymous, *Twelve Steps and Twelve Traditions* (New York: Alcoholics Anonymous World Services, 1987), 72.

p. 247 James Redfield, *The Celestine Prophecy* (New York: Warner Books, 1993).

p. 250 Caroline Myss, *Anatomy of an Illness* (New York: Three Rivers Press, 1966), 152.

CHAPTER SEVEN

p. 271-272 Raymond Moody, *Life After Life* (New York: Bantam Books, 1975).

p. 272 Melvin Morse, Paul Perry, *Closer to the Light* (New York: Villard Books, 1990), 118, 134.

p. 282 Deepak Chopra, *Journey into Healing* (New York: Harmony Books, 1994), 114.

p. 286 The study mentioned is described in *Closer to the Light.*

p. 286 Susan Blackmore, *Dying to Live* (Buffalo, N. Y. Prometheus Books, 1993), 263.

p. 286 Melvin Morse, Paul Perry, *Transformed by the Light* (New York: Ivy Books, 1992), 66.

About the Author

Lynn Woodland has devoted her entire professional life to promoting spiritually empowering alternatives to traditional human services. While still a teenager, she spent four years working for a spiritually-based Waldorf-styled preschool. Then in 1975 she joined an innovative state-funded counseling program in Baltimore, Maryland that offered transpersonal alternatives to traditional psychotherapy and addictions treatment. In her twelve years with this program (called the Janus Center), she worked with groups, families, and individuals, specializing in both general mental health issues and addictions treatment.

In 1983 she helped to found, and became the first Director of the Baltimore Center for Attitudinal Healing, modeled after the Center in Tiburon, California, founded by Gerald Jampolsky. It offered support services to children and adults dealing with life-challenging illnesses, and promoted an uplifting philosophy that quite simply defines healing as letting go of fear. During this time she specialized in helping people with illnesses to understand the connection between consciousness and health. In particular, she developed expertise in understanding the secondary gains of illness and addressing the complex emotional dynamics that affect the will to heal.

In 1987 she left this Center to lead seminars based on her own work. She now specializes in six-day long intensives that facilitate a deeply cathartic peak-life experience and help people to access their innate power, wisdom and capacity to heal.

As a writer, Lynn Woodland has contributed articles to dozens of growth and wellness papers around the country. She is also the founder of the Miracles of the Spirit Church, a nondenominational service dedicated to miracles. A native of Baltimore, Maryland, she currently lives in Minneapolis.

If you would like to experience more
of what you just read...

Call 651-642-5405 for information
about Lynn Woodland's *POWER!* intensive
and other seminars.

Also visit her web site, **www.lynnwoodland.com**, for free services on-line,
including: The Odyssey of Life Oracle (messages of spiritual guidance),
Miracles of the Spirit Prayer Request Service,
Schedule of Upcoming Events
and more.

To order copies of this book call 651-641-9996
or visit web site www.lynnwoodland.com.